"One might be tempted to think that, a̶   ̶.̶.̶.̶,̶ ̶t̶h̶e̶ Second Vatican Council has been sufficiently analyzed and understood. Gerald O'Collins dismisses this assumption in the preface of his book, acknowledging that 'the documents still astonish [him] in golden bits.' He maintains that much of what the Council taught remains to be understood, appreciated, and practiced. This is clearly an underlying theme throughout his latest book on Vatican II. As in all of O'Collins's writings, there is a theological preciseness in his treatment of the Vatican II documents. Such an approach is essential for every theologian who continues to probe and understand the teachings of the Council."

> Sr. Maureen Sullivan, OP
> Professor of Theology
> St. Anselm College

"By any measure Gerald O'Collins has been at the forefront of Catholic theology in the post–Vatican II era. His voluminous writings have put all those seeking a deeper understanding of Christian faith in his debt. *The Second Vatican Council: Message and Meaning* proceeds from O'Collins's conviction that 'much in what the Council taught remains to be appreciated and practiced.' These lucid, insightful, indeed, magisterial essays are a precious guide toward a fuller appreciation and appropriation of the significance and implications of this epochal Council."

> Robert P. Imbelli
> Boston College (Emeritus)
> Author of *Rekindling the Christic Imagination:*
>   *Theological Meditations for the New Evangelization*

"The understanding, interpretation, and implementation of the Second Vatican Council's teachings remains a task for the Church. Much of the Council's rich and deeply interconnected teachings is still to be appreciated and received, and the renewal and reform it called for is yet to be realized in practice.

"Gerald O'Collins, SJ, is one of the leading figures in the English-speaking theological world in our time and an eminent interpreter of the Council. In this volume, which brings together a number of previously published articles, his fifty years of penetrating and insightful scholarship are brought to bear on an examination of the radical changes, in some cases reversals, in teaching and policy that the Council announced and to questions of the message and meaning of the Council. He pays particular attention to the Constitution on the Sacred Liturgy, the role of Scripture, the approaches of *ressourcement and aggiornamento* of the Council, the revelatory and salvific dimensions of the divine self-communication, the paschal mystery, the universality of revelation and faith, the teaching on other living faiths, and issues of fundamental theology.

"O'Collins's scholarship rightly commands the attention of scholars as well as students worldwide, and this most welcome book will undoubtedly serve to further the reception of the Council and the trajectories it initiated."

> Anne Hunt
> Executive Dean, Faculty of Theology and Philosophy
> Australian Catholic University

"The work of Gerald O'Collins, particularly this book, is a wonderful example of the vitality of the theology of Vatican II in light of the New Evangelization. It is also a much-needed correction to the unnecessary controversy that has recently surrounded Vatican II in some ecclesiastical quarters."

> Massimo Faggioli
> Author of *True Reform: Liturgy and Ecclesiology in* Sacrosanctum Concilium

The Second Vatican Council

Message and Meaning

Gerald O'Collins, SJ

A Michael Glazier Book

LITURGICAL PRESS
Collegeville, Minnesota

www.litpress.org

A Michael Glazier Book published by Liturgical Press

Cover design by Jodi Hendrickson. Photo courtesy of Wikimedia Commons.

Translations of Scripture texts are the author's own.

1   2   3   4   5   6   7   8   9

Library of Congress Cataloging-in-Publication Data

O'Collins, Gerald.
    The Second Vatican Council : message and meaning / Gerald O'Collins, SJ.
      pages   cm
    "A Michael Glazier book."
    Includes bibliographical references and index.
    ISBN 978-0-8146-8311-8 — ISBN 978-0-8146-8336-1 (ebook)
    1. Vatican Council (2nd : 1962–1965 : Basilica di San Pietro in Vaticano)
    I. Title.
    BX8301962 .O28   2014
    262'.52—dc23   2014010615

Contents

Preface

Called by St. John XXIII of blessed memory on January 29, 1959, the Second Vatican Council (1962–65) was widely recognized as the most significant religious event in the twentieth century. Trusting utterly in the Holy Spirit, Pope John hoped that this assembly of Roman Catholic bishops, joined by observers from other Christian churches and communities, would bring about a new Pentecost. He wanted to update and renew spiritually the Catholic Church, heal divisions within Christendom, and alter the Church's reactionary attitude toward the world.

Vatican II forced Catholics to think hard and differently about their Church. No longer maintaining a vision of the Church as a perfect society, a model elaborated by St. Robert Bellarmine (1542–1621) that remained more or less standard among Catholics for well over three hundred years, the bishops at Vatican II acknowledged the need for that "continued reformation to which Christ always calls his Church" (Decree on Ecumenism, 6).

From his election in 1978, St. John Paul II (who as a bishop had himself taken part in the Council) repeatedly asked Jews, Muslims, Orthodox and Protestant Christians, and other groups to forgive crimes committed against them by Catholics. On the First Sunday of Lent 2000 in St. Peter's Basilica, he underlined the constant need for repentance as an integral part of the Church's celebration of the Great Jubilee Year. The confession of sins at the Eucharist on that Sunday featured seven representatives of the Roman Curia asking pardon for such sins of the past and of the present as intolerance, anti-Semitism, discrimination against women, and contempt for various cultures and religions.

On June 22, 2003, John Paul II visited Banja Luka in northern Bosnia and celebrated Mass near the ruins of a Franciscan convent destroyed in 1995 by Serbian forces, who were taking revenge for the evils perpetrated by Father Vjekoslav Filipovic, a Franciscan expelled from his order during the Second World War. He led a 1942 attack by Croatian fascists who butchered more than two thousand local Serbs, including hundreds of women and children. "From this city marked by so much suffering and bloodshed," the pope said in his homily, "I ask almighty God to have mercy on the sins committed against humanity, human dignity, and freedom by the Catholic Church." The words of John Paul II showed once again how the self-image of the Church has profoundly changed and is still changing as Catholics continue to assimilate two basic themes from Vatican II: (a) being a holy sign as repentant sinners, and (b) being at the service of the world.

The two constitutions on the Church approved by the Council understood the Church to be (a) a visible sign of what the invisible Christ does (the Dogmatic Constitution on the Church, *Lumen Gentium* [LG]) and to be (b) a servant Church that embraces a ministry of justice and peace for the whole of humanity (the Pastoral Constitution on the Church in the Modern World, *Gaudium et Spes* [GS]). The bishops at Vatican II saw the Church as a sacrament of what Christ has done and is doing through the Holy Spirit to bring together all human beings into the kingdom of God.

During the four sessions of the Council and its aftermath, many other Christians and those of other faiths followed with deep interest its progress and, in some cases, affected its achievements. Rabbi Abraham Heschel and Ernst Ludwig Ehrlich, the European director of B'nai B'rith, played a role, for instance, in promoting what would be said about Jews in the declaration *Nostra Aetate* (NA). Rabbi James Rudin compared this declaration to the Magna Carta or the US Constitution because "it broke new ground and provided the mandate for constructive change." Through the presence of John Moorman, Bishop of Ripon, and his fellow observers, the Anglican Communion made its voice heard at Vatican II, and the opening of the Anglican Centre in Rome in 1966 has assured a permanent representation of that communion at the Vatican. The ecumenical thrust of the Council, encouraged by the presence of observers from nearly every Christian denomination, led directly to the creation of many bilateral dialogues between the Roman Catholic Church and other Christian churches and ecclesial communities. That work continues, sometimes with momentous results. The Catholic-Lutheran dialogue produced such an achievement in the 1999 "Joint Declaration on the Doctrine of Justification," which was accepted by the Catholic Church and the Lutheran World Federation and officially laid to rest divisions over God's saving gift of righteousness.

Several chapters of this book will examine the radical changes and, indeed, reversals in teaching and policy toward the religious "others" that Vatican II embodied. This deep reform has evoked praise from the leaders of other churches and other faiths—including Rowan Williams who wrote an article for the Christmas 2012 issue of the London *Tablet*. The outgoing Archbishop of Canterbury highlighted the theological developments that made Vatican II possible, as well as the Council's legacy and unfinished business. Hence this book addresses not only Roman Catholics but also all "the others," Christians and non-Christians alike, who continue to be interested (a) in retrieving what the Council taught and mandated about ecumenical, interfaith, and further areas, and (b) in identifying how much of that should still be put into practice.

Vatican II set itself an enormous agenda and, in its sixteen documents, produced thirty percent of the written texts coming from the twenty-one general councils of Catholic Christianity. Understanding, interpreting, and implementing Vatican II's texts remain a still far-from-completed task. For fifty years I have been studying Vatican II; yet the documents can still astonish me with the golden bits. Much in what the Council taught remains to be appreciated and practiced.

Chapter 3 of this book, for instance, develops more fully a thesis recently proposed by Massimo Faggioli: the first document to be promulgated, the constitution on the liturgy, not only enjoys a chronological priority but also provides a theological key for interpreting what was to come at Vatican II. Chapter 9 explores for the first time the role of the Scriptures in nourishing and fashioning the documents of the Council. There are further items in this book which, I would argue, can help to advance our understanding of what Vatican II achieved.

The book begins by presenting in chapter 1 various currents in what came to be called *ressourcement* theology (or *nouvelle théologie*) which retrieved forgotten or neglected themes found in the Scriptures, the fathers of the church, the liturgy, and the works of classical theologians. After sketching five characteristics of the widespread manualist theology with which *ressourcement* theology had to contend, the chapter shows how the *ressourcement* approach transformed the Council's doctrine on revelation (*Dei Verbum* [DV]), on the Church (*Lumen Gentium* [LG]), and on the divine revelation reaching all human beings (*Ad Gentes* [AG]).

Chapter 2 takes up the challenge that comes from the far-reaching changes within the Catholic Church and in her relationship with others brought by Vatican II. These changes obviously involved a measure of discontinuity with past teaching and practice. Three of the Council's documents (*Sacrosanctum Concilium* [SC], *Perfectae Caritatis* [PC], and *Dignitatis Humanae* [DH]) drew explicitly on principles to justify the renewal and reform they mandated. This chapter argues that we best understand and interpret the changes as a matter of maintaining and renewing the apostolic identity of the Church.

In a 2010 article for *Theological Studies* and in a 2012 book *True Reform*, Massimo Faggioli put the case for seeing the 1963 Constitution on the Sacred Liturgy as initiating and setting the agenda for subsequent conciliar documents and decisions. Chapter 3 nuances and enlarges Faggioli's thesis. At least twelve themes in the constitution anticipate what was to come in later texts of Vatican II. It was the theological starting point for the Council's teaching and reforms.

Chapter 4 takes up and explores what *Sacrosanctum Concilium* proposed about five modes of Christ's liturgical presence (no. 7). It argues that such presence displays ten characteristics: as relational, mediated, personal, free, transformative, costly, bodily, multiform, feminine, and future-oriented. Understood that way, Vatican II's teaching on Christ's presence could prove a rich lode of reflection for sacramental theology.

Chapter 5 moves the focus to evaluate what the Council taught about other living faiths in *Nostra Aetate* and further documents. The current world situation adds a political urgency to retrieving what Vatican II said about Judaism, Islam, Hinduism, and other world religions. Right from *Sacrosanctum Concilium*, we can see how the salvation of all humanity stood high on the agenda for the Council. The positive teaching about the religious "others" that unfolded in *Lumen Gentium*, *Nostra Aetate*, *Ad Gentes*, and *Gaudium et Spes* prepared the way for groundbreaking initiatives in interfaith dialogue and collaboration.

Chapter 6, "Implementing *Nostra Aetate*," reflects on seven ways in which John Paul II (pope 1978–2005) creatively developed and applied the teaching of that conciliar declaration. The chapter also explores three issues which *Nostra Aetate* raises and which have not yet received adequate attention.

Chapter 7 shifts attention to *Dei Verbum* and six themes that it clearly develops about God's self-revelation. In passing, the constitution attends to the Jewish and Christian *experience* of that divine self-disclosure. But to grasp the full scope of the Council's teaching on revelation, we need to glean from its other documents four further themes: the human condition that is open to revelation; the credibility of revelation; divine revelation reaching those who do not inherit the special history of biblical revelation; and "the signs of the times" that can mediate the divine presence and intentions.

The Constitution on Divine Revelation, along with other conciliar documents, proved fruitful for those engaged with fundamental or foundational theology. Chapter 8 takes up ways in which Vatican II contributed to four trajectories of contemporary fundamental theology: understanding the self-revelation of God in biblical history; interpreting the conditions that open up human beings to this divine self-communication; establishing the credibility of faith; and reflecting on the role of tradition and Scripture in transmitting the message of revelation.

To round off these reflections on Vatican II, chapter 9 investigates the degree to which the Council did in fact hear the word of God "religiously" and "faithfully" proclaim it (DV 1). A careful examination of the place of the Scriptures in two constitutions, *Sacrosanctum Concilium* and *Lumen Gentium*, substantiates the conclusion that Vatican II practiced what it preached about the Scriptures being "the supreme rule of faith" (DV 21).

My concluding reflections (chap. 10) are followed by a select bibliography, an appendix on the reform of the Congregation for the Doctrine of the Faith, a biblical index, and an index of names.

In the London *Tablet* at Christmas 2002, the late Cardinal Franz König, former Archbishop of Vienna, wrote: "the crucial process of reception, that all-important part of any church council, can take several generations. It continues today." To the extent that this book can further the reception of Vatican II and help promote the trajectories it initiated, I will be very grateful. I dedicate the volume to friends and colleagues who continue to contribute toward understanding and promoting the Council's teaching: María Carmen Aparicio Valls, Christopher Bellitto, John Borelli, Nunzio Capizzi, Maryanne Confoy,

Elena Curti, Massimo Faggioli, Archbishop Rino Fisichella, Archbishop Michael Fitzgerald, Gabriel Flynn, Michael Paul Gallagher, Janette Gray, Michael Hayes, Michael Heher, William Henn, Peter Hünermann, Anne Hunt, Michael Keenan Jones, Cardinal Walter Kasper, Gerard Kelly, Daniel Kendall, Nicholas King, Joseph Komonchak, Nicholas Lash, René Latourelle, Bishop Brendan Leahy, Daniel Madigan, Bernard McGarty, John O'Malley, Neil Ormerod, Catherine Pepinster, Peter Phan, Archbishop John Quinn, Ormond Rush, David Schultenhover, Peter and Peggy Steinfels, Jane Steingraeber, Francis Sullivan, Maureen Sullivan, Peter Vaghi, Jared Wicks, John Wilkins, and others who work or have worked for *America* magazine, and the London *Tablet*.

By permission of Oxford University Press this book includes "*Ressourcement* and Vatican II," which originally appeared as chapter 24 in Gabriel Flynn and Paul D. Murray, eds., *Ressourcement: A Movement for Renewal in Twentieth-Century Catholic Theology* (Oxford: Oxford University Press, 2012), 372–91. I also thank Sage Publications for permission to republish "Does Vatican II Represent Continuity or Discontinuity?" (*Theological Studies* 73 [2012]), "Vatican II on the Liturgical Presence of Christ" (*Irish Theological Quarterly* 77 [2012]), "Vatican II and Other Living Faiths" (*Pacifica* 26 [2013]), and "Vatican II and Fundamental Theology" (*Irish Theological Quarterly* 74 [2009]).

Finally, I am grateful to *Asian Horizons* for permission to republish "*Dei Verbum* and Revelation" (*Asian Horizons* 7 [2013]) and to the editor of *The Tablet* for permission to republish "The Reform of the Congregation for the Doctrine of the Faith" (*The Tablet* [July 14, 2012]).

For their generous work in reading carefully this book, correcting errors, and making various suggestions, I wish to thank very warmly Christopher Willcock and several other (anonymous) referees. I am also very grateful to Hans Christoffersen, Lauren L. Murphy, Bill Kauffmann, and others at Liturgical Press for their courteous efficiency in seeing this book through to publication.

Gerald O'Collins, SJ, AC
Australian Catholic University
  and The University of Divinity (Melbourne)
Pentecost 2013

Abbreviations

Vatican II Documents

AA	*Apostolicam Actuositatem*, Decree on the Apostolate of Lay People
AG	*Ad Gentes*, Decree on the Church's Missionary Activity
CD	*Christus Dominus*, Decree on the Pastoral Office of Bishops in the Church
DH	*Dignitatis Humanae*, Declaration on Religious Liberty
DV	*Dei Verbum*, Dogmatic Constitution on Divine Revelation
GE	*Gravissimum Educationis*, Declaration on Religious Education
GS	*Gaudium et Spes*, Pastoral Constitution on the Church in the Modern World
IM	*Inter Mirifica*, Decree on the Means of Social Communication
LG	*Lumen Gentium*, Dogmatic Constitution on the Church
NA	*Nostra Aetate*, Declaration on the Relation of the Church to Non-Christian Religions
OE	*Orientalium Ecclesiarum*, Decree on the Catholic Eastern Churches
OT	*Optatam Totius*, Decree on the Training of Priests
PC	*Perfectae Caritatis*, Decree on the Up-to-date Renewal of Religious Life
PO	*Presbyterorum Ordinis*, Decree on the Ministry and Life of Priests
SC	*Sacrosanctum Concilium*, Constitution on the Sacred Liturgy
UR	*Unitatis Redintegratio*, Decree on Ecumenism

Other Abbreviations

AAS   *Acta Apostolicae Sedis*

DzH   H. Denzinger and P. Hünermann, eds., *Enchiridion Symbolorum,
       definitionum et declarationum*, 42nd ed. (Freiburg im Breisgau:
       Herder, 2009)

FT   *Fundamental Theology*

ND   J. Neuner and J. Dupuis, eds., *The Christian Faith*, 7th ed.
       (Bangalore: Theological Publications in India, 2001)

Note: I make my own translation of the Vatican II documents directly
from *Sacrosanctum Oecumenicum Concilium Vaticanum II, Constitutiones,
Decreta, Declarationes* (Vatican City: Typis Polyglottis Vaticanis, 1966).

Chapter 1

Ressourcement and Vatican II

From the late nineteenth century, various currents of what came to be called *ressourcement* theology emerged and aimed at retrieving forgotten or neglected themes found in the Scriptures, the fathers of the Church, the liturgy, and the works of classic theologians. This phenomenon included the biblical movement, the ecumenical movement, the liturgical renewal, the patristic renewal (championed, in particular, by those who had launched the *Sources chrétiennes* series), and the renewal of Thomism.[1] Various forms of *ressourcement* theology flowed into and enriched the achievements of the Second Vatican Council.

This impact on the Council's work was only to be expected. Some of those who led *ressourcement* theology (e.g., Yves Congar, Jean Daniélou, Henri de Lubac, and Karl Rahner) became *periti* or expert-consultants who collaborated closely with the bishops in producing the conciliar texts.[2] In his diary entry on the eve of the closing of the Council,

---

[1] Gabriel Flynn and Paul Murray, eds., *Ressourcement: A Movement for Renewal in Twentieth-Century Catholic Theology* (Oxford: Oxford University Press, 2012); see chapters on the renewal of biblical studies (B. T. Viviano), on contributions to ecumenism (G. Flynn, A. Louth, P. D. Murray, and J. Webster), on the renewal of the liturgy (K. F. Pecklers), on the patristic renewal (B. Pottier), and on the renewal of Thomism (S. Fields and F. A. Murphy).

[2] See chapters in ibid. on Congar (G. Flynn, J. Komonchak, J. Mettepenningen, and P. D. Murray), on Daniélou (B. Pottier), on de Lubac (D. Grummett), and on Rahner (R. Lennan). Some query the inclusion of Rahner among the leaders of *ressourcement*, since he often refrains from citing particular biblical and other sources. Yet repeatedly one can retrieve precise references that support what he proposes—e.g., to take one example among very many—on the theology of the death and resurrection of Jesus (*Foundations of Christian Faith*, trans. W. V. Dych [New York: Seabury Press, 1978], 264–85).

December 7, 1965, Congar listed what he had contributed—either as initial drafter or as editor of emendations subsequently proposed by the bishops—to eight of the sixteen documents issued by the Council.[3]

In tackling the impact of *ressourcement* theology on Vatican II, we will examine first what some conciliar texts say about retrieving valuable sources in the tradition that should revitalize the Church's teaching and practice. Second, we will describe a roadblock which initially hindered that retrieval from shaping the teaching of the Council: the widespread manualist theology, exemplified by textbooks published in Rome and the *Sacrae Theologiae Summa* authored by a number of Spanish Jesuits. Third, we investigate how *ressourcement* theologians worked with the bishops in challenging, revising, and replacing draft documents prepared by the "manualists." Sampling Vatican II texts will illustrate the way these texts frequently embodied some major and minor themes developed by *ressourcement* theology.

References by Vatican II to *Ressourcement*

Those who scour the sixteen documents of Vatican II for *explicit* references to *ressourcement* or the return to sources will find something to report. The clearest endorsement of *ressourcement* comes in the Decree on the Appropriate Renewal of Religious Life (*Perfectae Caritatis* of October 28, 1965). The decree emphasizes that "an appropriate renewal of religious life comprises *both* a continual return to the sources of the whole Christian life and to the original inspiration of the institutes *and* their adaptation to the changed conditions of the times." Starting from the "supreme rule," "the following of Christ proposed in the Gospel," the decree then spells out five principles for this renewal, which should be "promoted under the impulse of the Holy Spirit and the guidance of the Church" (no. 2; emphasis added).

Apropos of the life of prayer for religious, the decree recommends that they should "draw from the fitting sources of Christian spirituality."

---

[3] Yves Congar, *My Journal of the Council*, trans. Mary John Ronayne and Mary Cecily Boulding (Collegeville, MN: Liturgical Press, 2012), 870–71. On the original French edition of this diary (2002), see the reviews by G. Flynn, *Louvain Studies* 28 (2003), 48–70, and Jared Wicks, *Gregorianum* 84 (2003), 499–550; and J. J. Scarisbrick, "An Historian's Reflections on Yves Congar's *Mon Journal du Concil*," in *Yves Congar Theologian of the Church*, ed. G. Flynn (Louvain: Peeters Press, 2005), 249–75.

That means drawing not only from the Eucharist but also from daily contact with "the Sacred Scripture, so that by reading and meditating on the divine Scriptures they might learn the surpassing knowledge of Jesus Christ (Phil 3:8)" (no. 6).[4]

On the same day that *Perfectae Caritatis* (PC) appeared, Vatican II also promulgated the Decree on the Training of Priests, *Optatam Totius* (OT). It proposed a thoroughgoing revision of ecclesiastical studies, which involves seminarians studying biblical languages, Latin, and the liturgical language of their own rite. Knowing the original languages of "Sacred Scripture and Tradition" will facilitate their access to the sources and free them from the sometimes misleading medium of translation (no. 13). Those who teach theology are directed to use a genetic method (see below), which begins by drawing on the riches of the Scripture, the patristic tradition, and the best medieval authors as foundational for Catholic faith and doctrine (no. 16).

Three weeks later, in its Dogmatic Constitution on Divine Revelation (DV, promulgated on November 18, 1965), Vatican II called on all Christians, and not merely members of religious institutes, to be "nourished and ruled by Sacred Scripture," "the pure and perennial source of spiritual life" (no. 21; see no. 25). The day before the Council ended, in the Decree on the Ministry and Life of Priests (*Presbyterorum Ordinis* [PO] of December 7, 1965), Vatican II exhorted priests to return to the same biblical source: their "sacred knowledge" should be "drawn from reading and meditating on the Sacred Scripture." This knowledge should also be "fruitfully nourished by the study of the Holy Fathers and Doctors of the Church and other monuments of Tradition" (no. 19).

Two other documents also presented a creative return to biblical and traditional sources as the route to renew the life of the Church. Thus the Constitution on the Sacred Liturgy (*Sacrosanctum Concilium* of December 4, 1963) prescribed that texts set to music should be "drawn especially from Sacred Scriptures and from liturgical sources" (no. 121). Apropos of the special position of the Eastern Churches,

---

[4] On the return to the sources in PC, see F. Wulf, "Decree on the Appropriate Renewal of the Religious Life," in *Commentary on the Documents of Vatican II*, ed. H. Vorgrimler, trans. R. Walls, vol. 2 (London: Burns & Oates, 1968), 301–70, at 329, 333, 335–36, 348.

the Decree on Ecumenism (*Unitatis Redintegratio* [UR] of November 21, 1964) earnestly recommended that Catholics should "access more often the spiritual riches of the Eastern Fathers which lift the whole human person to contemplate divine matters" (no. 15).

While *Perfectae Caritatis* leads the way in spelling out what *ressourcement* involves, five other Vatican documents emphasize how a creative return to the sources will revitalize the Church's teaching and practice. Without ignoring other sources that should be retrieved (liturgical sources, the writings of the fathers and doctors of the Church, and, in particular, "the spiritual riches of the Eastern Fathers"), the conciliar documents repeatedly stressed the need to return to the Scriptures, the preeminent source for Christian faith and life.[5]

The Challenge of the Manualists

A sense of how the preconciliar manuals of theology worked can sharpen our appreciation of what *ressourcement* theology stood for and had to contend with when Vatican II was being prepared and began.[6] Manualist theology, which belonged to what many identify as "Neo-Scholasticism," was embodied in some of the nine drafts distributed (seven in August and two in November 1962) to the bishops attending the Council. Two of those drafts or "schemata" involved in a special way a manualist approach: on the moral order (*De Ordine Morali*, largely prepared by a subcommission led by Franz Xavier Hürth, who filled out a sketch composed by Sebastian Tromp)[7] and on the Church (*De Ecclesia*, largely prepared by Marie-Rosaire Gagnebet,[8] and Tromp, under the watchful eye of Cardinal Alfredo Ottaviani, the head of the Theological Commission).[9]

---

[5] For further discussion of *ressourcement*, see chap. 3 below.

[6] See J. Wicks, "Theology, Manualist," in *Dictionary of Fundamental Theology*, ed. René Latourelle and Rino Fisichella (New York: Crossroad, 1996), 1102–5.

[7] See J. A. Komonchak, "The Struggle for the Council during the Preparation of Vatican II," in *History of Vatican II*, vol. 1, ed. G. Alberigo and J. A. Komonchak (Maryknoll, NY: Orbis Books, 1995), 167–356, at 246–51.

[8] But see H. Donneaud on Gagnebet's work in retrieving Thomas Aquinas' understanding of theology as a science: "Gagnebet's Hidden *Ressourcement*: A Dominican Speculative Theology from Toulouse," in *Ressourcement*, 95–110.

[9] Komonchak, "The Struggle for the Council," 285–300, 311–13.

One might characterize manualist theology as (1) "regressive" in method, (2) conceptualist rather than historical and biblical, (3) legalistic and worried about errors, (4) non-liturgical, and (5) non-experiential. Let me take up in turn those five characteristics.

1. The "regressive" method began with the present teaching of the pope and bishops and returned to the past in order to show how this teaching was first expressed in the Scriptures, developed by the fathers and doctors of the Church, and deployed in official teaching. Manualist theologians read the sources but only in the light of what was currently taught and believed and with the intention of defending what came from the official teaching authority of the Church and, in particular, from the current pope. In the words of Pius XII, "it is for them [theologians] to show how the teaching of the living Magisterium is found in the Sacred Scriptures and in the divine tradition, whether explicitly or implicitly."[10]

Ressourcement theology used instead a "genetic" method, a return to the sources that studied *first* the biblical witness and then the subsequent history of doctrinal development. By starting from the Scriptures and the fathers, it tracked, along the lines of John Henry Newman's view of doctrinal development, the living tradition and what it embodied for growth and change in Church teaching and practice.

2. Largely indifferent to the claims not only of historical consciousness but also of critical biblical scholarship (which, encouraged by the 1943 encyclical of Pius XII, *Divino Afflante Spiritu*,[11] went beyond lifting "proof texts" from the Scriptures, and studied biblical passages in their full context), the manualists at their worst seemed to imagine that concepts had been transmitted unchanged from one generation of Church teachers and theologians to another. Ignoring the political,

---

[10] Pope Pius XII, encyclical letter *Humani Generis* (1950), no. 21; H. Denzinger and P. Hünermann, eds., *Enchiridion Symbolorum, definitionum et declarationum*, 42nd ed. (Freiburg im Breisgau: Herder, 2009), 3886 (hereafter DzH); J. Neuner and J. Dupuis, eds., *The Christian Faith*, 7th ed. (Bangalore: Theological Publications in India, 2001), 859 (hereafter ND). This encyclical was widely and correctly understood to repudiate the *ressourcement* approach of the *Nouvelle Théologie* of French Dominicans and Jesuits.

[11] This encyclical and further papal documents (e.g., from Paul VI and John Paul II), to which reference will be made later in this book, are all available on the Vatican website and in various printed versions.

social, and cultural developments of the modern world, they claimed "unprejudiced" access to an objective order and dealt with eternal truths and general laws, from which they felt justified in deducing particular applications. Thus the draft document *De Ordine Morali* drew commands and prohibitions from universal principles of morality, while largely neglecting the central role of love that the New Testament proposes as giving a specifically Christian orientation to life.

3. A legalistic mentality prompted the manualists to assign a wide range of "notes" or qualifications to theological propositions. In decreasing importance, these "notes" ran from the highest level "of defined faith" to the least authoritative, "offensive to pious ears." The propositions they had crafted allowed manualist authors to indulge in syllogistic deductions and, inevitably, to condemn errors of every kind, often a series of abstractions such as agnosticism, atheism, humanism, materialism, relativism, and subjectivism.

This legalistic mentality was also highly juridical, and in manuals of ecclesiology concerned with the validity of the sacraments and the supreme jurisdiction of the bishops and pope. Congar, de Lubac, and other *ressourcement* theologians privileged the sacramental character of the whole Church rather than the juridical approach of what Congar called "hierarchology."[12]

4. Following the seven fundamental principles and sources or *"loci theologici"* enumerated by Melchior Cano (1509–60), manualists made no room for liturgy and liturgical sources as an important and even essential "locus" for theology. De Lubac's principle of "the Eucharist makes the Church"[13] was alien to their theological imagination. By making the liturgy the theme of their first officially approved document, *Sacrosanctum Concilium*, the bishops at Vatican II were, one might say, endorsing the principle of "the liturgy makes the Council." They ranked the study of liturgy and liturgical sources among "the principal courses" for programs of theology (no. 16). Among the texts promulgated in the Council's final session, *Dei Verbum*, when recognizing "the divine Scriptures, taken together with Sacred Tradition, as the supreme

---

[12] See Hans Boersma, *"Nouvelle Théologie" and Sacramental Ontology: A Return to Mystery* (Oxford: Oxford University Press, 2009), 242–87; P. McPartlan, *The Eucharist Makes the Church: Henri de Lubac and John Zizioulas in Dialogue* (Edinburgh: T. & T. Clark, 1993).

[13] Boersma, *"Nouvelle Théologie,"* 247–55.

rule of faith" (no. 21), specifically mentioned the study of only two items belonging to "sacred Tradition": "the Fathers, both of the East and the West, and *the sacred Liturgies*" (no. 23; emphasis added). Much pre–Vatican II manual theology paid little more than lip service to the fathers and none at all to liturgical sources.[14]

5. The Gospel of John, the letters of St. Paul, the *Confessions* of St. Augustine, and other classical works established and encouraged an experiential approach to understanding and interpreting the divine-human relationship. A long line of spiritual and mystical authorities examined this relationship in the key of experience. William of Saint-Thierry (1085–1148) was one of very many Christians who explored in depth our spiritual experience. Nevertheless, two modern documents of the Catholic magisterium, *Dei Filius* (from the First Vatican Council in 1870) and *Pascendi* (from Pope Pius X in 1907) warned against denying that "external signs" could lend credibility to divine revelation, appealing only to the "internal experience" of individuals (DzH 3033; ND 127), making faith in God depend on the "private experience" of the individual, and maintaining that interior, immediate experience of God prevails over rational arguments (DzH 3484). A justified opposition to one-sided and partial versions of religious experience unfortunately encouraged among manualists the dangerous delusion that somehow we could encounter and accept the divine self-communication "outside" human experience.

Vatican II's *Dei Verbum* was to set the record straight. Through the special history of revelation and salvation, the Israelites "experienced the ways of God with human beings" (no. 14). In the post–New Testament life of the Church, so the Council acknowledged, their "experience" of "spiritual realities" has helped believers contribute to the progress of tradition (no. 8). The closing document from the Council, the Pastoral Constitution on the Church in the Modern World (GS of December 7, 1965), was nothing less than a profound reflection on the experience of the whole human family in the light of the cruci-fied and risen Christ. It is in the light of Christ's revelation that "the

---

[14] When citing fathers of the Church, many manualists simply lifted proof texts from a classic anthology: M. J. Rouët de Journel, ed., *Enchiridion Patristicum*, 23rd ed. (Barcelona: Herder, 1965). Not content with using anthologies, such leading figures of *ressourcement* theology as Jean Daniélou and Henri de Lubac were out-standing patristic scholars.

sublime calling and profound misery which human beings experience find their final explanation" (no. 13). Here and elsewhere *Gaudium et Spes* aimed to correlate "the light of revelation" with human experience (e.g., no. 33).

Pope John Paul II proved himself an authoritative commentator on *Gaudium et Spes*. Right from his first encyclical, *Redemptor Hominis* (1979), he drew on the constitution and repeatedly reflected on human experience. His 1980 encyclical, *Dives in Misericordia*, began by appealing to collective and individual experience (no. 4) and went on to use "experience" as a noun thirteen times and as a verb six times. His studies of phenomenologists and mystics also help explain the late pope's interest in human experience, both general and religious. But not many commentators have reflected on the theme of experience endorsed by Vatican II and then running through the teaching of John Paul II. Apart from George H. Williams,[15] only a few have drawn attention to this theme.[16]

Three Achievements of *Ressourcement* Theologians

After sketching five characteristics of the widespread manualist theology with which *ressourcement* theology had to contend, let me take up three dramatic examples of *ressourcement* theology transforming Catholic doctrine (1) on revelation (*Dei Verbum*); (2) on the Church (*Lumen Gentium*), and (3) on divine revelation reaching all human beings (*Ad Gentes*).

1. The Doctrine on Revelation

In August 1962, just six weeks before the Council opened on 11 October, the bishops received seven official drafts, which included

[15] George Hunston Williams, *The Mind of John Paul II: Origins of His Thought and Action* (New York: Seabury Press, 1981), 115–40.

[16] See Derek S. Jeffreys, "A Deep Amazement at Man's Worth and Dignity," in *The Legacy of John Paul II: An Evangelical Assessment*, ed. Tim Perry (Downers Grove, IL: IVP Academic, 2007), 37–56, at 39–42; Nancy R. Pearcey, "*Evangelium Vitae*: John Paul II Meets Francis Schaeffer," in ibid., 181–204, at 201–4; Kenneth L. Schmitz, *At the Center of the Human Drama: The Philosophical Anthropology of Karol Wojtyla/Pope John Paul II* (Washington, DC: Catholic University of America Press, 1993), 127, 134–35, 126–28.

a "schema" on "the Sources of Revelation" and another on the related topic of "Preserving the Purity of the Deposit of Faith." In November 1962, many of the bishops at Vatican II were to criticize strongly the first schema, and a majority voted to have the document returned to the Theological Commission for rewriting. Pope John XXIII intervened to confirm the majority view and set up a new joint commission to handle the work of revision. The members of the "mixed commission" were drawn from the Secretariat for Christian Unity and from the Theological Commission itself.[17] In its fourth and final session, the bishops were to approve the Dogmatic Constitution on Divine Revelation, *Dei Verbum*, a text that enjoys theological priority in the corpus of the sixteen documents of Vatican II. In the preparation of that final text, *ressourcement* theologians played a vital role, not only such well known ones as Daniélou, Rahner, and Joseph Ratzinger but also such lesser known ones as Pieter Smulders.[18]

Josef Frings, the cardinal archbishop of Cologne, asked Ratzinger as his theological *peritus* to evaluate the seven drafts, and then signed the response he received from Ratzinger and forwarded it to the Vatican. Ratzinger suggested that the schema "On Preserving the Purity of the Deposit of Faith" should be put aside. As for the draft text on "the Sources of Revelation," it needed an opening chapter on revelation itself and should be revised to avoid pronouncing authoritatively on topics debated among Catholics. In an address to German-speaking bishops on the day before the Council opened, Ratzinger criticized sharply the schema's version of revelation and its treatment of such controversial topics as the relationship between Scripture and tradition. Ratzinger's earlier study of Bonaventure's concept of revelation had allowed him to retrieve the notion that divine revelation is actualized in its outcome, human faith. God's self-revelation exists in living

[17] On the debate about "the Sources of Revelation," see Giuseppe Ruggieri, "The First Doctrinal Clash," in *History of Vatican II*, vol. 2 (1997), 233–66.

[18] On the input from these *periti* toward the genesis of *Dei Verbum*, see Jared Wicks, "Vatican II on Revelation—Behind the Scenes," *Theological Studies* 71 (2010): 637–50. Wicks supplies rich documentation about this work from the *periti*, not least the five articles he published on "Pieter Smulders and *Dei Verbum*," *Gregorianum* 82 (2001): 241–77; 559–93; 83 (2002): 225–67; 85 (2004): 242–77; 86 (2005): 92–134. See further Brian E. Daley, "Knowing God in History and in the Church: *Dei Verbum* and *'nouvelle théologie,'*" in Flynn and Murray, *Ressourcement*, 333–51.

subjects, those who respond with faith.[19] In a lecture given in 1963, Ratzinger was to insist that "revelation always and only becomes a reality where there is faith . . . revelation to some degree includes its recipient, without whom it does not exist."[20]

Around the time that Frings contacted Ratzinger in August 1962, the papal nuncio to the Hague, Archbishop Giuseppe Beltrami, consulted a Dutch Jesuit, Pieter Smulders, about the same seven schemas. Smulders strongly criticized the schema "on Preserving the Purity of the Deposit of Faith" for one-sidedly presenting revelation as word (*locutio Dei*) and not recognizing that divine works also belong to the event of revelation. Word and saving deeds belong inseparably together, above all in the supreme self-manifestation of God through Jesus Christ, witnessed by 1 John 1:2-3, a text which would appear three years later in *Dei Verbum* (no. 1).[21] Through his work as a *peritus* for the bishops of Indonesia in 1962 and 1963, as drafter of a paper for the "mixed commission" established by the pope in November 1962,[22] and then in 1964 as a drafter of some of chapter 1 of *Dei Verbum*, Smulders played a major role in the production of the constitution—not least in the "sacramental" view it adopted of divine self-revelation occurring through inseparably interrelated "words and works" (nos. 2, 4, 14, 17).

It has been more or less conventional to assign an ecumenical origin to this way of presenting God's saving and revealing self-communication, as if the bishops and their drafters consciously wanted to combine here the language of word-of-God theologians like Karl Barth and Rudolf Bultmann with that favored by Oscar Cullmann, Wolfhart Pannenberg, and George Ernest Wright about God's revealing and/or saving acts in history. But a year before the promulgation of *Dei Verbum*, the Council's Dogmatic Constitution on the Church had already used the scheme of "word/work" when recalling Jesus' proclamation of God's kingdom: "This kingdom shines out to human beings in the word, works, and presence of Christ" (LG 5). Even more significantly,

[19] On all this, see Wicks, "Vatican II on Revelation," 641–43.

[20] "Revelation and Tradition," in Karl Rahner and Joseph Ratzinger, *Revelation and Tradition*, trans. W. J. O'Hara (London: Burns & Oates, 1966), 26–49, at 36.

[21] In "Vatican II on Revelation," 643–45, Wicks summarizes the input that came from Smulders in fashioning the final text of *Dei Verbum*.

[22] See Gerald O'Collins, "At the Origins of *Dei Verbum*," *Heythrop Journal* 26 (1985): 5–13.

in November 1962, the language of "words" and "works" had already entered the making of *Dei Verbum* through the paper that Smulders drafted for the mixed commission and through the paper that Daniélou produced for Cardinal Garrone (see below).

The "sacramental" language of *Dei Verbum* applies equally to "the economy of revelation" and "the history of salvation." As with the administration of the sacraments, the words and deeds of persons interact to communicate God's revelation and salvation (nos. 2, 4, 14). Above all in the case of Jesus himself, the words and deeds of one person convey the saving self-manifestation of God (no. 17).

As with Ratzinger's thinking on revelation being shaped by a retrieval of Bonaventure, the *ressourcement* theology of revelation coming from Smulders was affected not only by biblical theology but also by Hilary of Poitiers. In the scheme of "words and deeds" as the vehicle of revelation, Smulders, a world-class expert on Hilary, echoed his language. In the opening article of his *Tractatus Mysteriorum*, Hilary wrote of the biblical "words (*dicta*)" and "facts (*facta*)" that, respectively, "announce (*nuntiare*)" and "express/reveal (*exprimere*)" the coming of Christ: *"et dictis nuntiat et factis exprimit."*[23]

During the first session of the Council, various *ressourcement* theologians, such as Edward Schillebeeckx, composed and circulated among the bishops critiques of the official schemas and even proposed alternate texts.[24] Rahner produced a critical *Disquisitio Brevis* on the question of Scripture and tradition.[25] Working with Ratzinger he wrote an alternative to the schema on "the Sources of Revelation," *De Revelatione Dei et Hominis in Iesu Christo Facta*. Two thousand copies of this document

[23] *Traité des mystères*, 1.1, ed. Jean-Paul Brisson, *Sources Chrétiennes* 19, 2nd ed. (Paris: Cerf, 2005), 71.

[24] Schillebeeckx can rightly be considered a *ressourcement* theologian, given his work on, e.g., revelation, theology, and the sacrament of marriage: see *Revelation and Theology*, 2 vols., trans. Norman David Smith (London: Sheed & Ward, 1967–68), a collection of preconciliar articles in which he retrieved themes from Scripture and Thomas Aquinas); and *Marriage: Secular Reality and Saving Mystery*, 2 vols., trans. Norman David Smith (London: Sheed & Ward, 1965; orig. 1963), a work in which he retrieved themes from Scripture and the history of the Church.

[25] H. Sauer published this text as an appendix to *Erfahrung und Glaube: Die Begründung des pastoralen Prinzips durch die Offenbarungskonstitution des II. Vatikanischen Konzils* (Frankfurt: Peter Lang, 1993), 657–68.

were circulated to the bishops in November just before they began discussing "the Sources of Revelation."[26]

Various themes from Rahner's *Disquisitio* and the draft he wrote with Ratzinger were to make their way into the final text of *Dei Verbum*: for instance, "the magisterium is not above the word of God but serves it" (no. 10), and the refusal to adopt the manualist language of Scripture and tradition being "two sources" of revelation. After all, the Council of Trent spoke of only one source, the Gospel itself, which is equivalent to God's self-revelation in Christ. Rahner, Ratzinger, and other *ressourcement* theologians prompted the language of *Dei Verbum* about Scripture and tradition flowing from the same divine source, functioning together inseparably, and moving toward "the same goal," the final revelation of God at the end of world history (no. 9).[27]

In the debate of November 1962, among the bishops who called for a radical revision of the schema on "the Sources of Revelation" was Cardinal Gabriel Garrone of Toulouse, who then became a member of the new joint commission. To supply a fresh prologue he turned to Daniélou, who supplied a draft "On Revelation and the Word of God" that Garrone presented to the commission on November 27, 1962. Many of the Daniélou/Garrone themes found their way into the final text of *Dei Verbum*: for instance, Christ as "the" Revealer of the triune God.[28]

The history of the genesis of *Dei Verbum* offers a dramatic case of the close collaboration of Daniélou, Rahner, Ratzinger, Smulders, and other theologians (and biblical scholars) with the bishops in producing a text that embodies some key themes of *ressourcement* theology. Before moving to a similar example, the transformed teaching on the Church that resulted in *Lumen Gentium*, let me summarize five major themes from *ressourcement* theology that *Dei Verbum* incorporated.

(a) First, where manualist theology understood revelation to be the disclosure by God of otherwise unattainable truths, an increase in "supernatural" knowledge making up the "deposit of faith" that is

---

[26] The text in its original Latin with a German translation was published by Elmar Klinger and Klaus Wittstadt, eds., *Glaube im Prozess: Christsein nach dem II. Vatikanum* (Freiburg im Breisgau: Herder, 1984), 33–50.

[27] On the content and influence of the Rahner and Rahner/Ratzinger documents, see Giuseppe Ruggieri, "The First Doctrinal Clash," 236–41, and Wicks, "Vatican II on Revelation," 646–47.

[28] On Garrone and Daniélou, see Wicks, "Vatican II on Revelation," 647–50.

"contained in" the inspired Scriptures and tradition, chapter 1 of *Dei Verbum* interpreted revelation as *primarily* the personal self-revelation of the triune God in Christ, who invites human beings to enter freely into a dialogue of love. As an interpersonal event, revelation evokes a response of faith, understood as a personal commitment of the whole human being inspired by the Holy Spirit (no. 5) and not merely an intellectual assent to the truths now revealed (which the manualists stressed when interpreting faith). *Dei Verbum* presented the divine self-revelation and the history of salvation as inseparably connected and interchangeable (2, 3, 4). To borrow language from St. John's Gospel, the *light* of revelation brings the *life* of salvation, and vice versa.

The climax of this divine self-communication[29] and its signs came with the death and resurrection of Christ, together with the outpouring of the Holy Spirit (no. 4).[30] Through the Spirit the divine revelation given, once and for all, remains a present reality repeatedly actualized (no. 8) until the final consummation of revelation at the end of time (no. 4). Thus *Dei Verbum*, not to mention other documents of Vatican II,[31] understands revelation to be a past, present, and future reality.[32]

---

[29] By speaking of God "manifesting" and "communicating" himself (DV 6), Vatican II introduced into official Catholic teaching the language of divine "self-communication," a term cherished by Rahner for holding together God's self-*revelation* and self-*giving* through saving grace. God's communication is not merely cognitive but constitutes a real self-communication of God that not only makes salvation known but also brings it in person. See Rahner, "Observations on the Concept of Revelation," in Rahner and Ratzinger, *Revelation and Tradition*, 9–25, at 14–15. John Paul II took up the language of divine "self-communication" in his 1980 encyclical *Dives in Misericordia* (no. 7) and then, repeatedly in his 1986 encyclical *Dominum et Vivificantem* (nos. 13, 14, 23, 50, 51, and 58).

[30] Manualist theology lacked any rich, doctrinal appreciation of the revelatory and salvific impact of Christ's resurrection; they left the resurrection aside or at best reduced it to a "proof" that lent credibility to his divine identity. Thus Jésus Solano, who wrote a standard manual on Christology that ran to 326 pages, devoted less than a page to the resurrection: *Sacrae Theologiae Summa*, vol. 3 (Madrid: Biblioteca de Autores Cristianos, 1956).

[31] On the teaching about revelation to be gleaned from other documents of Vatican II, see Gerald O'Collins, *Retrieving Fundamental Theology* (Mahwah, NJ: Paulist Press, 1993), 63–78.

[32] On "Revelation, Past, Present, and Future," see Gerald O'Collins, *Rethinking Fundamental Theology: Toward a New Fundamental Theology* (Oxford: Oxford University Press, 2011), 128–35.

Essentially completed (as to its "content," the "deposit of faith" [no. 10] or the "treasure of revelation entrusted to the Church" [no. 26]) in the past with Christ and the apostolic Church, revelation is repeatedly actualized in the event of human faith until its consummation in the face-to-face encounter with God at the end. Here *ressourcement* theology tells a different story from the manuals, which limited revelation to the past and allowed only for an ongoing understanding and interpretation of such past revelation. This was to ignore what one should draw from Bonaventure (see Ratzinger above) and the logic of faith presented by John's Gospel: since faith is an encounter "now" with God in Christ, so too must revelation be an actual, present self-disclosure of God who invites such faith. As reciprocal realities, faith and revelation occur together.

(b) Second, such teaching on revelation entailed a switch of language: from the manualist terminology of revealed "mysteries" (in the plural) to the terminology of "the mystery" or divine plan now personally disclosed in Christ (no. 2)—the *reductio in mysterium* popularized by Rahner[33] and other *ressourcement* theologians. Talk of "the mystery" forms a major *leitmotif* of *Dei Verbum*: five times this constitution speaks of "mystery" in the singular (nos. 2, 15, 17, 24, and 26) and never of "mysteries" in the plural.

The same tendency shows up in the other texts promulgated by Vatican II: the sixteen documents use "mystery" in the singular 106 times and "mysteries" in the plural only twenty-two times. While not totally avoiding talk of "mysteries" (see UR 11; OT 16), Vatican II preferred to retrieve the biblical language of the "mystery" of the triune God, revealed in the history of salvation and inviting human beings into a new relationship of eternal love (Eph 1:9). For that matter, right from his first encyclical John Paul II exemplified the same tendency. *Redemptor Hominis* (1979) speaks fifty-nine times of "the mystery of redemption," "the paschal mystery," "the mystery of Christ," and so forth, without ever using the term "mystery" in the plural. The pope's second encyclical, *Dives in Misericordia* (1980), uses "mystery" thirty-nine times but "mysteries" only twice.

---

[33] Karl Rahner, "The Concept of Mystery in Catholic Theology," *Theological Investigations*, vol. 4, trans. Kevin Smyth (London: Darton, Longman & Todd, 1966), 36–73, esp. 60–73; German original 1960.

(c) Third, I have already remarked above on the "sacramental" and historical approach that such *ressourcement* theologians as Daniélou and Smulders contributed to *Dei Verbum*. This approach understands revelation to be a living event communicated through words and deeds functioning together in the course of salvation history.

(d) Fourth, the presentation of revelation as primarily an encounter with the self-communicating God put into a new context the whole debate about tradition and sacred Scripture. They are inseparably related in their past origin (the living word of God or divine self-disclosure), present functioning, and future goal (the final revelation to come at the end of history) (DV 9). Revelation, as a living reality, is made known by the inspired Scriptures but cannot be "contained in" anything, not even in the inspired Scriptures.[34]

In 1546 the Council of Trent declared "the gospel" to be "the source of all saving truth and conduct," adding that "this truth and rule of conduct are contained in the written books [of the Bible] and the unwritten [apostolic] traditions" (DzH 1501; ND 210). Despite Trent's language about the gospel (= revelation) being "the source" (in the singular), manualist theology developed the "two-source" theory of revelation, according to which Scripture and tradition are two distinct sources for revealed truths. Tradition could and does supply some truths which are not found in Scripture. In other words, Scripture is not merely "formally insufficient" (= needing to be interpreted and actualized by tradition) but also "materially insufficient" (= not "containing" all revealed truths). This view obviously privileged a propositional notion of revelation: namely, the model of revelation as the communication of truths which would otherwise have remained hidden in God. Although *Dei Verbum* did not explicitly rule out the "two-source theory," that theory is certainly much more difficult to maintain in the face of Vatican II's understanding of revelation (as being primarily God's self-revelation) and its stress on the unity between Scripture and tradition.

(e) Fifth and finally, in great part the product of *ressourcement* thinking, *Dei Verbum* shows a profoundly biblical orientation. It comes as no surprise when it exhorts theologians to make the study of Scriptures the very "soul" of their work (no. 24). This recommendation, taken

---

[34] See Ratzinger, "Revelation and Tradition," 35–37.

from Leo XIII's 1893 encyclical *Providentissimus Deus*, drew on an early Jesuit tradition[35] and the practice of the best medieval theologians, which in their turn reflected the theological method of Church fathers, both Eastern and Western. The prayerful study of the Bible, both Old and New Testaments, was "the very soul" of their teaching; their work, which ran to nearly four hundred volumes in the Migne edition, could be described as one vast commentary on the Scriptures.

While Catholic scholars like Marie-Joseph Lagrange (1855–1938) carried forward critical biblical scholarship, de Lubac and other *ressourcement* figures reintroduced a "spiritual" interpretation of the Scriptures that retrieved the best of the patristic and medieval traditions. In its chapter on the interpretation of the Scriptures, *Dei Verbum* endorsed both critical and "spiritual" interpretation (no. 12).

The biblical component of *ressourcement* flowered, however, in the whole closing chapter of *Dei Verbum*, "Sacred Scripture in the Life of the Church" (nos. 21–26). Here the Council dreamed of the whole Church being nourished by the Bible at every level of her existence. A prayerful knowledge of the Scriptures would foster among all the baptized a living union with Christ and a life centered on him and blessed by the Holy Spirit.

Along with the five themes just described, one could scrutinize further the final text of *Dei Verbum* and note how it embodied other themes from *ressourcement* theology: for instance, a sense of biblical truth as truth "for the sake of our salvation" (no. 11), as well as an endorsement of a three-stage scheme in the formation of the Gospels spelled out in 1964 by the Pontifical Biblical Commission (no. 19). Add too the pastoral tone and ecumenical spirit of *Dei Verbum*, which embodied the desires and hopes of Pope John XXIII for the work of Vatican II. Here one should also honor Congar for having years before set out the pastoral and ecumenical needs of the Church.[36] But let us turn next to the ways in which *ressourcement* theologians, led not only

---

[35] See J. M. Lera, "*Sacrae paginae studium sit veluti anima Sacrae Theologiae* (Notas sobre el origen y procedencia de esta frase)," in *Palabra y Vida. Homenaje a José Alonso Díaz en su 70 cumpleaños*, ed. A. Vargas Machuca and Gregorio Ruiz (Madrid: Universidad Comillas, 1984), 409–22.

[36] Yves Congar, *Divided Christendom: A Catholic Study of the Problem of Reunion*, trans. M. A. Bousfield (London: Geoffrey Bles, 1938; French original 1937); id., *Vraie et fausse réforme dans l'Église* (Paris: Cerf, 1950).

by Congar[37] but also by Gérard Philips, helped transform teaching on the Church.

2. The Doctrine on the Church

Above I recalled how Gagnebet and Tromp, under the watchful direction of Cardinal Ottaviani, led the way in preparing a draft text, *De Ecclesia*. This schema of manualist inspiration highlighted the Church as a hierarchical society rather than as being a mystery and the whole people of God. Falling into line with the 1943 encyclical of Pius XII, *Mystici Corporis*, it identified the Mystical Body of Christ with the Roman Catholic Church and so used the term "church" exclusively of the Roman Catholic Church. In the final days of the first session of Vatican II, this schema was sharply criticized by the bishops (December 1–6, 1962).

Even before that, in October 1962, Cardinal Leo Jozef Suenens had asked Philips to "revise, complete, and improve" this schema on the Church.[38] As a result of the December debate, the schema was removed, and over several months (February–May 1963) a new draft was prepared on the basis of the revised text authored by Philips.[39] For some weeks in the spring of 1963, Congar also worked on the revision that resulted in a fresh draft mailed to the bishops in the middle of the year. In that revised schema, which eventually became the final text of *Lumen Gentium* (November 21, 1964), Congar worked on numbers 9, 13, 16, and 17 in chapter 2 ("The People of God") and contributed to chapter 1 ("The Mystery of the Church").

Number 16 of chapter 2, with its positive regard for Jews, Muslims, and others, prepared the way not only for *Nostra Aetate*, Vatican II's Declaration on the Relation of the Church to Non-Christian Religions (October 28, 1965), but also for a key doctrinal principle on the universal availability of revelation taught by *Ad Gentes*, the Decree on the Church's Missionary Activity (December 7, 1965) (see below). But it was in chapter 1 of *Lumen Gentium* that themes cherished by Congar

[37] See William Henn, "Yves Congar and *Lumen gentium*," *Gregorianum* 86 (2005): 563–92.

[38] Giuseppe Ruggieri, "Beyond an Ecclesiology of Polemics: The Debate on the Church," in *The History of Vatican II*, vol. 2, 281–357, 282–84.

[39] Jan Grootaers, "The Drama Continues between the Acts: The 'Second Preparation' and Its Opponents," in ibid., 359–514, at 399–412.

and other *ressourcement* theologians came through even more clearly. In richly biblical and patristic language, that chapter emphasized the sacramental reality of the Church, from which "shines" the "light" of Christ and which is "the sign and instrument of intimate communion with God and of unity among the whole human race" (no. 1). A full spread of biblical images (no. 6) illuminates "the mystery of the holy Church" (no. 5), which "subsists" (= continues to exist [fully]) in the Roman Catholic Church (no. 8) but is not simply identical with the Roman Catholic Church, as Tromp and other manualists claimed. To be sure, the meaning of "subsists" continues to be disputed, with the Congregation for the Doctrine of the Faith offering over the years varying translations, as Francis Sullivan has pointed out.[40] But the conclusion that the Church of God is not *tout court* identical with the Roman Catholic Church does not simply depend on the translation of *"subsistit"*; it emerges clearly from other passages in Vatican II documents.

Recognizing in this context how "many elements of sanctification and truth" are found outside the "visible" Roman Catholic Church (no. 8), *Lumen Gentium* would go on to specify some of these elements: "believing the Sacred Scripture" to be "the norm of faith and life," belief in the Trinity, and the reception of baptism and "other sacraments in their own Churches or ecclesial communities" (no. 15). Here the Council recognized as "Churches" bodies of Christian not (or not yet) in union with the Roman Catholic Church. Even more specifically in its Decree on Ecumenism (*Unitatis Redintegratio* of November 21, 1964), Vatican II recognized how the principle "the Eucharist makes the Church" operates also for the Eastern Churches not in communion with the Bishop of Rome: "through the celebration of the Eucharist of the Lord in each of these Churches, the Church of God is built up and grows" (no. 15). In other words, while the Church of God continues to exist fully in the Roman Catholic Church, it also continues to exist in other churches or ecclesial communities, above all in the

---

[40] For a magisterial guide to the meaning of "subsists" in this context and some of the controversy surrounding its meaning, see Francis A. Sullivan, "The Meaning of *Subsistit in* as explained by the Congregation of the Doctrine of the Faith," *Theological Studies* 67 (2006): 116–24; id., "A Response to Karl Becker, SJ, on the Meaning of *Subsistit in*," *Theological Studies* 67 (2006): 395–409; id., "Further Thoughts on the Meaning of *Subsistit in*," *Theological Studies* 71 (2010): 133–47.

Eastern Churches, which enjoy almost all the elements of Christian sanctification and truth.

As well as supplying the basic draft that became the eight chapters of *Lumen Gentium*, Philips played a major role, in particular, in developing chapter 4 ("The Laity") and the application of Christ's triple office (of priest, prophet, and king/shepherd) to bishops (and ordained priests), and to all the baptized. The teaching/prophetic, priestly, and pastoral/kingly office of the bishops, which had already appeared in the original schema, was further elaborated in chapter 3 ("The Church is Hierarchical"); the priestly, prophetic, and kingly role of all the baptized was introduced, above all, in chapter 4 ("The Laity"). Philips played a major role in these two developments.[41]

Before the Council opened, both Congar and Philips had written on both the triple office and on the laity. Congar had published a classic study on the laity;[42] and in that book he dedicated chapters 4, 5, and 6 to the way in which laypeople share the priestly, kingly, and prophetical (in that order) functions of Christ. In the year Vatican II opened, Philips published *Pour un christianisme adulte*, in which he expounded the three functions of the laity: "A Priestly, Prophetic, Royal People."[43] Yet, at the Council, neither Congar nor Philips seemed to have been involved, at least directly, with the drafting and emending of the Decree on the Apostolate of Lay People (*Apostolicam Actuositatem* of November 18, 1965). That document spoke of "the priestly, prophetic and kingly office of Christ", in which the laity "share" (no. 2). Consecrated as a "royal priesthood" (no. 3), they participate in "the function of Christ, priest, prophet and king" (no. 10). Congar and Philips had encouraged such a *ressourcement* theme   both of them through their publications and Philips through *Lumen Gentium*, promulgated a year earlier and containing in chapter 4 ("The Laity") a firm endorsement of the priestly, prophetic, and kingly role of all the baptized.

---

[41] Two years after the Council closed, Philips published *L'Église et son mystère au IIe Concile du Vatican: histoire, texte et commentaire de la Constitution "Lumen Gentium,"* 2 vols. (Paris: Desclée, 1967). Philips treats the threefold office of the bishops (1:254–57) and, at greater length, that of the laity (2:31–48).

[42] Yves Congar, *Jalons pour une théologie du laïcat* (Paris: Cerf, 1953); trans. Donald Attwater as *Lay People in the Church: A Study for a Theology of the Laity* (London: Bloomsbury, 1957).

[43] Trans. Eileen Kane as *Achieving Christian Maturity* (Dublin: Gill, 1966), 65–93.

In the genesis of *Lumen Gentium*, Congar had his significant role, but it was Philips who authored the initial draft, secured an entire chapter on the laity,[44] applied the scheme of "priest, prophet, and king/shepherd" to the hierarchy and the laity, defended the collegial character of bishops (who form with the pope an "apostolic college" [nos. 22–23]), and—more than any other expert-consultant—helped to shepherd *Lumen Gentium* through to its final form and promulgation in November 1964.[45]

Apropos of introducing into the Council's documents the *munus triplex* of "priest, prophet, and king," Congar's hand is most visible in the decree *Presbyterorum Ordinis*. He drafted the text (with the help of Joseph Lécuyer and Willy Onclin), was involved in the revisions, and composed the moving conclusion (no. 22). In this document on the ministry and life of ordained priests, numbers 4–6 take up and spell out in detail what the introduction states: "through the sacred ordination and mission that they receive from the bishops, priests are promoted to serve Christ the *Teacher, Priest*, and *King*" (no. 1; emphasis added). Number 4 details what is involved in priests being "ministers of God's Word"; number 5 expounds their function as "ministers of the sacraments and the Eucharist"; and number 6 describes their role as kingly "rulers of God's people" and "pastors" of the Church.

The triple office of Christ as priest, prophet, and king, in which all the faithful share through baptism and some through ministerial ordination, is a major theme of the 1964 Dogmatic Constitution on the Church and of two decrees that depended upon it and were promulgated in 1965: the Decree on the Apostolate of the Lay People and the Decree on the Ministry and Life of Priests. *Ressourcement* theology, represented by Congar and Philips, had retrieved this theme of the *munus triplex* from traditional and biblical sources. One can trace it back through John Henry Newman, John Calvin, Thomas Aquinas, and various fathers of the Church to its roots in the Scriptures, both Old Testament and New Testament.[46]

---

[44] In the Gagnebet-Tromp, 1962 schema *De Ecclesia*, Philips had largely authored the chapter on the laity. He tweaked this chapter a little for the revised text adopted in March 1963 that became the new base-text for *Lumen Gentium*.

[45] See Alberigo and Komonchak, eds., *History of Vatican II*, vols. 2–4, *passim*.

[46] See Gerald O'Collins and Michael Keenan Jones, *Jesus Our Priest: A Christian Approach to the Priesthood of Christ* (Oxford: Oxford University Press, 2010), *passim*.

3. Divine Revelation to All

This third section will address more briefly one further *ressourcement* theme that, thanks to Congar, found its place in the teaching of Vatican II: God's self-revelation to all people.

Sharply different views of Christian missionary activity led to many difficulties in the drafting, discussion, and revision of *Ad Gentes*.[47] At the end, however, 2,394 fathers voted yes and only five voted no—a dramatic tribute to the work of Congar and other experts in developing the Decree on the Church's Missionary Activity. He played a major role in developing the decree and, especially, in composing chapter 1 ("Doctrinal Principles"), his own work "from A to Z," as he put it.[48] This is the longest of the six chapters that make up *Ad Gentes*, as well as including more sources (cited or referred to) in the footnotes than all the other chapters put together. "The patristic references are particularly numerous and excellently chosen," Heinrich Suso Brechter wrote, "whereas the following chapters quote almost exclusively from conciliar texts and papal allocutions."[49] In a *tour de force* Congar quoted or referred to twenty-three fathers of the Church, some of them, like Irenaeus and Augustine, more than once, retrieving remarkable texts that illuminate principles that give life to the Church's missionary activity, itself based in the missionary activity of the Trinity for the salvation of human beings. Let me cite an example that concerns the divine self-revelation to all people.

To explain "the preparation for the Gospel" (no. 3), footnote two quotes two passages from Irenaeus' *Adversus Haereses*: "the Word existing with God, through whom all things were made . . . was always present to the human race"; hence "from the beginning the Son, being present in his creation, reveals (*revelat*) the Father to all whom the Father desires, at the time and in the manner desired by the Father" (*Adversus Haereses*, 3.18.1; 4.6.7). Thus *Ad Gentes* aligns itself with Irenaeus in recognizing the Word as the agent of all creation (see John 1:1-3, 10; 1 Cor 8:6; Col 1:16; Heb 1:2). Consequently the Word has

---

[47] See Heinrich Suso Brechter, "Decree on the Church's Missionary Activity," trans. W. J. O'Hara, in *Commentary on the Documents of Vatican II*, vol. 4 (1969), 87–181, at 98–111.

[48] Congar, *My Journal of the Council*, 870–71.

[49] Brechter, "Decree on the Church's Missionary Activity," 113.

"always" been "present to the human race," and not merely to certain groups or nations.[50]

Granted the Christological origin and character of creation, right "from the beginning" of human history the Son has been "revealing" the Father to human beings. In all the sixteen documents it is only here that Vatican II applies the verb "reveal" to the knowledge of God mediated through the created world. Clearly this revelation of God through creation and "ordinary" human history allows for endless variety, as "the Son reveals the Father to all whom the Father desires [and] at the time and in the manner desired by the Father." In contemporary terms, Irenaeus was speaking of the "general" history of revelation (and salvation), in which from the beginning of the human story the Son of God has been revealing the Father.

The two quotations from Irenaeus highlight the universal divine activity by which the word/Son of God was preparing people for the coming of the Gospel. The use of the term "reveal" implies the counterpart of faith: it is with true faith that human beings can respond to the initiative of the Son of God present in and through creation and revealing God to them.[51] The divine quest for all human beings takes precedence over any human quest for God. It is primarily due to this divine initiative and not to a human search that "elements of *truth* and *grace*," which constitute "a secret presence of God," are already found among peoples before they are evangelized and can accept Christ explicitly (AG 9; emphasis added).

The Decree on the Church's Missionary Activity echoes what had been said a year earlier in *Lumen Gentium* about those who had "arrived at an explicit recognition of God and who, not without divine grace, strive to live an upright life": "Whatever *goodness and truth* that

---

[50] From the time of Justin Martyr, this real but hidden presence of the Word *in* the created world and *to* the human race went under the name of "the seeds of the Word" (e.g., AG 11), another rich theme retrieved by *ressourcement* theology. See Jean Daniélou, *A History of Early Christian Doctrine*, vol. 2, *Gospel Message and Hellenistic Culture*, trans. John A. Baker (London: Darton, Longman & Todd, 1973), 41–44.

[51] This point (a faith response to revelation made by the non-evangelized) is expressly acknowledged in the chapter of AG for which Congar was responsible: "in ways known to himself God can lead those who, through no fault of their own, are ignorant of the Gospel to that faith without which it is impossible to please him (Heb 11:6)" (no. 7).

is found among them is considered by the Church to be a preparation for the Gospel and *given by Him who enlightens all human beings* that they may at length have life" (no. 16; emphasis added). As we noted above, Congar helped shape this article of *Lumen Gentium* about God preparing people for evangelization.[52]

Conclusions

I have concentrated on examples from *Dei Verbum*, *Lumen Gentium*, and *Ad Gentes* to illustrate the way in which *ressourcement* theology represented by Congar, Daniélou, Philips, Smulders, and others contributed to the making of the Vatican II's teaching. One could add many further examples and further names. Let me mention only three further items.

First, Marie-Dominique Chenu had retrieved, ultimately from the New Testament, the language of "the signs of the times" (Matt 16:3).[53] The last and longest document from Vatican II, the Pastoral Constitution on the Church in the Modern World (*Gaudium et Spes* of December 7, 1965) picked up this theme: "the Church carries the responsibility of scrutinizing the signs of the times and interpreting them in the light of the Gospel" (no. 4). It is the whole "people of God," led "by the Spirit of the Lord that fills the whole world," who try "to discern" in "the events, the needs, and the longings that it shares with other human beings of our age," what "may be true signs of the presence or of the purpose of God" (no. 11).

Second, the Decree on Ecumenism, *Unitatis Redintegratio*, included the important observation that "there exists an order or 'hierarchy' among the truths of Catholic doctrine" (no. 11). All truths of Catholic doctrine are important, but some truths (e.g., the Trinity and the

---

[52] On salvation and revelation being available outside the visible Church and on the Church's role in the divine plan for humanity, see Gabriel Flynn, *Yves Congar's Vision of the Church in a World of Unbelief* (Aldershot: Ashgate, 2004), 39–51.

[53] See Marie-Dominique Chenu, *Le Saulchoir: Une école de la théologie* (Paris: Étoilles, 1937), 142; id., "Les Signes des temps," in *L'Église dans le monde de ce temps: Constitution pastoral "Gaudium et Spes,"* ed. Yves Congar and Michel Peuchmaurd (Paris: Cerf, 1967), 205–25. Citing Matt 16:3, John XXIII introduced the theme of "the signs of the times" in his 1962 "bull" of convocation for Vatican II, *Humanae Salutis*, and a year later in the encyclical *Pacem in Terris* (nos. 126–29), but there no evidence that the pope directly drew this theme from Chenu.

incarnation) are more fundamental than others (e.g., the primacy of the Bishop of Rome). Even if Congar did not work on the drafting of that decree, he helped to originate the principle of a "hierarchy of truths," a principle ultimately based on his retrieval of the notion of truth and truths developed by Thomas Aquinas.[54]

Third, among the pioneering works of *ressourcement* theology, de Lubac's *Catholicism*[55] is preeminent. It came about when Congar invited de Lubac to put together some articles into a book published by the *Unam Sanctam* series, directed at the time by Congar himself. Some of the language of what became a classic article in *Gaudium et Spes* (and was to be cited by John Paul II) about Christ revealing human beings to themselves and all human beings being called to the "same destiny" (no. 22) echoed what de Lubac had written.[56]

Called by Pope John XXIII of blessed memory, Vatican II was the most significant religious event in the twentieth century. One generation has now passed, and a second is well established since the Council ended in 1965. Its teaching is still being received and tested in the lives of believers. In major ways that teaching was shaped by theologians of the *ressourcement* movement: Chenu, Congar, Daniélou, de Lubac, Philips, Rahner, Ratzinger, Smulders, and others. They left the whole Christian Church a life-giving legacy in what they retrieved from the Scriptures and the great tradition for the documents of Vatican II.

But how did the changes brought by this retrieval affect the identity of the worldwide Church? Did Vatican II bring discontinuity with the past, or did it rather strengthen a deeper continuity with apostolic Christianity? To that issue we turn in the next chapter.

[54] See William Henn, *The Hierarchy of Truths According to Yves Congar, OP* (Rome: Gregorian University Press, 1987).

[55] Trans. Lancelot C. Sheppard and Elizabeth Englund (San Francisco: Ignatius Press, 1988); French original, *Catholicisme: Les aspects sociaux du dogme* (Paris: Cerf, 1947).

[56] Ibid., 299 and 339. Paul McPartlan drew attention to this similarity in *Sacrament of Salvation: An Introduction to Eucharistic Ecclesiology* (Edinburgh: T. & T. Clark, 1995), 74; see also id., "John Paul II and Vatican II," in *The Vision of John Paul II: Assessing His Thought and Influence*, ed. Gerard Mannion (Collegeville, MN: Liturgical Press, 2008), 45–61, at 49–51.

Chapter 2

Does the Second Vatican Council Represent Continuity or Discontinuity?

On the occasion of the fiftieth anniversary of the Second Vatican Council (1962–65), publications, conferences, and other events have continued to probe and celebrate the Council's achievements. What has the Council represented in the history of Christianity, and how should it be evaluated? The Council obviously brought far-reaching changes within the life of the Catholic Church and in her relationship with "the others." Has this change involved discontinuity with past teaching and practice? Or are the changes compatible with claims about Vatican II being in (total?) continuity with what went before? An address by Benedict XVI to the Roman Curia on December 22, 2005 reinvigorated the debate about this issue.[1]

---

[1] AAS 98 (2006) 40–53; trans. as "Interpreting Vatican II: Address to the Roman Curia," *Origins* (January 28, 2006): 534–39. Apropos of this address, see Massimo Faggioli, *Vatican II: The Battle for Meaning* (Mahwah, NJ: Paulist Press, 2012), 109–12; Joseph A. Komonchak, "Novelty in Continuity: Pope Benedict's Interpretation of Vatican II," *America* (February 2, 2009): 10–16. An expanded version of this article ("Benedict XVI and the Interpretation of Vatican II") is found in Michael J. Lacey and Francis Oakley, eds., *The Crisis of Authority in Catholic Modernity* (New York: Oxford University Press, 2011), 93–110; the section of the pope's address that concerns interpreting Vatican II is reprinted in ibid., 357–62. See also John W. O'Malley, "Vatican II: Did Anything Happen?," *Theological Studies* 67 (2006): 3–33; id., *What Happened at Vatican II* (Cambridge, MA: Belknap Press of Harvard University Press, 2008); Neil Ormerod, "Vatican II—Continuity or Discontinuity? Toward an Ontology of Meaning," *Theological Studies* 67 (2010): 609–36.

In that address the pope contrasted two contrary hermeneutics: "a hermeneutic of discontinuity and rupture," over against "a hermeneutic of reform, of renewal in the continuity of the subject-church that the Lord has given us. She is the subject that increases in time and develops yet always remains the same." Yet he went on to bring together discontinuity, reform, and continuity, but not rupture when he said: "it is precisely" in a "combination of continuity and discontinuity at different levels that the very nature of reform consists."[2]

How might we understand and interpret continuity and discontinuity, as well as the closely related language of reform, renewal, review, revision, or rupture? What reasons have we to recognize continuity and discontinuity? We should pay adequate attention to *both* continuity *and* discontinuity,[3] unlike some contributors to *Vatican II: Renewal within Tradition* who failed to face up to the elements of discontinuity found in the sixteen documents of Vatican II.[4] Renewal and innovation are unthinkable without some measure of discontinuity, at least discontinuity with the recent or not so recent past. We need to examine in detail those texts if we are going to construct a well-founded position on the continuity and/or discontinuity that they embody. No position here will be convincing unless it recognizes the amount of change Vatican II ushered in. To introduce the discussion, let us turn first to what the Council itself had to say about continuity and discontinuity in the changes it mandated, and examine, in particular, three of its sixteen documents.

---

[2] Benedict XVI, "Interpreting Vatican II," 536, 538. As Komonchak remarks, "a hermeneutics of reform, it turns out, acknowledges some important discontinuities" ("Novelty in Continuity," 13). Without some discontinuity, there could not be any reform. Moreover, unless discontinuity amounts to *total* discontinuity, there could not be any real rupture or complete break. For a rich, historical reflection on the language of reform(ation), its partial equivalents, and its use by the pope in his December 2005 address, see John W. O'Malley, "'The Hermeneutic of Reform': A Historical Analysis," *Theological Studies* 73 (2012): 517–46.

[3] See Ormond Rush, *Still Interpreting Vatican II: Some Hermeneutical Principles* (Mahwah, NJ: Paulist Press, 2004), 79–80.

[4] Matthew L. Lamb and Matthew Levering, eds., *Vatican II: Renewal within Tradition* (New York: Oxford University Press, 2008); see Komonchak, "Benedict XVI and the Interpretation of Vatican II," 110, n. 22; and id., "Rewriting History," *Commonweal* (January 30, 2009): 22–24.

What the Council Said about Changes

1. The Constitution on the Sacred Liturgy

The first document to be approved and promulgated by Vatican II was the Constitution on the Sacred Liturgy, *Sacrosanctum Concilium* (December 4, 1963). It was in the liturgical changes prescribed by the Council and introduced later that the question of continuity/discontinuity would become most visible. How did Vatican II understand and express what it was doing in changing the liturgy and revising the rites?

When commenting on the constitution, Josef Jungmann wrote of its aiming at the "renewal of liturgical life," the "revival" and "reform" of the liturgy, and, in particular, the "reform of the Mass."[5] Yet, while closely related and often overlapping, "renewal," "revival," and "reform" are not strictly synonyms, if indeed any completely synonymous terms ever truly exist. Let us look at the terms used by the Council to describe its teaching on the liturgy and the changes ushered in by that teaching.[6]

In one place *Sacrosanctum Concilium* speaks of "reviewing/revising [*recognoscantur*]" the rites and "giving them new vigour [*novo vigore donentur*]" (no. 4). In another article, it prescribes that the "prayer of the faithful" should "be restored [*restituatur*]" (no. 53). But the term favored by the constitution was *instaurare*, which means "to renew" or "to restore."

Thus the very first article of *Sacrosanctum Concilium* speaks of the Council's commitment "to renew and foster the Liturgy [*instaurandam*

---

[5] Josef Jungmann, "Constitution on the Sacred Liturgy," trans. L. Adolphus, in *Commentary on the Documents of Vatican II*, ed. H. Vorgrimler, vol. 1 (London: Burns & Oates, 1967), 1–88, at 2, 6, 8, 31.

[6] SC, as M. Faggioli has argued, proved to be a "pillar" of the Council's eucharistic ecclesiology (*Ecclesia de Eucharistia*) which has rediscovered "the centrality of the Scripture" and, one can add, the central image of the Church as the (worshipping) People of God (see SC 33). Faggioli also recognizes how the liturgical constitution prepared the way for the *rapprochement* manifestoes of Vatican II (UR, NA, and GS) and initiated the Council's *ressourcement* procedure. In short, he champions "a hermeneutics of the Council based on *Sacrosanctum Concilium*." See M. Faggioli, "*Sacrosanctum Concilium* and the Meaning of Vatican II," *Theological Studies* 71 (2010): 337–52, at 350–52; see the next chapter of this book for a discussion of Faggioli's thesis.

atque fovendam Liturgiam]."[7] In reverse order the two verbs recur in article 3, when the constitution indicates that it will introduce principles and norms concerned "with the fostering and renewing of the Liturgy [*de fovenda atque instauranda Liturgia*]." Chapter 1 puts the same verbs into its title: "On general principles for the renewal and fostering of the sacred Liturgy [*De principiis generalibus ad sacram Liturgiam instaurandam atque fovendam*]." Later, in article 21 of chapter 1, *Sacrosanctum Concilium* uses the noun *instauratio* when indicating its "desire to undertake with great care the general renewal of the Liturgy itself [*ipsius Liturgiae generalem instaurationem sedulo curare cupit*]." Similar words provide the heading for section three: "on the renewal of the sacred Liturgy [*de sacrae Liturgiae instauratione*]." But two translations, those edited by Walter Abbott (with Joseph Gallagher) and Austin Flannery, both render the chapter heading as "the Reform of the Sacred Liturgy."[8] The translation edited by Norman Tanner rightly makes the heading "the renewal of the liturgy," but then presses on to render *Liturgiae generalem instaurationem* as "a general reform of the liturgy" (825). The constitution prefers, however, to present its task in the language of *instaurare* and *instauratio* and not in that of *reformare* or *reformatio*.

The Decree on Ecumenism, *Unitatis Redintegratio*, promulgated a year after the liturgical constitution, famously introduced the terminology of "reformation" when calling not only for a "renewal [*renovatio*]" of the

---

[7] *The Documents of Vatican II*, ed. Walter M. Abbott and Joseph Gallagher (London: Geoffrey Chapman, 1965), translates the passage as providing for "the renewal and fostering of the liturgy" (137). In Austin Flannery, ed., *Vatican II: The Conciliar and Post Conciliar Documents*, rev. ed. (Northport, NY: Costello Publishing Company, 1988), this becomes undertaking "the reform and promotion of the liturgy" (1). But the original text does not read *"reformandam atque promovendam liturgiam."* In Norman Tanner, ed., *Decrees of the Ecumenical Councils*, vol. 2 (London/Washington, DC: Sheed & Ward/Georgetown University Press, 1990), the phrase is rendered as "the renewal and growth of the liturgy" (820), and then *"de fovenda atque instauranda Liturgia"* (art. 3) is translated as "the renewal and progress of the liturgy" (820). But *fovere* means "foster" or "nourish"; its result can be "growth" and "progress." As I remain somewhat dissatisfied with the Abbott, Flannery, and Tanner translations, I prefer to translate the Council's texts for myself.

[8] Flannery (9) follows Abbott (146) in rendering *Liturgiae generalem instaurationem* as "a general restoration of the liturgy," and, when *instauratione* recurs later in art. 21, again both render it as "restoration." Where SC puts "Liturgy" in uppercase, Abbott, Flannery, and Tanner persistently reduce it to lowercase.

Church but also for her "constant reformation [*perennem reformationem*]" (no. 6). The lexical meaning of the Latin *reformare* is (a) "to transform" or "change radically for the better" and (b) simply and less dramatically, "to restore." Inevitably, however, in *Unitatis Redintegratio*, a decree dealing in part with Churches and ecclesial communities that came into existence in the sixteenth century, to speak of "reformation" inevitably conjures up nuances of "improving by removing faults and errors."

Putting matters within the focus of this chapter, however, one can ask: where the decision is taken through the liturgical constitution to give up some things, remove certain faults and even errors, and change matters radically for the better, are we not facing a situation of "reformation"? Without using the explicit language of "reformation" or "reform," *Sacrosanctum Concilium* gave up certain things (e.g., the obligatory use of the Latin language in the Roman rite, no. 36), prescribed the removal of such faulty things as "useless repetitions" in the liturgy (no. 34; see no. 50), and wanted to change liturgical matters radically for the better by, for instance, introducing the Scriptures more abundantly and with a better representation from all "the treasures of the Bible" (no. 51). In fact, by allowing the liturgy to be celebrated in the vernacular, by stressing "the table of God's word," along with the importance of the homily (no. 52), and by granting to the laity, under certain circumstances, communion "under both kinds" (no. 55), Vatican II conceded the demands of Martin Luther and other sixteenth-century Protestant reformers, albeit in the twentieth century. In short, while the liturgical constitution did not use explicitly the language of "reform" or "reformation," what it enacted can and should be described in those terms.[9]

In pressing for the renewal (or reform) of the liturgy, *Sacrosanctum Concilium* prescribed a revision "according to the mind of healthy tradition (*ad mentem sanae traditionis*)," which might give the rites new vigour "for the sake of today's circumstances and needs" (no. 4). The twin principles recurred in a later article, which spoke of both "retaining healthy tradition" and "opening the way to legitimate progress" (no. 23). This was to set up two procedures: retrieving healthy tradition

---

[9] Hence recent calling into question some changes mandated by SC have been widely called "the reform of the reform"; see Faggioli, *Vatican II: The Battle for Meaning*, 102–5.

inherited from the past and discerning what present conditions call for. Thus the two procedures, retrieval (*ressourcement*) and updating to meet pastoral needs in the new contexts of the modern world (the *aggiornamento* that John XXIII invited when convoking the Council), featured right in the introduction to the first document promulgated by Vatican II (SC 4). Some people continue to present "retrieval" and "aggiornamento" as if they were opposed principles and procedures. But this is a mistake: remembering and recovering forgotten or neglected teaching and practice from the Scriptures and the great tradition serve the Church's adaptation in the present and progress into the future. The postconciliar liturgical changes offer spectacular examples of the two procedures working in tandem: for instance, the Second Eucharistic Prayer retrieved from the *Apostolic Tradition* of St. Hippolytus (d. around 236);[10] the restoration of the ancient Rite of Christian Initiation of Adults (SC 64); and the reintroduction of the "prayer of the faithful," based on 1 Timothy 2:1-2 and now restored after the gospel and homily (SC 53). The process of "retrieval" concerns a major resource for renewal, whereas the task of *aggiornamento* may include "retrieval" but always involves discerning what should be changed and what should be introduced as being pastorally desirable. Thus *ressourcement* and *aggiornamento*, far from being in competition, are different but complementary principles and procedures, with the former often, but not always, making a major contribution to the latter.[11]

These two principles could be translated in terms of inherited *tradition* and contemporary *experience*. *Sacrosanctum Concilium* prescribes taking into account "the general laws of the structure and intention" of the liturgy (which obviously derive from Christian tradition), and doing so in the light of "the experience coming from more recent liturgical renewal" (art. 23). The spirit of *ressourcement* encourages retrieving healthy traditions that have fallen into abeyance,[12] while

[10] See "The Apostolic Tradition," in *The Oxford Dictionary of the Christian Church*, ed. F. L. Cross and E. A. Livingstone, 3rd ed. (Oxford: Oxford University Press, 2005), 92. Some scholars date *The Apostolic Tradition*, at least in part, to the fourth century.

[11] See Gabriel Flynn and Paul Murray, eds., *Ressourcement. A Movement for Renewal in Twentieth-Century Catholic Theology* (Oxford: Oxford University Press, 2012).

[12] Thus SC prescribed that valuable elements in the rites, which had been "lost" over the centuries, "should be restored [*restituantur*]" (no. 50).

the spirit of *aggiornamento* encourages discerning the life-giving, contemporary experience of liturgy and other areas of Christian life and practice, and promoting such experience.

When introducing norms for the renewal (or reform) of the liturgy and, in particular, what *aggiornamento* entailed, *Sacrosanctum Concilium* distinguished in the liturgy between (a) "a part that cannot be changed, inasmuch as it is divinely instituted [*parte immutabili, utpote divinitus instituta*]," and (b) "parts that are subject to change [*partibus mutationi obnoxiis*]." Apropos of (b), the constitution added at once that these parts can and indeed ought to be changed, "if by chance there have crept into them things that might respond less well to the inner nature of the liturgy or that might have become less suitable [than they once were]." After dealing with elements that might be inappropriate or unsuitable, the document pressed ahead to express what it positively expected from the renewal of the rites. They should, in their revised form, "express more clearly [*clarius exprimant*] the holy things that they signify," so that "the Christian people" can "understand [these things] easily and share in them through a community celebration that is full, active and proper" (no. 21). In this way *Sacrosanctum Concilium* set out the principles governing the changes in the liturgy that a discerning *aggiornamento* calls for.[13]

The document came back to these principles when treating in chapter 3 the sacraments (other than the Eucharist) and the sacramentals. It noted how "in the course of time, there have crept into the rites of the sacraments and sacramentals certain things by which their nature and purpose have become less clear [*minus eluceant*] in our days." Hence "there is much more need to adapt certain things in them [the rites] to the needs of our age" (no. 62). With the aim of purging what is unsuitable and fails to communicate clearly and of adapting to the needs of our times (*aggiornamento*), the constitution then enjoined

---

[13] In "Theologischer Kommentar zur Konstitution über die heilige Liturgie, *Sacrosanctum Concilium*," *Herders Theologischer Kommentar zum Zweiten Vatikanischen Konzil*, ed. Peter Hünermann and Bernd Jochen Hilberath, vol. 2 (Freiburg im Breisgau: Herder, 2004), Reiner Kaczynski sums up the prescriptions of SC 21: "the outer form of the liturgical celebration must allow its inner content to be experienced, in order that the community can in the easiest way possible grasp [this content] and celebrate the divine service with a fuller, more active, and more community [oriented] participation" (87; trans. mine).

that the rites of baptism, confirmation, penance, the "anointing of the sick" (a new name to replace "extreme unction"), ordination, marriage, and various sacramentals (e.g., the rites for burial) should be "reviewed/revised [*recognoscantur*]" (nos. 66–82). Over and over again the reason given for such changes was to let significant elements at the heart of the rites "become clearer [*magis pateant*]" (no. 67), to indicate them "more openly and more suitably [*apertius et congruentius*]" (no. 69), to express them "more clearly [*clarius*]" (no. 72), and to "signify more clearly [*clarius*] the grace of the sacrament" (no. 77). The desire for the rites to exercise more successfully their pedagogical function motivated and fashioned the far-reaching changes being prescribed.

Finally, two further principles were consciously operative to shape the changes the constitution envisaged. First, there were to be "no innovations unless a true and certain advantage of the Church requires it [*innovationes ne fiant nisi vera et certa utilitas Ecclesiae id exigat*]." In other words, changes were not to be admitted unless obvious needs demanded them; and still less did the constitution tolerate change for its own sake. Second (and more importantly for the scope of what we are examining), "new forms should in some way *grow organically* from the already existing forms [*novae formae ex formis iam exstantibus organice quodammodo crescent*]" (no. 23; emphasis added).[14]

The first principle enshrines the good sense expressed by the proverbial wisdom of the question: "If it works, why fix it?" The second moves us toward Blessed John Henry Newman's first "note of a genuine development, preservation of type," which is "readily suggested by the analogy of physical growth." Newman explains this analogy of organic development as follows: "the parts and proportions of the developed form, however altered, correspond to those which belong to its rudiments. The adult animal has the same make as it had on its birth; young birds do not grow into fishes, nor does the child degenerate into the brute, wild or domestic, of which he is by inheritance lord." To clinch his case, Newman quotes St. Vincent of Lerins who adopted the same analogy to illustrate the development of doctrine:

---

[14] When commenting on SC 23, Kaczynski, has nothing to say about the "organic" analogy of development; he contents himself with remarking that "liturgical renewal stands in the field of tension between the preservation of healthy tradition and courageous, justified progress" ("*Sacrosanctum Concilium*," 89; trans. mine).

"Let the soul's religion imitate the law of the body, which, as years go on, develops indeed and opens out its due proportions, and yet remains identically what it was. Small are the baby's limbs, a youth's are larger, yet they are the same."[15] Thus organic growth illustrates classically how, along with many obvious changes in size, in the capacity to do things, and in other regards, animals, birds, and human beings remain the same, identical beings. While passing through radical alterations, a certain correspondence persists between their rudimentary shape and their mature form. An unbroken succession or organic continuity links together the different stages of their lives and maintains their uninterrupted identity. Along with innumerable "alterations," which we might call secondary discontinuities, at no point do they suffer a radical discontinuity, a deep break or "rupture" that would sever the connection with their past and cause them to go out of existence.

To sum up, *Sacrosanctum Concilium* never explicitly raises the question of continuity versus discontinuity. Nevertheless, on the one hand, the comprehensive and far-reaching changes it mandates cannot be reconciled with any thesis of total continuity. On the other hand, it obviously rules out any suggestion of total discontinuity, in particular by insisting that "the divinely instituted part of the liturgy cannot be changed."[16] After mediating between tradition (*ressourcement*) and experience (from which discerning eyes can draw suitable and even necessary changes), the constitution aims at giving the rites new vigor and enhancing their pedagogical function. Throughout, *Sacrosanctum Concilium* embodies a deep pastoral desire to renew the Church by renewing her liturgy. Like a growing organism, the liturgy can preserve an unbroken continuity with the past, but it will be a continuity amenable to widespread external adaptations and inner changes.

---

[15] John Henry Newman, *An Essay on the Development of Christian Doctrine* (New York: Doubleday, 1960), 177; Newman cites Vincent's *Commonitorium*, 9. After proposing "preservation of type" as his first "note of a genuine development," Newman suggests a second, which also enjoys obvious relevance to the issue of appropriate liturgical change: "the continuity of principles" (*Essay*, 183–89), or what he calls "the continuous identity of principles" (309–36, at 312).

[16] SC does not specify what comes under such a "divinely instituted part," but presumably it would include, for example, the trinitarian formula of baptism (Matt 28:19).

2. The Decree on the Up-to-Date Renewal of Religious Life

In the immediate aftermath of the Second Vatican Council, Friedrich Wulf wrote prophetically about one major area of renewal: "the Decree on the Appropriate Renewal of Religious Life, despite its shortness and shortcomings, is a turning point in the history of religious orders" and "will, indeed, initiate that turning, the full sweep of which cannot yet be seen."[17] Whatever we conclude if we work our way through the stories of various religious institutes over the past fifty years, Wulf was correct in observing that the decree, *Perfectae Caritatis*, introduced into those institutes "a new theological and spiritual mentality."[18] In fashioning and promoting such a mentality, this decree clearly endorsed two principles for change: *ressourcement* and *aggiornamento*. It emphasized that "an updated renewal of religious life comprises *both* a continual return to the sources of the whole Christian life and to the original inspiration of the institutes *and* their adaptation to the changed conditions of the times." Starting from the "supreme rule," "the following of Christ proposed in the Gospel," the decree spelled out norms for this renewal, which should be "promoted under the impulse of the Holy Spirit and the guidance of the Church" (no. 2; emphasis added).

The role of *ressourcement* comes into view constantly. Apropos of the prayer life for religious men and women, *Perfectae Caritatis* recommends that they should "draw from the fitting sources of Christian spirituality." That means drawing not only from the Eucharist but also from daily contact with "the Sacred Scripture, so that by reading and meditating on the divine scriptures they might learn the surpassing knowledge of Jesus Christ (Phil. 3:8)" (no. 6). The return to the sources also involves "faithfully recognizing and observing the spirit and particular aims of the founders, as well as the healthy traditions; all of these constitute the patrimony of each institute" (no. 2).

While stressing the indispensable role of "spiritual renewal" (PC 2), the decree called on religious to take into account "the conditions of the

---

[17] Friedrich Wulf, "Decree on the Appropriate Renewal of the Religious Life," trans. Roland Walls, in *Commentary on the Documents of Vatican II*, vol. 2 (1968), 301–70, at 370.

[18] Ibid., 330. See also the way Joachim Schmiedl has characterized PC as one component in a larger paradigm shift to be found in Vatican II: Schmiedl, *Das Konzil und die Orden: Krise und Erneuerung des Gottgeweihten Lebens* (Vallendar-Schönstatt: Patis Verlag, 1999), 472.

times," "the needs of the Church" (no. 2), "the present-day physical and psychological condition of the members," "the requirements of the culture" (no. 3), and so forth. All of this amounted to acknowledging the place of *aggiornamento* in changing the legislation and customs that guide the life of religious institutes. *Perfectae Caritatis* spoke of "right updating/adaptation [*recta accommodatio*]" and of "the norms of an updated/adapted renewal [*normas accomodatae renovationis*]" (no. 4).

"Up-to-date renewal [*accommodata renovatio*]" entered, of course, into the very title of the decree. The Abbott translation renders the two Latin words as "the Appropriate Renewal," whereas the Tanner version moves further away from the Latin and has "the Sensitive Renewal." Flannery's "the Up-to-date Renewal" opens up memories of John XXIII's call for *aggiornamento* and fills out what kind of "*accommodatio* [updating/adapting]" was intended. The words from the title, "up-to-date renewal [*accommodata renovatio*]," were to recur once in article 2 and twice in article 4.

Perfectae Caritatis initiated wide-ranging changes in religious life. Whatever one's verdict on those changes in postconciliar history, Vatican II fashioned the decree in the light of two principles: *ressourcement* and *aggiornamento*, which amounted to retrieving life giving traditions and acting on a prayerful discernment of present experience. As with *Sacrosanctum Concilium*, these two principles brought about continuity-in-discontinuity, or what Newman might call "preservation of type" in a situation of far-reaching development.

3. Declaration on Religious Freedom

A third Vatican II document not only introduced change but also explicitly reflected, albeit more briefly, on the dramatic change it was mandating. In *Dignitatis Humanae*, promulgated on December 7, 1965, according to Basil Mitchell, the Catholic Church "finally abandoned the traditional doctrine that 'error has no rights' and embraced a more liberal theory based upon the rights of the person, and the individual's duty to follow his conscience."[19] This Declaration on Religious Freedom

---

[19] Basil Mitchell, "The Christian Conscience," in *The Oxford Illustrated History of Christianity*, ed. John McManners (Oxford: Oxford University Press, 1990), 602–27, at 602–3.

went through six drafts before being finally approved on the last working day of the Council, with 2,308 votes in favor and seventy votes against. An article that appeared in the Turin-based daily paper *La Stampa* spoke, not of the Church "abandoning" a traditional doctrine and "embracing" a "more liberal theory," but of a development of doctrine: "the schema which deals with religious freedom constitutes by itself a genuine development of doctrine, perhaps the greatest and most characteristic progress achieved by the Council."[20]

In teaching the right of individuals to religious liberty—that is to say, their freedom in civil society to worship God according to their conscience—the Council "intended to develop [*evolvere*] the teaching of more recent popes about the inviolable rights of the human person and about the juridical regulation of society" (no. 1). The declaration ended by calling this religious freedom "the greatest of the duties and rights of human beings" (no. 15). When, however, we recall how the *Syllabus of Errors*, published by Pius IX in 1864, excluded public religious freedom, how could the Council allege that its declaration represented a development in official teaching? In a footnote that accompanied article 2, *Dignitatis Humanae* cited prior teaching by John XXIII, Pius XII, Pius XI, and Leo XIII. But, pointedly, it did not attempt to enlist any support from Pius IX. The "more recent popes" stopped at Leo XIII (pope 1878–1903). *Dignitatis Humanae*, when set over against the *Syllabus of Errors*, looks more like a reversal rather than a development of doctrine.[21]

In the *Syllabus of Errors*, Pius IX had condemned the proposition that "everyone is free to embrace and profess the religion which by the light of reason one judges to be true" (DzH 2915; ND 1013/15). Compare this with the statement from *Dignitatis Humanae* that "the

---

[20] Quoted by Pietro Pavan, "Declaration on Religious Freedom," trans. Hilda Graef, in *Commentary on Vatican II*, vol. 4 (1969), 49–86, at 62. For a thorough treatment of the making of DH, see Silvia Scatena, *La fatica della libertà: l'elaborazione della dichiarazione "Dignitatis humanae" sulla libertà umana del Vaticano II* (Bologna: Il Mulino, 2003).

[21] See Francis A. Sullivan, "Catholic Tradition and Traditions," in *The Crisis of Authority in Catholic Modernity*, 113–33, at 126–27. Cardinal Ratzinger called DH, along with NA and GS, "a revision of the *Syllabus* of Pius IX, a kind of counter syllabus" (*Principles of Catholic Theology: Building Stones for a Fundamental Theology*, trans. Mary Frances McCarthy [San Francisco: Ignatius Press, 1987], 381).

human person has the right to religious freedom" (no. 1). The *Syllabus* rejected the notion of the Catholic Church surrendering or losing its position where it enjoyed a monopoly as state church, and so condemned the proposition: "in our age it is no longer advisable that the Catholic religion be the only State religion, excluding all the other cults" (DzH 2977; ND 1103/77).[22] For *Dignitatis Humanae,* however, "the other cults" were not to be "excluded" in countries where the Catholic Church or any other religious group was constitutionally recognized: "if in view of the particular circumstances of peoples, special recognition is assigned in the constitution to one religious community, the right of all citizens and religious communities to freedom in religious matters must at the same time be recognized and respected" (no. 6).

Earlier in its introduction, our document showed its readiness to hear the voices of our times (see GS 44) and, in particular, the widespread "desires [*appetitiones*]" for "the free exercise of religion in society." The Council "declared" these desires to be "in conformity with truth and justice" (DH 1). Later the text observed not only that "people of today want to be able to profess their religion in public and in private," but also that "religious liberty is already declared a civil right in many constitutions and solemnly recognized in international documents" (no. 15).[23] When *Dignitatis Humanae* disclosed its intention of catching up with the true and just concerns of contemporary humanity, the spirit of *aggiornamento* came into view.

But then at once, in the spirit of *ressourcement*, the Council announced that it would "examine the sacred tradition and doctrine of the Church, from which it produces new things always consistent [*congruentia*] with the old" (DH 15).[24] Obviously the declaration produced

[22] In the spirit of "error has no rights," the *Syllabus* also condemned the proposition: "it is praiseworthy that in some Catholic regions the law has allowed people migrating there to exercise publicly their own cult" (DzH 2978; ND 1013/78).

[23] There is an obvious reference to article 18 of the 1948 Universal Declaration of Human Rights: "Everyone has the right to freedom of thought, conscience, and religion; this right includes freedom to change his religion or belief, and freedom either alone or in community with others and in public or private, to manifest his religion or belief in teaching, practice, worship and observance."

[24] Talking of *nova et vetera* inevitably conjures up the implied signature of the author of Matthew's gospel, when he speaks about a "scribe trained for the kingdom of heaven bringing out of his treasure what is new and what is old" (Matt 13:52).

something strikingly "new," by insisting that governments should safeguard religious freedom. But what could be "the old things" that were consistent with this new teaching on religious freedom? They were certainly not "old things" authorized by the *Syllabus of Errors*, but rather things known "through the revealed word of God and reason" (no. 2). A later article reversed this order and first clarified the role of "reason": (a) "the demands [of human dignity] have become more fully known to human reason through the experience of centuries." (b) Furthermore, "this doctrine of [religious] freedom has roots in divine revelation" (no. 9).

When articles 2–8 expressed what "centuries" of experience had made known, the declaration appealed to philosophical anthropology and insights into a constitutional order of society, based on justice (no. 3) and "human dignity." Those two words formed the title of the document and recurred in articles 2, 3, and 9. It was from the dignity of the human person created in the divine image that John XXIII in his 1963 encyclical *Pacem in Terris* had drawn his extensive treatment of natural rights which concerned such matters as life, education, and religious freedom (DzH 3956–72; ND 2026–42). This encyclical, cited four times in the footnotes to articles 2–8, provided a major witness supporting the case for civil authority protecting the inviolable rights of citizens—in particular, the religious freedom and equality of all before the law. The *ressourcement* at work in establishing "the general principle of religious freedom" (nos. 2–8) retrieved past teaching but only as far back as Leo XIII.

The process of retrieval showed up much more clearly in what came next, in the theological appeal to the revelation mediated through Christ and his apostles (nos. 9–15). Christ always respected human freedom and, specifically, the religious freedom of human beings, which meant that their faith could not be coerced. His disciples followed him by maintaining that the human response to God must be free, as well as by asserting their own right to proclaim the good news (nos. 9–11).[25] As part of this theological defence of religious

---

But the evangelist does not (explicitly) claim that the "new" will be consistent with the "old."

[25] Commenting on this example of *ressourcement*, Benedict XVI judged that DH had "recovered the deepest patrimony of the Church" by being "in full harmony with the teaching of Jesus himself'" ("Interpreting Vatican II," 538).

freedom, *Dignitatis Humanae* cited the teaching of four fathers of the Church (from Lactantius to Gregory the Great), as well as that of two medieval popes (Clement III and Innocent III). Here the document might also have referenced Pope Nicholas I. In a letter sent to the ruler of Bulgaria, he rejected any violent means for forcing people to accept the Christian faith which had just been officially accepted in the country (DzH 647–48).

Retrieving the past also involved acknowledging that, while the Church maintained the teaching that "no one should be coerced into believing," it had at times behaved in ways "not in keeping with the spirit of the Gospel and even opposed to it" (DzH 12). Notoriously in 1252 Pope Innocent IV (in *Ad extirpanda*) authorized the use of torture to force suspected heretics to "confess," retract their errors, and reveal the names of "other heretics."[26] Catholic Christianity countenanced torture during the thirteenth-century anti-Albigensian crusade and later—all in the cause of maintaining religious unity which under-pinned social and political stability. Through the sixteenth century and beyond, faith commitments were woven into the fabric of life: bishops, rulers, and their officials felt themselves answerable to God for supporting what they believed to be the true religion. Those who spread "heresy" brought eternal ruin on any who accepted their false views, and hence were deemed worse than thieves and murderers.[27] It took, as *Dignitatis Humanae* confessed, "the course of time" for "the leaven of the Gospel" to contribute to the conviction that "in religious matters" the human person should be free from any "coercion" (DH 12). This section of our document, when retrieving the past, acknowledged past practice that must be judged incompatible with the Christian Gospel. The principle of *ressourcement* can operate negatively as well as positively.

By retrieving the teaching and practice of Jesus, *Dignitatis Humanae* showed how Scripture can correct distorted and false traditions: in particular, the long-standing conviction that "error has no rights." Where the Dogmatic Constitution on Divine Revelation, *Dei Verbum*,

---

[26] "Innocent IV, Pope," *Oxford Dictionary of the Christian Church*, 840.

[27] For a cross-confessional study of (mainly) sixteenth-century Protestant, Anabaptist, and Catholic martyrs, see Brad S. Gregory, *Salvation at Stake: Christian Martyrdom in Early Modern Europe* (Cambridge, MA: Harvard University Press, 1999).

did not offer guidance about the role of the Scriptures in evaluating and criticizing particular traditions, we find such guidance embodied in *Dignitatis Humanae* and other Vatican II documents. They illustrated effectively how particular traditions can be corrected and even eliminated by the retrieval of the Scriptures.

Thus far we have examined three documents of Vatican II, which, respectively, mandated changes in the liturgy, updated religious life, and reversed nineteenth-century papal teaching to support religious freedom in civil society. We have seen how, when introducing these changes and so creating some discontinuity with the past, the Council consciously invoked two complementary principles: that of *ressourcement* (retrieval of past tradition) and *aggiornamento* (an updating in the light of experience and contemporary society). We can turn now to two further documents, which brought far-reaching changes but with less self-conscious attention to the underlying principles involved when they embraced innovation.

Some Changes Introduced by Two Further Documents

1. Lumen Gentium

Albert Outler called the Dogmatic Constitution on the Church (*Lumen Gentium*), promulgated on November 21, 1964, "the first full-orbed conciliar exposition of the doctrine of the Church in Christian history."[28] As a perceptive observer of the work of Vatican II, he also judged that "the Council intended the Constitution to be the major resource in the renovation and reform of the Catholic Church."[29] Through what changes did this "renovation and reform" express themselves in *Lumen Gentium*? Let me single out four changes, which concerned, respectively, sharing in Christ's triple "office" as priest, prophet, and king; the collegial authority of bishops; a positive vision of non-Catholic,

---

[28] Albert C. Outler, "A Response," in Abbott, *The Documents of Vatican II*, 102–10, at 102.

[29] Ibid., 106. On LG see P. Hünermann, *"Lumen Gentium,"* in *Herders Theologischer Kommentar*, vol. 2 (2004), 269–563; G. Philips, "History of the Constitution [*Lumen Gentium*]", trans. K. Smyth, in *Commentary on the Documents of Vatican II*, vol. 1 (1966), 105–37; id., *L'Église et son mystère au IIe Concile de Vaticane: histoire, texte et commentaire de la Constitution "Lumen Gentium,"* 2 vols. (Paris: Desclée, 1967).

Christian Churches and communities; and the religious situation of Jews, Muslims, and followers of other faiths.

First, earlier work by John Henry Newman, Joseph Lécuyer, Yves Congar, Gérard Philips, and others on Christ's triple office as priest/prophet/king or shepherd had prepared the way for the constitution to incorporate this major theme in its new vision of the Church.[30] (We initiated a discussion of the triple office in chap. 1.) Vatican II wished Catholics at large to relearn the long-neglected or even forgotten truth that each of the baptized shares in the dignity and responsibility of Christ's triple office. They are all priests, prophets/teachers, and kings/shepherds; some of them are ordained to ministry as deacons, priests, and bishops.[31]

Lumen Gentium names Christ as "Teacher, Shepherd and Priest" (no. 21) or, introducing one equivalent title ("Teacher") when expressing his threefold office, calls him "Teacher, King and Priest" (no. 13). Distinguishing "the common priesthood of the faithful" from "the ministerial or hierarchical priesthood," *Lumen Gentium* adds that "each in its own proper way shares in the one priesthood of Christ," which is a "*royal* priesthood" (no. 10; emphasis added). The constitution completes the threefold scheme when it moves on to say that "the holy people of God shares also in Christ's prophetic office" (no. 12).

Given its scope as a document on the Church, *Lumen Gentium* does not set itself to explore and define the triple office of Christ himself. It is concerned rather to illustrate in detail how others participate in his priestly, prophetic, and kingly office. Nevertheless, before doing that it sets out the living presence and continuous activity of "the Lord Jesus Christ": in "the person of the bishops, to whom the priests render assistance," this "supreme High Priest is present in the midst of the faithful. Though seated at the right hand of God the Father, he is not absent." But, through the service of the bishops, he "preaches the Word of God to all peoples, administers ceaselessly" the "sacraments of faith," and "directs and guides the people of the New Testament on their journey toward eternal beatitude" (no. 21). This fresh vision of Christ as the

---

[30] For the ways in which Newman and others had already developed the triple office, see Gerald O'Collins and Michael Keenan Jones, *Jesus Our Priest: A Christian Approach to the Priesthood of Christ* (Oxford: Oxford University Press, 2010), 206–34.

[31] Ibid., 273–91.

ever-active prophet, priest and shepherd/king shapes what the constitution wishes to say about the bishops as "teachers of doctrine, ministers of sacred worship, and holders of office in government" (no. 20).[32]

The document invests further time in unpacking the prophetic, priestly, and kingly role of *bishops* as, first, preachers, teachers, and "heralds of the faith" (no. 25); as, second, "stewards of the grace" of the fullness of priesthood (no. 26); and as, third, "*vicars* and legates of Christ" who "govern the particular churches assigned to them" (no. 27; emphasis added).[33] The text then applies the threefold office to *priests*: "they are consecrated in order to preach the Gospel and shepherd the faithful, as well as to celebrate divine worship" (no. 28). Where the bishops are pictured in their prophetic, priestly, and kingly roles, at least here the order is varied for priests: they "preach," "shepherd," and "celebrate divine worship."

Finally, chapter 4 of *Lumen Gentium* elaborates the threefold office of the laity as priests, prophets, and kings (in that order). First of all, "Christ Jesus, the supreme and eternal Priest," "intimately joins" all the baptized to "his life and mission," and gives them "a share in his priestly office" to offer spiritual worship in the Holy Spirit "for the glory of the Father and the salvation of the world" (no. 34). Second, Christ, "the great prophet who proclaimed the kingdom of the Father," now "fulfills this prophetic office not only by the hierarchy who teach in his name . . . but also by the laity." He "establishes them as witnesses" and "powerful heralds of the faith" (no. 35). Third, "the Lord also desires that his kingdom be spread by the lay faithful," through their kingly office that is described at even more length than their priestly and prophetic office (no. 36).

In its fourth and final session, the Second Vatican Council promulgated six decrees, three of which concern us here: the Decree on the

---

[32] In the Decree on Ecumenism, Vatican II pictures the triple office of the bishops and its hoped-for outcome: "through their faithful *preaching* of the Gospel, administrating the *sacraments*, and *governing in love*, Jesus Christ wishes his people to increase, under the action of the Holy Spirit, and he perfects his people's communion in unity: in the confession of one faith, in the common celebration of divine worship, and in the fraternal harmony of God's family" (UR 2; emphasis added).

[33] Here LG corrected the long-standing habit of limiting the title "vicar of Christ" to the bishop of Rome (see no. 19 on the pope as the vicar of Christ).

Pastoral Office of Bishops in the Church (*Christus Dominus*), the Decree on the Apostolate of Lay People (*Apostolicam Actuositatem*), and the Decree on the Ministry and Life of Priests (*Presbyterorum Ordinis*). These three decrees developed *Lumen Gentium* by spelling out in detail what sharing in the threefold office of Christ entailed in the lives of bishops, laypersons, and priests, respectively. Never before in the history of Roman Catholicism had a general council published documents dedicated to the life and ministry of bishops, laypeople, and priests.[34] Never before had a council attended to the royal priesthood and prophetic office conferred on all the baptized. Even if the Council of Trent in its decrees on the Mass and the sacrament of order taught something about the ordained priesthood (DzH 1743, 1763–78; ND 1548, 1706–21), *Presbyterorum Ordinis* and *Lumen Gentium* went beyond the limited view of priesthood offered by Trent. Most importantly, Vatican II insisted that preaching the Word is an essential and, indeed, primary obligation of ministerial priests.

A second change that *Lumen Gentium* introduced and that caught the imagination of many commentators was its teaching about all the Catholic bishops around the world forming with the Bishop of Rome a college (nos. 22–23), like "the one apostolic college constituted by St. Peter and the rest of the apostles" (no. 22).[35] What grounds membership in this college for local bishops is their episcopal ordination and "communion with the head and members of this college" (no. 22).

Expressing the organic unity between pope and bishops and their joint responsibility for the universal church, this new doctrine of collegiality did not subordinate the pope to the bishops (even when they all meet in a general council) or make the episcopal college merely a gathering of equals (as happens in such bodies as national colleges of surgeons). Attention to the college of bishops filled out the one-sided picture left by the First Vatican Council with its definitions of papal primacy and infallibility. Episcopal collegiality complements rather than challenges the primacy of the pope.

Lumen Gentium reasserted the collegial authority of the bishops, who in communion with the pope and united among themselves share

---

[34] To this we can add that no previous council had ever recognized the priestly, prophetic, and royal offices entrusted by God to missionaries (AG 15).

[35] See also the "explanatory note [*nota previa*]" added by the Council's doctrinal commission (at the prompting of Paul VI) to clarify the nature of collegiality.

responsibility for the "shepherding" of the whole Church. While primarily exercised by all the bishops meeting in an ecumenical council, collegiality also applies, analogously, to national bishops' conferences[36] and to other groups and situations: for instance, to the co-responsibility of laypeople, priests, and religious who constitute parishes.[37] How well or badly has collegiality functioned in the primary case of the worldwide episcopate and, in particular, through three organs: the synods of bishops held in Rome, the national episcopal conferences, and such international bodies as CELAM (the Consejo Episcopal Latinoamericano) and FABC (the Federation of Asian Bishops' Conferences)? Neither the synods nor the bishops' conferences show collegiality to be already functioning fully.[38]

A third strikingly new development, initiated by *Lumen Gentium* and provisionally presented in chapter 1 above, concerned relations with other Christians. Apropos of the identity of the Roman Catholic Church as "the holy Church" founded by Christ (no. 5), the constitution famously left behind the 1943 encyclical of Pope Pius XII, *Mystici Corporis*, by saying that the holy Church "continues to exist [*subsistit*]" fully in the Roman Catholic Church but is not simply identical with it. The meaning of *subsistit in* remains controversial, with the Congrega-

[36] LG 23 states: "the episcopal conferences can today make a manifold and fruitful contribution to the concrete application of the collegial disposition."

[37] In a 1968 article that attacked the wide scope of collegiality, Archbishop Marcel-François Lefebvre recognized what was involved, even if he dismissed collegiality as a modern introduction rather than acknowledging it as retrieving what we find, e.g., in the Acts of the Apostles (esp. chaps. 1–15): "The democratization of the magisterium has been naturally followed by the democratization of government. Modern ideas on this point have been translated into the Church by the famous [he meant 'infamous'] slogan of 'collegiality.' It is supposed to be necessary to 'collegialize' the government: that of the pope or that of the bishops with a presbyteral college, that of the parish priest with a pastoral college of lay persons, all of it flanked by commissions, councils, assemblies, etc., . . . before authorities can think of giving orders and directives. The battle of collegiality, supported by the whole Communist, Protestant, and progressive press, will remain famous [he meant 'infamous'] in the annals of the Council" (*"Un peu de lumière sur la crise actuelle de l'Église"*), accessed at http://lacriseintegriste.typepad.fr/weblog /1968/03/article-de-mgr-lefebvre-dans-rivarol.html, trans. mine.

[38] On the counter-collegial current, see Faggioli, *Vatican II: The Battle for Meaning*, 10, 13–15, 24, 87; and Gerald O'Collins, *Living Vatican II: The 21st Council for the 21st Century* (Mahwah, NJ: Paulist Press, 2006), 35–38, 154–56.

tion for the Doctrine of the Faith offering over the years varying translations, as Francis Sullivan has pointed out.[39] But the conclusion that
the Church of God is not *tout court* identical with the Roman Catholic
Church does not simply depend on the translation of *subsistit in*; it
emerges from several passages in Vatican II documents.

Recognizing how "many elements of sanctification and grace" are
found outside the "visible" Roman Catholic Church (no. 8), *Lumen
Gentium* went on to specify some of these elements present among
other Christian Churches and communities: "believing the Sacred
Scripture" to be "the norm of faith and life"; faith in the Trinity; and
the reception of baptism and "other sacraments in their own Churches
and ecclesial communities" (no. 15).[40] Here the Council acknowledged as "Churches" various bodies of Christians not (or not yet) in
union with the Roman Catholic Church. Even more emphatically in
its Decree on Ecumenism, which was promulgated on the same day
as *Lumen Gentium* (November 21, 1964) and extended and applied to
practice the teaching of the constitution, Vatican II broke new ground
by recognizing how the principle "the Eucharist makes the Church"
operates *also* for the Eastern Churches not in communion with the
Bishop of Rome: "through the celebration of the Eucharist of the Lord
in each of these Churches, the Church of God is built up and grows"
(UR 15).[41] While the Church of God continues to exist fully in the
Roman Catholic Church, it also continues to exist in other churches

---

[39] For a guide to the meaning of "subsists" in this context and some of the
controversy surrounding its meaning, see Francis A. Sullivan, "The Meaning of
Subsistit in as Explained by the Congregation for the Doctrine of the Faith," *Theological Studies* 67 (2006): 116–24; id., "A Response to Karl Becker, SJ, on the Meaning of *Subsistit in*," *Theological Studies* 67 (2006): 395–409; id., "Further Thoughts
on the Meaning of *Subsistit in*," *Theological Studies* 71 (2010): 133–47. Alexandra
von Teuffenbach, using the council diaries of Sebastian Tromp, has argued for a
narrow version of "*subsistit in*" (simply "is") in *Die Bedeutung des "Subsistit in" (LG
8). Zum Selbstverständnis der katholischen Kirche* (Munich: Herbert Utz, 2002).

[40] Apropos of LG 15, the official *relatio* explained that the "elements of sanctification and grace" belong primarily not to individuals but to the heritage and
life of the ecclesial communities, which were now turning to each other through
dialogue and in quest of visible unity: *Acta Synodalia Sacrosancti Concilii Oecumenici
Vaticani II*, III/I (Vatican City: Typis Polyglottis Vaticanis, 1973), 204.

[41] On this principle, see the encyclical by John Paul II, *Ecclesia de Eucharistia*,
AAS 95 (2003), 433–75.

or ecclesial communities, especially in those Eastern Churches, which, while not in communion with the Bishop of Rome, enjoy almost all the elements of Christian sanctification and truth. Here Vatican II innovated by officially recognizing that, beyond the visible Roman Catholic Church, the Church of God also lives and grows among those whom the Council of Florence and the Council of Trent had labelled "heretics" and "schismatics"—language never used by *Lumen Gentium* or any other Vatican II document.

A sea change had taken place. The Catholic Church was a late-comer to the ecumenical movement in which many members of other Churches were far ahead. There had been some Catholic trailblazers like Abbé Paul Couturier (1881–1953).[42] Through his vast correspondence and tracts on prayer for Christian unity, Couturier enjoyed contacts with Christians around the world and encouraged innumerable people to pray for "the unity Christ wills, by the means he wills." Nevertheless, praying with other Christians remained forbidden by the official Catholic Church. The 1928 encyclical of Pius XI, *Mortalium Animos*, forbade Catholics even to take part in conferences with non-Roman Christians; such participation, he feared, would imply that the Catholic Church was but one of the denominations. When the World Council of Churches began, Catholic observers were not allowed to attend the first assemblies (Amsterdam in 1948 and Evanston in 1954).

Vatican II expressed and approved an "important change to a positive vision of non-Catholic Christian communities,"[43] a change deeply desired by John XXIII and his great collaborator, Cardinal Augustin Bea. *Unitatis Redintegratio* strongly endorsed theological dialogue with "the separated brethren" (no. 9), and opened the way for the establishment of numerous ecumenical commissions at an international, national, and diocesan level. It recommended that Catholics join in prayer with other Christians, not least at ecumenical gatherings and, in particular, services for Christian unity (no. 8).

With its positive statements first about Jews and then about Muslims, *Lumen Gentium* (no. 16) signalled a fourth change, which closely paralleled the official "about face" on relations with other Christians.

---

[42] "Couturier, Paul Irénée," in *Oxford Dictionary of the Christian Church*, 428.

[43] Joseph Feiner, "Commentary on the Decree [*Unitatis Redintegratio*]," trans. R. A. Wilson, in *Commentary on the Documents of Vatican II*, vol. 2 (1968), 57–164, at 61.

For the first time in the story of Catholic Christianity, an ecumenical council had something positive to say about Jews. Citing Romans 11:28-29, the constitution declared that the chosen people remain "most dear" to God, who never "repents" of his "gifts and calling." Commenting on the Declaration on the Relation of the Church to Non-Christian Religions, *Nostra Aetate*, promulgated on October 28, 1965, John M. Oesterreicher wrote: "It is the first time that the Church has publicly made her own the Pauline view of the mystery of Israel," and "given glory to God for his enduring faithfulness toward this chosen people, the Jews."[44] Beyond question, *Nostra Aetate* had more to say about Paul's view of the mystery of Israel. Nevertheless, it was a year earlier, when promulgating *Lumen Gentium* in November 1964 that for "the first time the Church publicly made her own the Pauline view."

Apropos of Muslims, Georges C. Anawati correctly observed that "up to the beginning of the twentieth century, the constant attitude of the Church toward Islam was one of condemnation." But he ignored the official change embodied a year earlier in *Lumen Gentium* (November 1964), when he attributed to *Nostra Aetate* (October 1965) "a change in the Church's attitude to Islam."[45] Eleven months before (in LG)—and for the first time since Muhammad (d. 632) founded Islam—an ecumenical council of the Catholic Church offered some positive teaching on Muslims.[46] This teaching highlighted common ground: the divine "plan of salvation also embraces those who acknowledge the Creator, in the first place among whom are the Muslims. They profess to hold the faith of Abraham, and together with us they adore the one, merciful God, who will judge human beings on the last day" (no. 16).[47] While describing Muslims as those "who

---

[44] John M. Oesterreicher, "Declaration on the Relation of the Church to Non-Christian Religions," trans. Simon Young, Erika Young, and Hilda Graef, in *Commentary on the Documents of Vatican II*, vol. 3 (1969), 1–136, at 1.

[45] Georges C. Anawati, "Excursus on Islam," trans. Simon and Erika Young, in *Commentary on the Documents of Vatican II*, vol. 3 (1969), 151–54, at 151.

[46] Meeting soon after the failure of the fifth and final (major) crusade, the Second Council of Lyons (1274) described "the Saracens" as "blasphemous," "faithless," and "the impious enemies of the Christian name." See *Decrees of the Ecumenical Councils*, 1:309.

[47] In no. 107 of his first encyclical, *Ecclesiam Suam* (August 6, 1964), Paul VI had anticipated by a few months the positive teaching on Islam found in LG. He wrote of Muslims, "whom we do well to admire on account of those things that

profess to hold the faith of Abraham" rather than simply state that Muslims hold the faith of Abraham, the Council agreed that they "acknowledge the Creator," "adore with us the one, merciful God," and also share with Christians an expectation of a general judgment "on the last day." A year later in *Nostra Aetate*, Vatican II would fill out its positive view of Islam and Judaism.

After the Muslims, the same article (LG 16) turns to other believers in God: "nor is this God distant from others who in shadows and images seek the unknown God, since to all he gives life and breath and all things (cf. Acts 17:23–28) and since the Savior wills all human beings to be saved (cf. 1 Tim 2:4)." Because God is both the Creator who gives life to all human beings and the Savior who wishes all to be saved, the Council holds that the divine presence also enfolds all God-seekers, even if it is "in shadows and images" that they seek "the unknown God." Hence "those who through no fault [of their own] do not know Christ's Gospel and his Church and who, nevertheless, seek God with a sincere heart and, under the influence of grace, try in their actions to fulfil his will made known through the dictate of their conscience—those too may obtain eternal salvation."

When this article in *Lumen Gentium* considers believers in God other than Jews and Muslims, it prioritizes the divine initiative. It is God who comes close to all (as Creator) by giving them life and (as Savior) by willing them to be saved. It is through "the influence of grace" that these "others" can try to follow their conscience and do God's will. But when they "seek the unknown God" and "seek God with a sincere heart," can they do this only because God draws them? When they seek God, is this only because God has first found them? While not clearly stated, an affirmative answer seems presupposed when article 16 speaks earlier of "all human beings without exception" being "called by God's grace to salvation."

While speaking of their salvation, the constitution remains silent about the other, inseparable dimension of the divine self-communication revelation. This particular passage of *Lumen Gentium* has nothing to say, at least explicitly, about divine revelation and its correlative in human faith. Nevertheless, we should ask: while the voice of conscience dic-

---

are true and commendable [*vera et probanda*] in their worship" (AAS 56 [1964], 609–59, at 654).

tates what the "God-seekers" should do, how has the will of God been "made known" to them at the heart of their conscience? Does the "making known" imply some measure of revelation? Although they can be described as seeking "the unknown God" and doing so "in shadows and images," this language suggests that something has been disclosed to them. Shadows are not equivalent to total darkness, and images imply some resemblance to truth and reality.

These reflections in *Lumen Gentium* on the religious situation of those who are neither Jews nor Muslims retrieved teaching from Acts and 1 Timothy and broke new ground in the history of ecumenical councils. Writing about a later conciliar document (*Nostra Aetate*), Oesterreicher forgot that *Lumen Gentium* had already acknowledged "the universal presence of grace and its activity in the many religions of mankind." It was in this constitution (and not in NA) that a general council had "for the first time in history" "honoured the truth and holiness in other religions as the work of the one living God."[48] Unquestionably, *Nostra Aetate* would have more to say, but it was a year earlier that *Lumen Gentium* had spoken up positively on the other religions.

Thus far we have recalled four pieces of new teaching found in *Lumen Gentium*: all Christians share in Christ's "triple office" as priest, prophet, and king; the bishops enjoy universal, "collegial" authority; a positive vision of non-Catholic Christian communities committed the Catholic Church firmly to the ecumenical movement; the Council recognized the work of God in other living faiths and in all who seek God. All four changes affected (a) life within the Catholic Church (through the teaching on the triple office and on episcopal collegiality), and (b) her relationship with "others" (through a transformed vision of non-Catholic Christians and followers of other faiths). Furthermore, these changes, as well as embodying something new, also drew on ancient testimony—notably the Scriptures (e.g., biblical teaching on the triple office). Thus the very changes themselves express a radical continuity with the past.

Obviously one could press on and list further changes of doctrine and practice incorporated in *Lumen Gentium*: the many biblical images that express the mystery of the Church (no. 6); the universal call to holiness of all the baptized (nos. 39–42) which retrieves teaching from

---

[48] Oesterreicher, "Declaration on the Relationship," 1.

St. Paul and other ancient sources; the restoration of the permanent diaconate[49] in the Latin rite; and much else besides. But let us turn to the remarkable changes found in *Nostra Aetate*.[50]

2. The Declaration on the Relation of the Church to Non-Christian Religions

While *Lumen Gentium* 16 had already broken new ground in the history of the twenty-one ecumenical councils of Catholic Christianity by its positive remarks about Judaism and Islam, *Nostra Aetate* took matters further by reflecting on other religions (in particular, on Hinduism and Buddhism) and by considering the human condition and "the riddles of the human condition" to which different religions provide an answer (no. 1). The opening words of the declaration (on human beings drawing closer together) loomed large as the first time any ecumenical council had ever reflected on the state of global humanity.[51] Popes had done so, notably John XXIII in *Pacem in Terris* (1963), but never before was that kind of pronouncement to be found

---

[49] If Vatican II had met today, it might well have proposed the restoration of the diaconate for women. See Phyllis Zagano, "Remembering Tradition: Women's Monastic Rituals and the Diaconate," *Theological Studies* 72 (2011): 787–811; and the International Theological Commission, *From the Diakonia of Christ to the Diakonia of the Apostles* (London: Catholic Truth Society, 2003); the English title tendentiously translates the original French, "*Le Diakonat: Évolution et perspectives,*" *La Documentation Catholique* (January 19, 2003): 58–107. See also Gerald O'Collins, "Unlock the Door: The Case for Women in the Diaconate," *The Tablet* (May 25, 2013): 4–5.

[50] On the making of NA, see Giovanni Miccoli, "Two Sensitive Issues: Religious Freedom and the Jews," in *History of Vatican II*, vol. 4 (2003), 135–93; Riccardo Burigana and Giovanni Turbanti, "The Intersession: Preparing the Conclusion of the Council," in ibid., 4:546–59; Mauro Velati, "Completing the Conciliar Agenda," in *History of Vatican II*, vol. 5 (2006), 185–273, at 211–31. On the theological impact of the declaration, see the following articles in *Gregorianum* 87 (2006): Michael L. Fitzgerald, "*Nostra Aetate*, A Key to Interreligious Dialogue," 700–713; Daniel A. Madigan, "*Nostra Aetate* and the Questions It Chose to Leave Open," 781–96; Gerald O'Collins, "Implementing *Nostra Aetate*," 714–26; and Jacques Scheuer, "The Dialogue with the Traditions of India and the Far East," 797–809; see also Roman A. Siebenrock, "Theologischer Kommentar zur Erklärung über die Haltung der Kirche zu den nichtchristlichen Religionen *Nostra Aetate*," in *Herders Theologischer Kommentar*, vol. 3 (2005), 591–693.

[51] LG, albeit very briefly, had already adverted to "the conditions of this time," and the way "all human beings are more closely joined today by various social, technical, and cultural bonds" (no. 1; see also the closing words of no. 28).

in any ecumenical council. *Nostra Aetate* named three basic reasons for acknowledging what all nations have in common, to the point of making them "one community": their origin in God, the divine providence that extends to all, and their common, heavenly destiny.

On the basis of the unity between all human beings finding its deepest foundation in what God has done, is doing, and will do, *Nostra Aetate* turns next to the common self-questioning that also—but this time, on the side of humanity—bonds everyone (no. 1). The declaration's eloquent exposé of the deep questions that haunt human beings has no precedent in the teaching of earlier councils. The same is true when the document reflects explicitly and positively on some aspects of Hinduism and Buddhism, two religious ways of life that existed centuries before the coming of Christ himself. In the history of Catholic Christianity no previous ecumenical council had ever reflected on these ancient Asian religions.

Before moving to Islam and Judaism, *Nostra Aetate* observes that "the Catholic Church rejects nothing of those things which are true and holy in these [other] religions." Rather, "it is with sincere respect that she considers those ways of acting and living, those precepts and doctrines, which, although they differ in many [respects] from what she herself holds and proposes, nevertheless, often reflect a ray of that Truth, which illuminates all human beings" (no. 2). By recognizing what is "true and holy" in other religions, the declaration follows the lead of *Lumen Gentium* in using a Johannine, double-sided terminology that distinguishes (but does not separate) the two dimensions of the divine self-communication: revelation and salvation. What or rather who has given rise to "those things which are true and holy" in the other religions? *Nostra Aetate* responds by pointing to the person of Christ.

Without condemning various "ways of acting and living," as well as various "precepts and doctrines" to be found in other religions, but simply noting that they may "differ" in many respects from what the Catholic Church teaches, the declaration then acknowledges something extraordinarily positive: the beliefs and practices of other religions "often reflect a ray of that Truth that illuminates all human beings" (no. 2; see John 1:9). Since what is "true" among the others reflects "the Truth" that is the Word of God, presumably what is "holy" among them also comes from the Word who is the life of humankind (John 1:4). If Christ is "the truth" for everyone, he is also "the life" for them. This paragraph does not expressly state that Christ is both universal Revealer and universal Savior, but what it says amounts to that. How can he "illuminate" all human beings, without conveying to them (through a personal divine self-disclosure) something of God's self-revelation and hence also the offer of salvation? All of this teaching, which retrieves and applies what we find in John's gospel, boldly develops doctrine and, in fact, reverses the ugly way the Council of Florence in its decree for the Copts had indiscriminately relegated "pagans" (as well as "Jews, heretics, and schismatics") to eternal damnation.[52]

After its fuller treatment of Islam (no. 3) and Judaism (no. 4), *Nostra Aetate* recalls a theme from the Book of Genesis that fills out what has already been said about all people having a common origin in God (no. 5). Right from the very first human beings, they have all been "created in the image and likeness of God" (Gen 1:26-27). Seeing all men and women as not only created by God but also created in the divine image will prove an effective mind-set; it dramatically puts back on display how we should interpret and understand "the religious others," whoever they may be. The declaration draws a practical conclusion from the doctrine of all people being created in the divine image: there is no basis for any "discrimination" that offends or curtails "human dignity and the rights that flow from it" (NA 5). "Human dignity" would become the title of the Declaration on Religious Liberty, promulgated a few weeks later on December 7, 1965. The Pastoral Constitution on the Church in the Modern World, promulgated on the same day, would insist at greater length on "the extraordinary dignity of the human person" and the basic rights that flow from that dignity (no. 26; see no. 29). The use that *Nostra Aetate* (briefly) and *Gaudium et Spes* (more fully) made of Genesis 1:26-27 enjoys no precedent in any earlier councils. Here once again Vatican II innovates, this time by applying a basic biblical theme about the creation of humanity.

Understanding and Interpreting Changes

Thus far this chapter has set itself to illustrate how Vatican II introduced sweeping changes in liturgical practice and religious life, reversed set positions about religious freedom and relations with other

[52] DzH 1351; ND 810.

Christians, and, for the first time in the story of general councils, offered positive teaching on Judaism, Islam, Hinduism, Buddhism, and other religions. *Lumen Gentium*, as we saw, besides breaking new ground with its positive vision of other Christian communities and other living faiths, also innovated by teaching that all the baptized share in the triple office of Christ and that the bishops enjoy universal, "collegiate" authority.

Much more could be added about the extent and nature of change in doctrine and practice brought by Vatican II. For example, it retrieved the central importance of Sacred Scripture for liturgy, theology, and the whole life of the Church (SC 24, 51–52; DV 21–26), and encouraged a theology of the local Church (e.g., AG 19–23). It rejected the institution of slavery and the use of torture (GS 27), both of which the Catholic Church had found acceptable for centuries.[53] A dramatic language shift involved not only dropping such standard talk about "pagans," "heretics," and "schismatics," but also introducing such positive terms as "collegiality," "dialogue," and "dignity." *Ressourcement* also meant retrieving biblical language that had long been neglected. In giving the Decree on the Ministry and Life of Priests the name of *Presbyterorum Ordinis* (of the order of presbyters), Vatican II retrieved from early Christianity a typical term for Church leaders.[54] We could amass further examples inspired by *aggiornamento* and *ressourcement*—not least the extent to which the retrieval of biblical themes such as creation in the divine image impacted deeply on two conciliar documents, *Nostra Aetate* and *Gaudium et Spes*.[55]

---

[53] On the Church's longstanding approval or at least tolerance of slavery, see John T. Noonan Jr., *A Church That Can and Cannot Change: The Development of Catholic Moral Teaching* (Notre Dame, IN: University of Notre Dame Press, 2005), 110–23; Sullivan, "Catholic Tradition and Traditions," 118–25. The 1948 Universal Declaration of Human Rights outlawed slavery and torture (nos. 4 and 5).

[54] See Friedrich Wulf, "Decree on the Ministry and Life of Priests: Commentary on the Decree," trans. R.Walls, in *Commentary on the Documents of Vatican II*, vol. 4 (1969), 210–14; and Gerard Kelly, "Ordination in the Presbyteral Order," *Australasian Catholic Record* 73 (1996): 259–72.

[55] Significantly in opposing Vatican II and its implementation, Archbishop Lefebvre appealed to his own vision of "the Church" and "tradition" but avoided the challenge of the Scriptures. Thus in an interview which appeared in *Newsweek* for December 19, 1977, he spoke thirteen times of "the Church" but never referred to the New Testament or to Jesus Christ.

But what should we make of all these changes brought by Vatican II? Let me respond by citing Neil Ormerod and Benedict XVI and then adding two suggestions of my own.

First, Ormerod rightly warns that, when we locate the changes within any "larger theory" of social and cultural crisis and change, we face something "extremely complex."[56] He himself speaks of "authentic" or "inauthentic" developments. Old ways of promoting the Church's mission have become dysfunctional and need, after discernment, to be discarded and replaced. Ormerod also applies the language of Bernard Lonergan and speaks of the Church being called to an intellectual, moral, and religious conversion.[57]

Second, in his 2005 address to the Roman Curia, Pope Benedict uses the scheme of permanent principles and changing forms to interpret the changes brought by Vatican II. In the "innovation in continuity," "only the principles" express "the permanent aspect." While he allows that "the practical forms depend on the historical situation and are therefore subject to change," he maintains "the continuity of principles."[58] This proposal opens up memories of John Henry Newman's "continuity of principles," his second "note" for distinguishing between "the genuine development of an idea" and its corruption." While "doctrines grow and are enlarged," principles are "permanent."[59]

Along with the scheme of permanent principles and changing forms, the pope also introduced a term, "identity," when remarking: "in apparent discontinuity it [the Church] has actually preserved and deepened her inmost nature and true identity."[60] That brief remark opens the way to my closing observations. But, before examining "identity," I want to explore briefly the possibility of distinguishing between essentials and nonessentials.

The widespread innovations sanctioned by Vatican II inevitably meant many discontinuities with the past—often with the more recent past but sometimes (e.g., in the case of the toleration of torture and slavery) with a past that reached back to the early centuries of Christendom. One might comment that in all these changes no es-

[56] Ormerod, "Vatican II—Continuity or Discontinuity?," 611, 612.
[57] Ibid., 613, 633.
[58] Benedict XVI, "Interpreting Vatican II," 538.
[59] Newman, *Essay*, 183–89, at 183; see also ibid., 309–36.
[60] Benedict XVI, "Interpreting Vatican II," 538.

sential or substantial belief (e.g., faith in the Trinity) or practice (e.g., baptism) was dropped, and so substantial continuity remained intact. Following *Sacrosanctum Concilium* (no. 21), one might then distinguish between the permanence of essentials from change in nonessentials. Nothing essential has been lost or removed, and nothing essentially or substantially new has been added. Thus a scheme of "essential" and "nonessential" (or "substantial/substantive" and "accidental") could be pressed into service.

Yet Pope Benedict's term "identity" may offer a richer theme to pursue and could lead us to ask: is the pre–Vatican II and post–Vatican II Church one and the same corporate subject? Has there been a loss of identity? Or has the Church retained her authentic identity, so that all the faithful can continue to participate in a fellowship structured by the same values and goals and living by the same essential beliefs and practices? There can be only one reply: the indwelling Holy Spirit maintains the Church's true, deep, and lasting trinitarian identity as the Body of Christ and the People of God.

Far from threatening the enduring continuity of the Church, change makes possible that continuous identity of this corporate subject profoundly shaped by the tripersonal God. As with any living organism, for the Church not to change would be to die. Or, making this point positively and with Newman's words, one can say: "in a higher world it is otherwise, but here below to live is to change and to be perfect is to have changed often."[61]

Finally, we need to enlarge our vision of the identity between the pre–Vatican II and post–Vatican II Church. The continuous identity at stake is nothing less than *apostolic* identity. Newman admitted "the abstract possibility of extreme changes" that would bring a loss of "identity" and a kind of "counterfeit Christianity." But he argued for a "real continuity" that made Christianity of later centuries "in its substance the very religion which Christ and his apostles taught in the first, whatever may be the modifications for good or for evil which lapse of years, or the vicissitudes of human affairs, have impressed upon it."[62]

[61] Newman, *Essay*, 63.
[62] Ibid., 33.

   What Newman calls "real continuity" is nothing less than apostolic identity. Far from threatening that "real continuity," the Second Vatican Council renewed the Church's apostolic identity or its "real continuity" (through the guidance of the Holy Spirit) with what the crucified and risen Christ and the original witnesses did in founding and propagating the Church. With a reverential nod toward Newman, some have understood "development" to be *the* issue underlying both the events that constituted the Council and the texts that it produced. Yet one goes closer to the heart of the matter by naming as *the* conciliar challenge that of maintaining and renewing the *apostolic identity* of the Church.[63]

[63] On the apostolic character and identity of the Church, see Lutheran–Roman Catholic Commission on Unity, *The Apostolicity of the Church: Study Document of the Lutheran–Roman Catholic Commission on Unity* (Minneapolis: Lutheran University Press, 2006).

Chapter 3

Sacrosanctum Concilium as a Hermeneutical Key for Vatican II

Right from the closing session of the Second Vatican Council, notable commentators have assigned a primary importance to the Dogmatic Constitution on the Church, *Lumen Gentium* (promulgated on November 21, 1964). Whether or not they invoked the technical language of hermeneutical theory, they understood and interpreted *Lumen Gentium* as the key for understanding and interpreting the other fifteen documents. Thus in December 1965 Karl Rahner presented this text as conveying the Church's fundamental understanding of herself. He put it in a separate, opening section, with the further documents arranged under two, subordinate headings: "the inner life of the Church" and "the exterior commission of the Church."[1]

Other commentators, for instance, an anonymous referee of this chapter, have noted how *Lumen Gentium* exercised a major influence on such subsequent documents of ecclesiological application as *Christus Dominus*, *Apostolicam Actuositatem*, *Ad Gentes*, and *Presbyterorum Ordinis* (all promulgated in 1965). Together they refer sixty times to *Lumen Gentium* but only eleven times to the 1963 *Sacrosanctum Concilium*, while *Lumen Gentium* itself makes little explicit use of *Sacrosanctum Concilium*, introducing it only three times in 170 notes.

Massimo Faggioli has, nevertheless, argued that the Constitution on the Sacred Liturgy, *Sacrosanctum Concilium* (promulgated on December 4, 1963), proved one of the "pillars" of the Second Vatican Council's

---

[1] For details, see Herbert Vorgrimler, ed., *The Documents of Vatican II*, vol. 1 (London: Burns & Oates, 1967), viii.

eucharistic ecclesiology (*Ecclesia de Eucharistia*), rediscovered "the centrality of Scripture and the Eucharist," prepared the way for the *rapprochement* manifestos (*Unitatis Redintegratio, Nostra Aetate,* and *Gaudium
et Spes*), and initiated the Council's *ressourcement* (or retrieval) procedure.
In short, he championed "a hermeneutics of the Council based on *Sacrosanctum Concilium*" and not on *Lumen Gentium*.[2] Faggioli subsequently
put this case briefly in *Vatican II: The Battle for Meaning,* and then developed it further in *True Reform: Liturgy and Ecclesiology in* Sacrosanctum
Concilium.[3] The second book, examining the reception of *Sacrosanctum
Concilium* by Vatican II itself, proposed that the liturgical constitution's
vision of the Church helped to set the agenda for many of the later conciliar documents and affected their content and formulations.

While valuing Faggioli's proposal, I think it needs nuancing and
enlarging. First, although he cites Peter Hünermann's approval of a
hermeneutical scheme (involving authors, texts, and recipients) for
interpreting the conciliar documents proposed by Ormond Rush,[4]
Faggioli does not set out his own hermeneutics and, significantly,
does not even include "hermeneutics" in the index of subjects for *True
Reform.* His thesis requires the support of a hermeneutical theory. Second,
Faggioli names seven themes where he finds *Sacrosanctum Concilium*
setting the agenda for subsequent documents of Vatican II. Below I
will argue that we need to add at least a further five themes to this list.
Before spending most of this chapter on these twelve themes, I need to
take a position on what is involved in interpreting the conciliar texts.

The Authors, the Readers, and the Texts

Over thirty years ago I first proposed a triple scheme for interpreting
biblical texts: the *intentio auctoris,* the *intentio legentis,* and the *intentio
textus ipsius.* While maintaining this scheme, I have come to nuance it
somewhat,[5] and would now speak more simply of (a) the author(s),

---

[2] M. Faggioli, "*Sacrosanctum concilium* and the Meaning of Vatican II," *Theological
Studies* 71 (2010): 437–52, at 450–52.

[3] M. Faggioli, *Vatican II: The Battle for Meaning* (Mahwah, NJ: Paulist Press,
2012), 5, 102–5; id., *True Reform: Liturgy and Ecclesiology in* Sacrosanctum Concilium
(Collegeville, MN: Liturgical Press, 2012).

[4] For details, see Faggioli, *True Reform,* 13.

[5] Gerald O'Collins, *Fundamental Theology* (New York: Paulist Press, 1981), 251–
58; id., *Rethinking Fundamental Theology: Toward a New Fundamental Theology* (Oxford:
Oxford University Press, 2011), 254–61.

(b) of the readers, and, above all, (c) of the texts themselves when interpreting biblical, conciliar, and other texts. One needs to investigate as far as possible (a) the sources and intentions of authors and (b) to recognize that all texts remain incomplete without their readers, with the interests and questions that drive them to read these texts. While we presume some meaning(s) to be present in the mind of the original author(s), we should also look for the meaning(s) grasped by those who read the texts that have been produced. Nevertheless, (c) the texts themselves are more than a mere bridge between the intentions of the original author(s) and the response of later readers. Any text, once written and published, begins its own history when people in different situations read, interpret, and apply it to their lives. Texts can often communicate more than their authors ever consciously knew, and their meaning(s) may go beyond what the authors intended when they drew on various sources to write in particular situations for specific audiences, as well as beyond what readers may have brought to their reading on the texts.[6]

When tackling documents produced by Vatican II, some limit the work of interpretation to what the authors—and this above all means those bishops and others who worked on the conciliar commissions—consciously intended to convey by the texts they composed and then revised (in the light of criticisms and suggestions coming from the assembled bishops and others). They carefully evaluated what things were to be included, how they were to be expressed, and on what basis they could be said. When they distributed the texts and then presented them in the Council, they justified their sources and formulations through the "notes" provided and the "relations" delivered in a conciliar session. All of this (and more) can be studied in the acts of the

---

[6] On texts being relatively independent from their original authors and readers, see Hans-Georg Gadamer, *Truth and Method*, trans. Joel Weinsheimer and Donald G. Marshall, 2nd ed. (New York: Crossroad, 1989). He states a universally valid principle: "not just occasionally, but always, the meaning of a text goes beyond its author." When repeating this point, he adds that texts also become independent from their original addressees: "the horizon of understanding cannot be limited either by what the writer originally had in mind or by the horizon of the person to whom the text was originally addressed." Hence he argues that "reconstructing what the author really had in mind" is at best "a limited undertaking" (296, 395, 373). For a similar hermeneutics, but one influenced by Hans Robert Jauss, see Ormond Rush, *Still Interpreting Vatican II: Some Hermeneutical Principles* (Mahwah, NJ: Paulist Press, 2004).

Council, the (unpublished) records from the commissions (available in a special Vatican archive), and in the "genetic" studies of particular documents.[7]

Such an approach, which limits itself to the evidence that discloses the intentions of the original authors or the "minds" behind the texts, naturally evaluates any connections *between* conciliar documents on the basis of connections made to earlier documents through footnotes provided by the later ones. Only *explicitly* indicated influences of an earlier on a later text count. Would such a restriction when detecting influences be widely accepted?[8] Is interpretation to be governed solely by (a) the intentions of the authors, without reference to any input from (b) (the questions and experiences of) subsequent readers, and from (c) the recognizable place of some newly published text vis-à-vis what had been written earlier and what would be written later?

Everyone should acknowledge that *Sacrosanctum Concilium* stands out as the first in a series of new departures. In the sixteenth century, the Council of Trent published teaching on the seven sacraments, but *Sacrosanctum Concilium* is the first liturgical document ever to be produced by an ecumenical or general council in the history of Catholic Christianity. It also marks the point of entry into official teaching of such themes as "the paschal mystery," the sacramental nature of salvation and revelation, and the procedures of *aggiornamento* and *ressourcement*. These and other themes were "on the books" after *Sacrosanctum Concilium* was promulgated in December 1963. Launched by its authors, this text could now enjoy a life of its own in provoking questions, suggesting connections, and being available for subsequent interpretation and actualization.

Even though at the time of its publication few of the bishops and their collaborators may have glimpsed the implications of *Sacrosanctum Concilium*, this relatively short document (less than half the length of *Lumen Gentium* and only about a third the length of *Gaudium et Spes*) prefigured much of what was to come in later documents of the

---

[7] See, e.g., Riccardo Burigana, *La Bibbia nel concilio. La redazione della costituzione "Dei Verbum" del Vaticano II* (Bologna: Il Mulino, 1998).

[8] In biblical studies confining attention to explicitly conscious references would not command wide acceptance. To take one example: in his letters St. Paul often cites the Jewish Scriptures, but exegetes may detect influences at work even where the Apostle does not explicitly quote earlier texts.

Council.[9] *Sacrosanctum Concilium* anticipated at least twelve themes, some more fully and others more briefly. That is the case this chapter will argue.

The Centrality of the Paschal Mystery

Right from its opening chapter, *Sacrosanctum Concilium* highlights the centrality of the paschal mystery, the dying and rising of Christ that was the principal "work" of redemption and that gave birth to the Church (no. 5). Baptism means being "inserted" into "the paschal mystery of Christ"—that is to say, "dying with him, being buried with him, and rising with him," to receive "the spirit of adoption" (no. 6). Coming together to hear the Scriptures and share in the Eucharist likewise involves "celebrating the paschal mystery" (no. 6). From its origins the Church has dedicated Sunday or "the Lord's day" to commemorate in a special way "the paschal mystery" (no. 106). All in all, *Sacrosanctum Concilium* speaks of "the paschal mystery" eight times (nos. 5, 6 [twice], 61, 104, 106, 107, and 109).

A lyric passage, perhaps the most famous passage from *Sacrosanctum Concilium,* calls the celebration of the paschal mystery in the liturgy "the summit towards which the activity of the Church aims and simultaneously the fountain from which all her strength flows." Hence it is "from the liturgy, and especially from the Eucharist as from a fountain that grace is drawn upon us, and the sanctification of human beings and the glorification of God are obtained with greatest effectiveness" (no. 10).

The centrality of Christ's resurrection from the dead (i.e., the paschal mystery) and its supreme celebration in the Eucharist do not, however, lead *Sacrosanctum Concilium* to gloss over what came before

[9] On SC, see Rita Ferrone, *Sacrosanctum Concilium* (Mahwah, NJ: Paulist Press, 2007); Josef Jungmann, "Constitution on the Sacred Liturgy," trans. L. Adolphus, in *Commentary on the Documents of Vatican II*, 1:1–88; Reiner Kaczynski, "Toward the Reform of the Liturgy," in *History of Vatican II*, ed. Giuseppe Alberigo and Joseph A. Komonchak, vol. 3 (Maryknoll, NY: Orbis, 2000), 192–256; id., *"Theologischer Kommentar zur Konstitution über die heilige Liturgie, Sacrosanctum Concilium,"* in *Herders Theologischer Kommentar zum Zweiten Vatikanischen Konzil*, ed. Peter Hünermann and Bernd Jochen Hilberath, vol. 2 (Freiburg im Breisgau: Herder, 2004), 1–227; Mathijs Lamberigts, "The Liturgy Debate," in *History of Vatican II*, 2:107–66.

(with the incarnation) and what is to come later (in the final kingdom of heaven). It is in terms of Christ's priesthood that the document vividly evokes the incarnation: "Jesus Christ, the High Priest of the New and Eternal Covenant, when he assumed a human nature, introduced into this land of exile the hymn that in heaven is sung throughout all ages. He unites the whole community of humankind with himself and associates it with him in singing this divine canticle of praise." Thus *Sacrosanctum Concilium* pictures Christ's liturgical activity starting when he takes on the human condition and joins all men and women to himself (no. 83).

Reflecting the kind of link which the Book of Revelation drew long ago between the earthly liturgy and the heavenly liturgy,[10] *Sacrosanctum Concilium* recognizes that "in the earthly liturgy we share in advance in that heavenly liturgy which is celebrated in the holy city of Jerusalem, toward which we move as pilgrims" (no. 8). Our present liturgical life is not yet definitive; it is a foretaste of what is to come in the heavenly liturgy. In other words, the centrality of the eucharistic celebration of the paschal mystery remains, but it is qualified by the expectation of the definitive liturgy to be celebrated in the heavenly Jerusalem.

The language of "the paschal mystery" that characterized *Sacrosanctum Concilium* would (consciously or unconsciously) be taken up by the Decree on the Pastoral Office of Bishops in the Church, *Christus Dominus* (promulgated on October 28, 1965): "they [the bishops] should strive that the Christian faithful know and live the paschal mystery more deeply through the Eucharist" (no. 15). According to the Decree on the Training of Priests, *Optatam Totius* (also promulgated on October 28, 1965), those preparing for ministerial ordination "should live the paschal mystery in such a way that they will know how to initiate into it the people committed to them" (no. 8).

The Decree on the Church's Missionary Activity, *Ad Gentes* (promulgated on December 7, 1965), mandated that the liturgy of Lent "should be restored in such a way as to prepare the hearts of the catechumens to celebrate the paschal mystery, in whose solemn ceremonies they are reborn to Christ through baptism" (no. 14). This progressive initiation

---

[10] For details, see Gerald O'Collins and Michael Keenan Jones, *Jesus Our Priest: A Christian Approach to the Priesthood of Christ* (Oxford: Oxford University Press, 2010), 38–42.

for which the Council called was embodied in the Rite of Christian Initiation of Adults, a Lenten course of preparation introduced in 1972. Article 14 of *Ad Gentes* references and applies what *Sacrosanctum Concilium* had enjoined two years earlier (nos. 64–65; see also no. 109)—a striking example of the liturgical constitution being explicitly received by later texts of the Council.

Finally, Vatican II's last document, the Pastoral Constitution on the Church in the Modern World, *Gaudium et Spes* (promulgated on December 7, 1965) envisions the impact of the paschal mystery not only on baptized Christians but also on all human beings. In "struggling against evil," the Christian does so as "one who has been made a partner [*consociatus*] in the paschal mystery, is configured to the death of Christ and, strengthened by hope, and runs toward the resurrection." But sharing in the paschal mystery is also a possibility for all those who have not (or have not yet) been baptized: "the Holy Spirit offers to all, in a way known to God, the possibility of being made partners [*consocientur*] in the paschal mystery" (no. 22). The relevance of the paschal mystery extends beyond the baptized gathered by the Holy Spirit to celebrate the death and resurrection of Christ. The grace and power of the paschal mystery touch the whole human race.

Without referencing the thirteen places where the Second Vatican Council used the term, Faggioli follows Reiner Kaczynski and Angelus Häussling in calling the "paschal mystery" not only central for *Sacrosanctum Concilium* but also a "heart word" for the Council.[11] Here a major theme for the "law of praying [*lex orandi*]" that shaped *Sacrosanctum Concilium* became a significant theme for "the law of believing [*lex credendi*]" in four subsequent conciliar documents (CD, OT, AG, and GS).

Before leaving the way in which the teaching of *Sacrosanctum Concilium* on the paschal mystery was taken up in subsequent conciliar documents, we should not neglect some links with the Dogmatic Constitution on Divine Revelation, *Dei Verbum* (promulgated on November 18, 1965). While this constitution does not introduce the term "paschal mystery" as such, it refers equivalently to "the mystery of our salvation" (no. 15), "the mystery of Christ" (no. 24), and "the eucharistic

---

[11] Faggioli, "*Sacrosanctum Concilium* and the Meaning of Vatican II," 445; id., *Vatican II: The Battle for Meaning*, 102, 174; id., *True Reform*, 9, 68, 83.

mystery" (no. 26). *Dei Verbum* understands Christ's death and glorious resurrection to "complete and perfect" the divine self-revelation (DV 4), just as for *Sacrosanctum Concilium* that death and resurrection constitute centrally "the work of our redemption" (SC 2) and make possible its liturgical celebration in the Eucharist.

The language of "revelation" and "salvation" link and differentiate *Sacrosanctum Concilium* and *Dei Verbum*. *Sacrosanctum Concilium* does not neglect the language of revelation; it refers, for instance, to God "speaking through the prophets" and to Christ "preaching the good news" (no. 5). But it is the language of salvation that characteristically shapes the liturgical constitution. *Dei Verbum* also introduces the language of salvation. It speaks not only of "the history of salvation" (no. 2) and Christ's "saving work" (no. 4) but also specifies the redemptive import of what he disclosed through the crucifixion, resurrection, and sending of the Holy Spirit. All this revealed "that God is with us, to liberate us from the darkness of sin and death and resurrect us to eternal life" (DV 4). But, in general, the focus of *Sacrosanctum Concilium* remains on salvation and the focus of *Dei Verbum* on revelation. Nevertheless, the teaching of *Sacrosanctum Concilium* about the liturgical celebration of the paschal mystery (as "the summit toward which the activity of the Church aims and the fountain from which all her strength flows") anticipated the way *Dei Verbum* was to expound the same paschal mystery as the completion and perfection of the divine self-revelation.

While the paschal mystery remains the summit in the history of salvation (the emphasis of SC) and revelation (the emphasis of DV), neither constitution neglected what preceded and what followed the paschal mystery. In particular, we saw above how *Sacrosanctum Concilium* both (a) reflected on the incarnation as initiating the liturgical activity of Christ as High Priest and (b) looked forward to the definitive liturgy to be celebrated in the final kingdom of God. Two years later *Dei Verbum* followed suit. While the dying and rising of Christ "completed and perfected" revelation, the constitution referred to John 1:14 and quoted Hebrews 1:1-2 (DV 2 fn. 2; 4) to (a) recognize the divine self-disclosure already embodied in the event of the incarnation. Likewise, *Dei Verbum*, referencing 1 Timothy 6:14 and Titus 2:13 spoke of (b) "the glorious manifestation of our Lord Jesus Christ" to come (DV 4). Once again we find *Sacrosanctum Concilium* prefiguring two important themes to be developed subsequently in the constitution on divine revelation. We come at once to further examples of *Dei Verbum* following the teaching of the liturgical constitution, by teaching the sacramental nature of salvation and revelation and by emphasizing the centrality of the Scriptures.

The Sacramental Nature of Salvation and Revelation

When describing how "the faith of those taking part is nourished" and how they offer worship to God, *Sacrosanctum Concilium* highlights the liturgy as word and action. "In the liturgy God *speaks* to his people [and] Christ is still *proclaiming* the Gospel," while "the Church prays, sings, or *acts*" (no. 33; emphasis added). The constitution calls the Eucharist "the sacred action," in which all the faithful should participate "consciously, devoutly, and actively" (no. 47). *Sacrosanctum Concilium* distinguishes but never separates word and action: "the two parts" of the Mass, "the liturgy of the word and the eucharistic liturgy, are so closely connected with each other that they form one act of worship" (no. 56).Throughout its teaching on liturgical renewal, *Sacrosanctum Concilium* employs a sacramental language of word and deed.

When expounding the interplay between word and action, the constitution states. "it is from it [the Sacred Scripture] that the lessons are read and explained in homilies, that psalms are sung, that the prayers, collects and liturgical songs draw their impulse and inspiration, and that *actions and signs* derive their significance" (no. 24; emphasis added). "Actions and signs" work together sacramentally with the word expressed in homilies, psalms, prayers, and hymns.

Sacrosanctum Concilium also enunciates the sacramental nature of liturgy by contrasting its visible and perceptible words and deeds with the invisible action of God. "Visible signs [*signa visibilia*]" are used "in the sacred liturgy for signifying invisible, divine realities" (no. 33).

Subsequent documents of Vatican II use and develop the sacramental language we find in *Sacrosanctum Concilium*. It was in such terms that the Dogmatic Constitution on the Church recalled Jesus' preaching of God's kingdom: "this kingdom was manifested to human beings in the word, deeds, and presence of Christ" (LG 5).

Dei Verbum repeatedly applied sacramental language to "the economy of revelation" and "the history of salvation." The "economy of revelation occurs through deeds and words [*gestis verbisque*] intrinsically connected with each other, so that the works [*opera*] performed by God in the history of salvation manifest and corroborate the doctrine and realities signified by the words, while the words proclaim the works and the mystery they contain" (no. 2). This sacramental language of words and deeds/actions recurs when *Dei Verbum* described the divine self-revelation in the Old Testament as happening "by words and deeds [*verbis ac gestis*]" (no. 14), and spoke of Christ's public ministry: he inaugurated "the kingdom of God on earth," and "by deeds and words [*factis et verbis*] manifested his Father and himself" (no. 17).[12]

In the passage cited above from *Lumen Gentium* we find the Council adding "presence" alongside words and deeds: God's kingdom was manifested "in the word, deeds, and presence of Christ" (no. 5). *Dei Verbum* also picks up the sacramental language of "presence," when it speaks of Christ effecting revelation "by the total presence and manifestation of himself [*tota Suiipsius presentia ac manifestatione*], [and] by words and deeds [*verbis et operibus*]" (no. 4). In a memorable passage, *Sacrosanctum Concilium* had already adverted to the manifold ways in which Christ is "present [*praesens*]" in the liturgy (no. 7).[13] *Lumen Gentium* and *Dei Verbum* took up this liturgical theme and applied it more broadly to Christ's presence in the history of divine self-revelation.

At no point does *Dei Verbum* explicitly receive and apply the liturgical constitution. But, in elaborating the sacramental dynamism of revelation, it applies the teaching of *Sacrosanctum Concilium* to the communication of divine salvation in Jesus Christ. This forms a second example of the way in which the "law of praying" of the liturgical constitution became "the law of believing" in the constitution on divine revelation.

Before leaving the sacramental teaching of *Sacrosanctum Concilium* and its reception in later conciliar documents, we should note how its

---

[12] Above and beyond SC, the "sacramental" language of DV had further sources or at least precedents in the works of Herman Schell, St. Hilary of Poitiers, and others: see Gerald O'Collins, *Retrieving Fundamental Theology* (Mahwah, NJ: Paulist Press, 1993), 54, 160. On the entry of this language into what became DV, see chap. 1 above.

[13] On Christ's liturgical "presence," see chap. 4 below. SC recognizes the whole Church as "sacrament" (nos. 5, 26), a theme recurring subsequently (e.g., in LG 1, 9), but the liturgy constitution also has something particular to say about the sacramental force of words, actions, and presence. Faggioli attends to the way SC proposes, in general, the sacramental nature of the Church (*True Reform*, 62, 66–68), but not to the particular way the constitution expounds the liturgy in terms of "words," "actions," and "presence"—an exposition that opened the way for some of what came later in LG, DV, and, as we shall see at once, in GS 4 and 11.

language of "visible signs signifying invisible divine realities" enjoyed a late echo in what *Gaudium et Spes* was to say about "the signs of the times," which need to be interpreted "in the light of the gospel" (no. 4). "In the events, needs, and longings" of our times there can be "genuine signs of the presence or purpose of God" (no. 11). To be sure, the Pastoral Constitution on the Church in the Modern World drew on further sources when speaking in this way—Pope John XXIII, others, and ultimately Jesus himself (Matt 16:3). Nevertheless, through its teaching on liturgical signs, *Sacrosanctum Concilium* had also opened a door for a wider use of this language. The signs of the times, whether at first glance positive or negative, may reveal to us something about where Christ is present in a special way and what God aims to bring about in our world.[14]

The Centrality of the Scripture

Influenced in part by the modern biblical movement and by Pius XII's 1943 encyclical *Divino Afflante Spiritu*, the liturgical constitution of Vatican II firmly endorsed the central significance of the Scripture for Christian worship and life. Containing thirteen quotations from the Bible and thirty-three references to it, *Sacrosanctum Concilium* showed, from the start of the Council, how the Scriptures could "nourish and rule" (DV 21) its teaching.[15]

In particular, the liturgical constitution mandated a richer selection of Scripture readings for the divine office (no. 92). Here it followed what it had already prescribed for the celebration of the Eucharist: "the treasures of the Bible are to be opened up more lavishly, so that a richer table of God's word may be prepared for the faithful. Thus a more representative part of the Holy Scriptures will be read to the people in the course of a determined number of years" (no. 51).

Subsequent conciliar documents and, in particular, *Dei Verbum*, followed the lead of the liturgical constitution when drawing on the resources of contemporary biblical studies and applying the Scriptures

---

[14] Apropos of "signs," we should respect the difference between sacramental signs and the phenomena of modern life (reviewed in GS 4–10) that can reveal to us divine intentions.

[15] On the earlier currents of biblical theology that had an impact on the conciliar documents, see chap. 1 above.

to the magisterium, theology, preaching, personal prayer, and the whole life of the Church. *Dei Verbum* began by describing the Council as "religiously hearing the Word of God and faithfully proclaiming it" (no. 1). With reference to the transmission of divine revelation, the same constitution said that the magisterium "devotedly hears, reverently guards, and faithfully expounds the Word of God" (no. 10). This set the stage for the final chapter of *Dei Verbum* to state that the Church "has always treated [the divine Scriptures] and treats them, together with Sacred Tradition, as the supreme rule of her faith." Hence "the entire preaching of the Church, like the Christian religion itself, should be nourished and ruled by Sacred Scripture" (no. 21).

More than any other chapter in the sixteen documents of Vatican II, chapter 6 of *Dei Verbum* puts on display the biblical mind-set that *Sacrosanctum Concilium* had already introduced into the conciliar teaching. For example, through the images of foundational, strengthening, and rejuvenating functions, the constitution presents the impact of the Scriptures in theology: "it [theology] rests upon the written Word of God, together with Sacred Tradition, as on a permanent foundation, and is most firmly strengthened and always rejuvenated by it [the Word of God]." Hence "the study of the Sacred Page should be, as it were, the soul [*anima*] of Sacred Theology" (no. 24). The Council drew this vivid description of the role of the Scriptures from the 1893 encyclical of Pope Leo XIII, *Providentissimus Deus*. It had already introduced this description a few weeks earlier in the Decree on the Training of Priests, *Optatam Totius:* "the study of Sacred Scripture . . . ought to be, as it were, the soul of the whole of theology" (OT 16).[16]

Faggioli's judgment that *Sacrosanctum Concilium* opened the way for the other conciliar documents to "rediscover" the centrality of the Scriptures can be convincingly vindicated. In particular, the authors of *Lumen Gentium* and *Dei Verbum* (consciously or unconsciously) took up and expanded the biblical mind-set of the liturgical constitution.[17] At the General Congregations of Vatican II, all held in St. Peter's Basilica, the

---

[16] On the origin of calling Scripture "the soul of theology," see José M. Lera, "*Sacrae paginae studium sit veluti anima Sacrae Theologiae* (Notas sobre el origen y procedencia de esta frase)," in *Palabra y vida. Homenaje a. José Alonso Diaz*, ed. José Antonio Vargas Machuca and Gregorio Ruiz (Madrid: Universidad Pontificia Comillas, 1983), 409–22.

[17] On this see chap. 9 below.

Book of the Gospels was enthroned each day right through the four sessions. Symbolizing the presence of Christ, the book displayed what *Dei Verbum* announced about the bishops' teaching office: "the magisterium is not above the word of God but serves it" (no. 10).[18] The authority of the Scriptures permeated the deliberations and documents of the Council.

Sacrosanctum Concilium, while setting in general a standard through clearly endorsing the centrality of the Scriptures, prepared the way in particular for *Dei Verbum*, *Lumen Gentium*, and *Nostra Aetate*. First, while containing thirteen quotations from the Bible and thirty-three references to it, *Sacrosanctum Concilium* also included twelve further quotations drawn from liturgical texts (seven), the Council of Trent (three), and the fathers (two), as well as ten references, drawn from liturgical texts (two), Trent (two) and the fathers (six). This spread of quotations and references mirrored a long and rich tradition, and showed the tradition applying and actualizing the divine revelation normatively recorded and interpreted in the Scriptures. The unity and interplay of Scripture and tradition to which *Sacrosanctum Concilium* witnessed in "practice" would be explained in "theory" by the chapter on tradition in *Dei Verbum* (nos. 7–10). Where *Sacrosanctum Concilium* had spoken of "sound [*sana*]" (nos. 4, 22) or "venerable [*venerabilis*]" (nos. 24, 89) tradition, *Dei Verbum* speaks of "sacred [*sacra*]" tradition and its functioning with "sacred Scriptures" (nos. 9, 10 [twice], 24).

Second, by mandating a liturgical use of "the treasures" of the whole Bible, *Sacrosanctum Concilium* recalled the indispensable place of the Jewish Scriptures and heritage in the life of Christians. This opened the way for the *rapprochement* with the Jewish people developed in later conciliar texts (LG 16; NA 4).

The (Worshipping) People of God

Sacrosanctum Concilium first quotes 1 Peter 2:9 about "the Christian people [*populus*]" being "a holy nation and a people [*populus*] of

---

[18] See Romeo de Maio, *The Book of the Gospels at the Oecumenical Councils* (Vatican City: Biblioteca Apostolica Vaticana, 1963); this *Book of the Gospels* was also published in French, German, Italian, and Spanish. Yves Congar mistakenly writes of the Bible being enthroned at the Council's sessions: see *My Journal of the Council*, trans. Mary John Ronayne and Mary Cecily Boulding (Collegeville, MN: Liturgical Press, 2012), 87.

[God's] possession," and then speaks of "the whole people [*populus*]" assembled for worship (no. 14). The constitution understands "liturgical actions" to be "celebrations" of "the holy people [*plebs*]" united with their bishop (no. 26). In the liturgy "God speaks to his people [*populus*], . . . [and] the people [*populus*] reply to God with songs and prayer" (no. 33). This paves the way for the prominent fashion in which the Dogmatic Constitution on the Church privileges "people of God" as an image for understanding the Church.

Before doing so, *Lumen Gentium* sets itself in chapter 1 to ponder the "mystery of the Church." It cites from the Scriptures various images of the Church drawn from sheep farming, the cultivation of olives and vineyards, the construction of buildings, family life, and marriage (no. 6). It moves to provide more elaborated teaching about the Church as the Body of Christ (no. 7), and then dedicates an entire chapter (nos. 9–17) to "the people of God" (also called "the messianic people," "the new people of God," "the one people of God," "the holy people of God," or, simply, "the people"). As a doctrinally rich account of the Church, "people of God" introduces the history of salvation (no. 9), the priestly and prophetic character of the Church (nos. 10–12), and the different ways in which human beings can be incorporated in, connected with, or related to this people (nos. 14–17).

This chapter in *Lumen Gentium* adds a further image, the Church as "communion" (nos. 9, 13 [three times], and 15).[19] The same chapter also speaks of the Holy Spirit dwelling in the Church as in a temple (no. 9). This prepared the way for ending the chapter on a trinitarian note and calling the Church "the People of God, the Body of the Lord [Jesus Christ], and the Temple of the Holy Spirit" (no. 17).The whole of chapter 2 is richly biblical, containing twelve quotations from the Scriptures and fifty-three references to them with six quotations coming from New Testament epistles and twenty-seven references being made to them. Chapters 1 and 2 should encourage us to identify the ecclesiology of Vatican II as a "biblical ecclesiology," which pays special

---

[19] The theme of the Church "as a communion of life, love, and truth" (no. 9) was to prove popular in the post–Vatican II situation, not least at the 1985 Extraordinary Synod of Bishops; see Jean-Marie-Roger Tillard, "Final Report of the Last Synod," in *Synod 1985: An Evaluation*, ed. Giuseppe Alberigo and James Provost (Edinburgh: T. & T. Clark, 1986), 64–77, at 71–73.

attention to the Church as "the People of God, the Body and Christ, and the Temple of the Holy Spirit."

All of this raises doubts when Faggioli first expounds *Sacrosanctum Concilium* as preparing the way for the "eucharistic ecclesiology" of the Council.[20] Then he modifies this judgment by acknowledging "the gap between the accomplished and coherent ecclesiology of the liturgical constitution and the ecclesiologies [plural] of *Lumen Gentium* and *Gaudium et Spes* and the decrees *Christus Dominus, Unitatis Redintegratio,* and *Actuositatem Apostolicam*."[21] The natural outcome of the eucharistic ecclesiology of *Sacrosanctum Concilium*, Faggioli rightly argues, was an ecclesiology of the local Church.[22] A eucharistic ecclesiology logically highlights the local community gathered around the local bishop.

Unquestionably, the liturgical constitution expounds at length the Eucharist (e.g., nos. 47–58). But *Lumen Gentium* hardly emphasizes a eucharistic ecclesiology. To be sure, it understands "the unity of the faithful to be expressed and effected" by the Eucharist (LG 3), and, when describing "the People of God," it speaks of them being strengthened in their "eucharistic communion" (no. 11). Later it mentions briefly the eucharistic ministry of bishops (no. 26)[23] and priests (no. 28), but stresses their function as preachers and teachers (nos. 25 and 28, respectively). The Decree on the Pastoral Office of Bishops in the Church likewise privileges their teaching role (nos. 12–14) over

---

[20] Faggioli, *"Sacrosanctum Concilium* and the Meaning of Vatican II," 441, 450. In developing his thesis about a "eucharistic ecclesiology," Faggioli endorses earlier work by Giuseppe Dossetti; see *True Reform,* 6 and 18.

[21] Faggioli, *True Reform,* 62; see 68, 71.

[22] Ibid., 75–79, 85–86.

[23] The constitution speaks of "the Eucharist by which the Church continually lives and grows" (LG 26). In *"Ressourcement,* Vatican II, and Eucharistic Ecclesiology," in *Ressourcement: A Movement for Renewal in Twentieth-Century Catholic Theology,* ed. Gabriel Flynn and Paul D. Murray (Oxford: Oxford University Press, 2012), 393–404, Paul McPartlan, without citing either Faggioli or Dossetti, argues that in LG the Council showed its intention to embrace a eucharistic ecclesiology. However, while texts drawn from Henri de Lubac and Nicholas Afanasíev (the theologian who coined the term "eucharistic ecclesiology") expressing such a eucharistic ecclesiology appeared in drafts of LG, none of these texts made it through to the final version that Vatican II promulgated. One might argue that precisely by leaving aside such citations the Council showed that in LG it did not want to embrace too closely a eucharistic ecclesiology.

that of "sanctifying" through the Eucharist and the other sacraments (no. 15). Remarkably the strongest statement supporting a eucharistic ecclesiology occurs in the Decree on Ecumenism, *Unitatis Redintegratio* (promulgated on November 21, 1964), when it comments on the sacramental life of Eastern Churches *not* in union with the Bishop of Rome: "through the celebration of the Eucharist of the Lord in each of these Churches, the Church of God is built up and grows in stature" (no. 15). This statement, without using the term, endorses the principle of "the Church from the Eucharist [*Ecclesia de Eucharistia*]."[24]

Sacrosanctum Concilium might have encouraged a more eucharistic ecclesiology and presented the Church as the "product" of the Eucharist. That could have been the happy outcome of its teaching about the liturgy, and supremely the Eucharist, being "the summit [*culmen*] toward which the activity of the Church aims and the fountain [*fons*] from which all her strength flows" (no. 10).[25] *Lumen Gentium* echoed this passage when it spoke of the "eucharistic sacrifice" as "the fountain and summit of the whole of Christian life" (LG 11). But, in fact, the authors of *Lumen Gentium* (consciously or unconsciously) followed other passages in *Sacrosanctum Concilium* (see SC 14 and 33) to develop the image of "the People of God," which it crafted into a trinitarian ecclesiology (*Ecclesia de Trinitate*) by adding the themes of the Body of Christ and the Temple of the Holy Spirit.[26]

Beyond question, a trinitarian ecclesiology and a eucharistic ecclesiology are not mutually exclusive. The public worship of Christians is unthinkable without its trinitarian *anamnesis* (remembering the saving actions of the incarnate Son), *epiclesis* (invoking the Holy Spirit), and *doxology* (giving glory to God the Father). Nevertheless, emphases differ. What we read in *Lumen Gentium* looks more like a trinitarian ecclesiology. Add to that the later Decree on the Church's Missionary Activity which famously opened by founding that activity in a thoroughly trinitarian way (AG 2–9).

---

[24] Faggioli quotes this passage from UR in *True Reform*, 71 n. 43.

[25] The daily celebration of the Eucharist in the council hall (St. Peter's Basilica) before Vatican II began its business at the plenary sessions could also have encouraged giving prominence to a eucharistic ecclesiology in the spirit of *Concilium de Eucharistia*. But this did not happen.

[26] See Anne Hunt, "The Trinitarian Depths of Vatican II," *Theological Studies* 74 (2013): 3–19.

The Holy Spirit

Faggioli has nothing to say about the (admittedly modest) teaching on the Holy Spirit offered by *Sacrosanctum Concilium*. The constitution appreciates how those who share in the daily liturgy are built up "into a dwelling place of God in the Spirit" (SC 2). The Christocentrism of *Sacrosanctum Concilium* involves representing Jesus being "anointed by the Holy Spirit" for his ministry (SC 5). On their side, the faithful, "through the power of the Holy Spirit," can give thanks to God for "the unutterable gift" of Jesus Christ (SC 6). This is as close as *Sacrosanctum Concilium* ever comes to naming the Holy Spirit as acting on the faithful in the Eucharist and other sacraments—something that would be explicitly stated by *Lumen Gentium* 50.

Lumen Gentium filled out the conciliar teaching on the Holy Spirit with its trinitarian ecclesiology (see above) and with considerable attention paid to the Spirit in particular sections: for instance, chapter 7 on the pilgrim people of God.[27] The Pastoral Constitution on the Church in the Modern World looked beyond the baptized faithful to the activity of the Holy Spirit in the world. The Spirit gives all human beings "the light and strength" needed "to respond to their supreme calling" (GS 10; see also nos. 15, 22, 38). Yet we can question whether the later conciliar texts nuanced sufficiently the Christocentrism of *Sacrosanctum Concilium*, which highlights Christ as the primary subject of the liturgy (SC 7) and largely leaves it at that, without paying much attention to the Holy Spirit.

Dei Verbum may refer to the Holy Spirit thirty-three times but remains very Christocentric. Despite the statistics, the constitution illustrates a Latin tendency to subordinate the work of the Spirit to that of the Son. The chapter on the Old Testament (DV 14–16), for instance, is oriented toward Christ and says nothing about the Spirit. On October 5, 1964, during a debate on the revised text of *De Divina Revelatione*, what was to become *Dei Verbum*, an Eastern archbishop, Néophytos Edelby, indicated the need to recognize more fully the role of the Spirit in revelation and its transmission through the Scriptures and tradition.[28] Unfortunately, Edelby's comments came too late and

---

[27] LG 48–51; these four articles name the Holy Spirit seven times.

[28] *Acta Synodalia Sacrosancti Concilii Oecumenici Vaticani Secundi*, III/III (Vatican City: Typis Polyglottis Vaticanis, 1974), 306–8.

hardly affected the final shape of *Dei Verbum*. Neither *Dei Verbum* nor other conciliar texts rose to the challenge left on the agenda by the somewhat one-sided Christocentrism of *Sacrosanctum Concilium*.

Priests, Prophets, and Kings

A sixth line of development from *Sacrosanctum Concilium* (but one not expounded by Faggioli[29]) opened when the constitution quoted 1 Peter 2:9 to picture the Christian people as being "a royal priesthood" (no. 14). This prepared the way for a major theme to be developed in *Lumen Gentium* and other documents: through baptism (all Christians) and ordination (the ministers), the faithful share in Christ's triple function as priest, prophet, and king/shepherd.

Admittedly, *Sacrosanctum Concilium* spoke only of "the exercise of the priestly office of Jesus Christ [*Iesu Christi sacerdotalis muneris exercitatio*]" in the liturgy and of "the work [*opus*] of Christ the priest" (no. 7), as well as of "the ministry of priests" through whom he is present (no. 7). This language recurred in chapter 4, which presented "the priestly work [*sacerdotale munus*]" of Christ being continued in the celebration of the Eucharist and in other ways, especially in the divine office (no. 83). *Sacrosanctum Concilium*, while being thus quite explicit about Christ's priestly function, left his prophetic and kingly roles implicit. The former was implied when the constitution referred to Christ "proclaiming his Gospel" (no. 33). His kingly/shepherding function was evoked when *Sacrosanctum Concilium* spoke of "pastors" and "pastors of souls" (nos. 14, 19) who lead Christ's "flock" (no.19).

Sacrosanctum Concilium hints at sharing in the priesthood of Christ when it states that every liturgical celebration is exercised by Christ the priest *and* the members of his "mystical Body" (no. 7). By virtue of their baptism all the faithful have "the right and the duty [*ius et officium*]" to participate actively in the liturgy (no. 14). The constitution speaks twenty-three times of such active participation.[30] As regards

---

[29] Faggioli mentioned the priesthood of Christ only in passing (*True Reform*, 31–32, 131). In a global way he affirmed, but without developing the statement, that "Christ's priestly, kingly, and prophetic offices are represented in the understanding of the church offered by the liturgical constitution" (*True Reform*, 70).

[30] For the noun (*participatio*) or the verb (*participare*), see SC 8, 10, 11, 12, 14 (twice), 17, 19, 21, 27, 30, 33, 41, 48, 50, 53, 55, 56, 79, 113, 114, 121, 124.

the ordained, it repeatedly implies that they share in a distinct and special way in Christ's priesthood (e.g., SC 7 and 41). By implication, ordained ministers also share in Christ's prophetic and kingly functions (e.g., SC 52 and 14, respectively).

But it was left to later documents of Vatican II to spell out fully the triple function of Christ and sharing in it through baptism and ordination. Distinguishing "the common priesthood of the faithful" from "the ministerial or hierarchical priesthood," *Lumen Gentium* adds that "each in their own proper way shares in the one priesthood of Christ," which is a "royal/kingly priesthood" (no. 10). The constitution completes the threefold scheme when it moves on to say that "the holy people of God also shares in Christ's prophetic office" (no. 12). *Lumen Gentium* opened the way for five further conciliar documents to repeat and develop the teaching about sharing in the triple office of Christ: *Unitatis Redintegratio* (no. 4), *Christus Dominus* (nos. 12–21), *Apostolicam Actuositatem* (nos. 2, 10), *Ad Gentes* (no. 15), and *Presbyterorum Ordinis* (nos. 1–6).

Thus the Council deployed in six documents what sharing in Christ's office as priest, prophet, and king/shepherd involves. In developing this teaching, the bishops and their advisors could draw on various sources—and not least the work of Blessed John Henry Newman.[31] But *Sacrosanctum Concilium* had led the way, and its brief teaching flowered when massively expanded in six subsequent texts of Vatican II.

Eschatology

In its introduction *Sacrosanctum Concilium* described the whole Church as a "pilgrim" people moving toward a "future city that we seek" (no. 2). Among the general principles that should shape the reform of the liturgy *Sacrosanctum Concilium* recalled the eschatological hope of Christians: "in the earthly liturgy we share in and have a foretaste of that heavenly liturgy which is celebrated in the holy city of Jerusalem toward which we move as *pilgrims*." The constitution added:

---

[31] For some major sources in the Scriptures and tradition for teaching about the triple function of priest, prophet, and king/shepherd, see O'Collins and Jones, *Jesus Our Priest, passim*.

"venerating the memory of the saints, we hope for some part and fellowship with them; we await the Saviour, Our Lord Jesus Christ, until he, our life, shall appear and we too shall appear with him in glory" (SC 8; emphasis added). Naturally when it comes to the Eucharist, *Sacrosanctum Concilium* cited the antiphon from the Feast of Corpus Christi about the Eucharist being "the paschal banquet" in which "a pledge of future glory is given to us" (SC 47). The mystery of Christ, unfolded in the liturgical year, nourishes "the expectation of blessed hope and of the coming of the Lord" (SC 107).

Through this teaching on the shape of things to come, *Sacrosanctum Concilium* prepared the way for expressions of Christian hope found in subsequent documents of Vatican II. *Lumen Gentium* dedicated a notable chapter to the "pilgrim people of God" (LG 48–51). The Constitution on the Church in the Modern World ended its first part by expressing hope in Christ, "the Alpha and the Omega." the beginning and end of all things (GS 45). The whole document concluded with a vivid expectation of the world's final fulfilment through Christ in a "homeland radiant with the glory of the Lord" (GS 93).[32]

The Collegiality of Bishops

The collegial authority of bishops proved an eighth area in which Vatican II went on to develop the teaching of the liturgy constitution. *Lumen Gentium* caught the imagination of many commentators by its doctrine of the Catholic bishops around the world forming with the Bishop of Rome a college (nos. 22–23), like "the one apostolic college constituted by St. Peter and the rest of the apostles" (no. 22). This teaching expressed the organic unity between pope and bishops and their joint responsibility for the universal Church.

While never dealing with collegiality in that clear sense, *Sacrosanctum Concilium* repeatedly assigned the authority for liturgical change to "bishops' conferences of various kinds, in given territories" (no. 22.2). "Competent ecclesiastical authority in given territories" should decide

---

[32] Faggioli mentions in passing "liturgy and eschatology,," but has nothing to say about SC initiating the Council's teaching on Christian hope. But he is not silent about the way in which SC helped prepare for the teaching on collegiality and the further themes we will discuss; on collegiality, see Faggioli, *True Reform*, 51–52, 61, 73, 80, 89, 103, and so forth.

"whether, and to what extent, the vernacular language is to be used." That involves consulting "with bishops of neighbouring regions which have the same language" and approving the translations for use (no. 36.3 and 4). *Sacrosanctum Concilium* acknowledged the authority of local bishops over liturgical adaptations (no. 39). In the case of "more radical adaptation of the liturgy," suggested by "the traditions and natural mentality [*ingenio*] of individual peoples," the local bishops should consult the Bishop of Rome over the adaptations that could be "useful or even necessary" (no. 40.1 and 2). Without employing the specific language of "collegiality," *Sacrosanctum Concilium* mandated here joint, collegial action of bishops' conferences when translating and adapting the liturgy. The constitution went on to encourage neighboring dioceses to act collegially and, where necessary, establish joint liturgical commissions (no. 45).

Promulgated a year later, *Lumen Gentium* was to spell out the collegial responsibility that bishops exercise "with Peter and under Peter" for the good of the whole Church. The two articles dedicated to collegiality ended by remarking that "bishops conferences can contribute manifold and fruitful help to the concrete application of the collegiate spirit [*collegialis affectus*]" (no. 23). It was precisely such a specific realization of collegiality which *Sacrosanctum Concilium* had mandated a year earlier and which *Lumen Gentium* received and developed.

Other Rites

From the outset, *Sacrosanctum Concilium* showed itself sensitive to the liturgical rites and traditions of Eastern Catholics that set them apart from the Roman or Latin rite. In Eastern Christianity, there are seven such major rites: the Armenian, the Byzantine (the rite of the Melkites), the Coptic, the East-Syrian (sometimes called Assyro-Chaldean), the Ethiopian, the Maronite (or Syro-Maronite), and West Syrian (or Antiochene). The constitution recognized that among "the principles and norms" that affect the reform of the liturgy, "some can and should be applied to the Roman rite and also to all other rites." But it added at once that "the practical norms" it would propose "should be taken as applying only to the Roman rite, except for those which, in the very nature of things, affect other rites as well" (no. 3).

Since different rites celebrated the daily Eucharist in the hall of the Council, the Latin rite bishops were encouraged to grow in a proper

sensitivity to the Eastern rites. Many Western bishops had never before participated in an Eastern-rite liturgy. They had said Mass only
in Latin, and now they were confronted with eucharistic liturgies
celebrated in different languages and some of them in modern languages. All of that became part of the learning experience at Vatican
II of many Latin-rite bishops.[33]

The respectful acknowledgment of Eastern Catholics in the introduction to *Sacrosanctum Concilium* flowered in two subsequent texts of
Vatican II, both promulgated on the same day (November 21, 1964):
the Decree on the Catholic Eastern Churches, *Orientalium Ecclesiarum,*
and the Decree on Ecumenism with its special section devoted to the
estranged Churches of Orthodoxy and Oriental Orthodoxy (UR 14–
18).[34] *Orientalium Ecclesiarum* (no. 20 n. 25) repeated the desire already
expressed in an appendix to *Sacrosanctum Concilium*, to fix with other
Christians the celebration of Easter on the same Sunday. It legislated
for some matters concerning the discipline of the sacraments (nos.
11–18). While "confirming and praising the ancient discipline about
the sacraments which exists in the Eastern Churches, and also the
practice concerning their celebration and administration," it wished
this "to be renewed where such a case arises" (no. 12). The decree left
to the synodical government of each of the seven Eastern rites any decisions about the languages to be used in liturgical celebration (OE 23).

Apropos of *Sacrosanctum Concilium* and non-Roman rites, Faggioli
reports what Eastern bishops contributed to a liturgical awareness in
general and to the debate on the text of *Sacrosanctum Concilium* in particular.[35] He also attends to adapting the liturgy and the role played by
the liturgical constitution in developing the subsequent conciliar teaching in the whole area of what came later to be called inculturation.[36]

[33] One should recall that certain bishops of the Latin rite (e.g., some from
France, Germany, and India) were already familiar with the liturgical use of the
vernacular.

[34] "Oriental Orthodox" is a modern term for those Eastern churches that accept
only the first three ecumenical councils, unlike the "Eastern Orthodox" churches
which accept the first seven.

[35] Faggioli, *True Reform*, 32, 34–35, 39, 63, 67, 118, 133, 140.

[36] Ibid., 38–43, 55, 56, 68, 82, 120, and so forth.

Adaptation (and Inculturation)

We saw above the provisions that *Sacrosanctum Concilium* made for local Churches to translate and adapt the liturgy (nos. 36, 37, 39). The constitution envisaged a "more radical adaptation of the liturgy," which, in the light of "the traditions and mentality of individual peoples" could be "useful or even necessary" (no. 40). It wanted to "honour and promote the qualities and gifts of various nations and peoples," and, where appropriate, incorporate those traditions into the liturgy (no. 38).

This teaching was received and developed by the constitution on the Church and then by the decree on missionary activity. They called for adaptations that included not only the liturgy but also ways of life. First, *Lumen Gentium* stated what had actually been accomplished and was taking place. The Church "fosters and adopts, insofar as they are good, the abilities, resources, and customs of peoples. In adopting [them], she purifies, strengthens, and elevates [them]" (no. 13). Using equivalent terms, the constitution went on to say that through missionary activity, "whatever good is found sown in the heart and mind of human beings or in the particular rites and cultures of peoples, so far from being lost, is healed, elevated, and consummated for the glory of God" (no. 17).

A year later, *Ad Gentes* quoted *Lumen Gentium* word for word by saying: "whatever good is found sown in the heart and mind of human beings or in the particular rites and cultures of peoples, so far from being lost, is healed, elevated, and consummated for the glory of God" (no. 9). A later passage in the missionary decree references (but without quoting) LG 13 when it speaks of "the young churches" taking over "all the riches of the nations. . . . They borrow from the customs and traditions of the peoples, from wisdom and doctrine, from the arts and disciplines everything which could contribute to confessing the glory of the Creator, to manifesting the grace of the Saviour, and to the right ordering of Christian life" (AG 22).

This led the missionary decree to call for theological experts to examine "by which ways faith could seek understanding through keeping in mind the philosophy and wisdom of the peoples," and by what means their "customs, sense of life, and social order" could be put together with divine revelation. All this "will open ways for a more profound adaptation in the whole sphere of Christian life." Thus

"Christian life will be adapted to the mentality and character of each culture, and particular traditions together with the special qualities of each family of nations, illuminated by the light of the Gospel, will be taken up into a Catholic unity" (AG 22). What Vatican II named here as adaptation overlapped with what was later to be called "inculturation," a new term for the old obligation to contextualize and indigenize the Christian way of life in the various cultures of our world.[37]

The Pastoral Constitution on the Church in the Modern World in its chapter on the proper development of culture reflected on the "links" between the message of salvation and various cultures: "when revealing himself to his people through to the full self-manifestation in the incarnate Son, God spoke according to the culture proper to different ages. Likewise the Church . . . has used the resources of different cultures in its preaching to spread and explain the message of Christ to all nations, to examine and understand it more deeply, and to express it better *in the liturgical celebration* and in various aspects of the life of the faithful." At the same time, *Gaudium et Spes* insisted that, "so far from being tied exclusively and indissolubly" to any particular culture, the Church "can enter into communion with different forms of culture, thereby enriching both herself and the various cultures themselves" (no. 58; emphasis added).

The constitution confidently announced that "the good news of Christ" never ceases to "purify and elevate the morality of peoples. It takes the spiritual qualities and endowments of every people and age," and causes them "to flower, as it were, from within; it strengthens, completes and restores them to Christ." In this way the Church "stimulates and advances human and civil culture, as well as contributing by its activity, including *liturgical activity*, to the interior freedom of human beings" (no. 58; emphasis added).

Thus at the close of Vatican II, *Gaudium et Spes* completed a trajectory initiated by what *Sacrosanctum Concilium* briefly taught on the liturgical adaptations required by "the traditions and mentality of individual peoples." Sets of verbs describe what such adaptation involves: "purifying, strengthening, and elevating" (LG 13), "healing, elevat-

---

[37] The literature on inculturation is vast; for an introduction see Gerald A. Arbuckle, *Culture, Inculturation, and Theologians: A Postmodern Critique* (Collegeville, MN: Liturgical Press, 2010).

ing, and consummating" (LG 17), "purifying and elevating" (GS 58), "strengthening, completing, and restoring to Christ," or "completing and advancing" (GS 58). This adaptation includes but presses beyond liturgical celebration to embrace wide aspects of Christian life.

The work of adaptation coincides in part with the *missionary* activity of the Church, an activity clearly stated in *Sacrosanctum Concilium* 9. Here what we recalled above from *Sacrosanctum Concilium* 36 and 38–40 prefigured the teaching on missionary activity that would be articulated fully in *Ad Gentes*.[38]

Dialogue with the Others

Faggioli rightly observed how the liturgical constitution prepared the way for what he called "the *rapprochement* manifestos" of Vatican II: the decree on ecumenism (UR), the declaration on other religions (NA), and the pastoral constitution (GS). Let us first see how *rapprochement* expressed itself in *Sacrosanctum Concilium*.

Right from the opening article, a worldwide mind-set distinguished the constitution. It named four related concerns that motivated the whole work of the Council: (a) fostering growth in the life of Roman Catholics; (b) updating those institutions that are subject to changes; (c) promoting "union" among all Christians;[39] and (d) strengthening "whatever can help to call all human beings into the bosom of the Church" (no. 1). These four concerns provided cogent reasons for "the renewal and promotion of the liturgy" (no. 1). Unlike the Council of Trent, Vatican II presented its teaching on the liturgy within the context not only of all Christianity but also of the entire human race.

The second article reflected the same mind-set. Through the liturgy and especially through the Eucharist, "the faithful express and *manifest to others* the mystery of Christ and the genuine nature of the true Church." As well as feeding their spiritual lives and bringing them to "the fullness of Christ," the Eucharist "strengthens their power to

---

[38] On the "missionary" link between SC and later documents, see Faggioli, *True Reform*, 37–46.

[39] The *ecumenical* thrust of the liturgical reform mandated by SC expressed itself through the importance assigned to the Scriptures (nos. 34, 51), the emphasis on preaching (nos. 35, 50), the introduction of the vernacular (no. 54), and communion under both kinds (no. 55). See Faggioli, *True Reform*, 110–11.

preach Christ and thus show forth, *to those who are outside*, the Church as a sign lifted up among the nations under which the scattered children of God may be gathered into one" (no. 2; emphasis added).[40] Thus, from the outset, the constitution presented the Eucharist as *also* involving an open desire to "preach Christ" and "manifest" his mystery to the world. *Sacrosanctum Concilium* signalled a commitment to the whole human race and a desire to share with everyone the life of Christ and the fellowship of the Church.

In a similar vein, chapter 1 (on "general principles for renewing and promoting the sacred liturgy") opens by quoting the classic New Testament text about God wanting "all human beings to be saved and come to the knowledge of the truth" (1 Tim 2:4). It refers at once to Christ coming as "the Mediator between God and human beings" (with 1 Tim 2:5 being referenced rather than quoted). The constitution then sums up the work of Christ as "redeeming human kind and giving perfect glory to God" (SC 5). Thus over and over again the opening chapter reveals the same encompassing vision and desire that "all human beings should know the one true God and Jesus Christ whom he has sent" (SC 9).

Given the world-encompassing mind-set of the constitution, we should not be surprised that chapter 2 (dedicated to the Eucharist) restores the "prayer of the faithful," an old tradition which had never been given up in the East, but which had disappeared in the Roman liturgy except on Good Friday.[41] This prayer was to be restored "after the gospel and homily, especially on Sundays and holidays of obligation." Recalling in a footnote 1 Timothy 2:1-2 (which enjoins a similar form of prayer), *Sacrosanctum Concilium* explains: "in this prayer in which the people are to take part, intercessions are made for the holy Church, for those who lead us politically, for those oppressed by various needs, for *all human beings*, and for *the salvation of the whole world*" (no. 53; emphasis added).

---

[40] Here SC evokes John 11:52 (about Jesus "gathering into one the scattered children of God"). This text will also be referenced when the constitution on the Church attends to all the "outsiders" (LG 13).

[41] See Adolf Adam, *The Eucharistic Celebration: The Source and Summit of Faith*, trans. Robert C. Schultz (Collegeville, MN: Liturgical Press, 1994), 49–51; Gerard Moore, *Lord, Hear Our Prayer: Praying the General Intercessions* (Strathfield, NSW: St. Paul's Publications, 2008), 11–17.

There is a further article in the constitution that witnesses to its universal outreach. The chapter on the divine office opens by saying: "Jesus Christ, the High Priest of the New and Eternal Covenant, when he assumed a human nature, introduced into this land of exile the hymn that in heaven is sung throughout all ages. He unites the whole community of human kind with himself and associates it with him in singing the divine canticle of praise" (SC 83). Earlier the constitution had taught that the risen Christ is present "when the Church prays and *sings psalms*" (SC 7; emphasis added). Now the document speaks of singing one "divine canticle of praise," led by the incarnate "Cantor" himself, who gathers together the entire human race in sharing the heavenly hymn that he has brought to earth. Christ is pictured here as associating with himself not merely those who come to know and believe in him but also the whole human community. Together they all form a choir of which he is the leader. The High Priest of the New and Eternal Covenant continues his priestly work through the Church, which is "ceaselessly engaged in praising the Lord [presumably understood here as God the Father] and interceding for the salvation of the whole world" (SC 83).

This prayerful openness to the whole human race was received and developed first of all by *Lumen Gentium* 16–17 and then by *Unitatis Redintegratio*, which set down Catholic principles on ecumenism (nos. 2–4) before sketching what their practice could and should involve (nos. 5–12) and respectfully describing the situation of Churches and ecclesial communities separated from the Catholic Church. This decree reversed centuries of polemic and embraced ecumenism. The presence in the "aula" of the Council of observers and guests—fifty-four in the first session and up to 182 in the fourth and final session—symbolized the dramatic change.[42] This decree prepared the way for ceremonies held on December 7, 1965 simultaneously in the Vatican and at the ecumenical patriarch's residence in Istanbul. Explaining in a joint declaration the significance of what they were doing, Pope Paul VI and Patriarch Athenagoras lifted the mutual excommunications between the Orthodox and Catholic Churches.

---

[42] The observers, being seated close to the presiders' table, enjoyed even better seats than the cardinals. Their presence, comments, and advice helped to shape UR and some other documents. See John W. O'Malley, *What Happened at Vatican II* (Cambridge, MA: The Belknap Press of Harvard University Press, 2008), 23, 33.

The Declaration on the Relation of the Church to Non-Christian Religions, *Nostra Aetate* (promulgated on October 28, 1965), whether consciously or not, took the *rapprochement* mind-set of *Sacrosanctum Concilium* into the area of interfaith relations.[43] *Nostra Aetate* opened with a vision of the one world, in which all human beings share the same origin, deep questions, divine providence, and final destiny (no. 1). The document then considered Hinduism, Buddhism (no. 2), Islam (no. 3), and Judaism (no. 4). It exhorted Catholics, while acting "with prudence and charity" and "witnessing to Christian faith and life," to take up "dialogue and collaboration with followers of other religions."[44] Such dialogue and collaboration, which involved Catholics in "recognizing, protecting, and promoting those spiritual and moral goods, as well as those socio-cultural values," embodied a loving concern for the religious others. But by "recognizing, protecting, and promoting" these goods and values, were Catholics to receive some of these "spiritual and moral goods" for themselves, as well as being blessed by the "socio-cultural values" of the others? No reply was given in *Nostra Aetate*. We could look for an answer in the mutual fruits of the dialogue and collaboration that emerged around the world in the aftermath of Vatican II.[45]

Finally, the Pastoral Constitution on the Church in the Modern World took the universal mind-set of *Sacrosanctum Concilium* to its fullest conclusion.[46] Let me single out two themes in the teaching of *Gaudium et Spes*. First, four affirmations concerning the mission of the Holy Spirit touch the deepest motivation for an all-encompassing outreach. The Holy Spirit gives all human beings "the light and strength" needed "to respond to their supreme calling" (GS 10). Through the

[43] On NA, see Gerald O'Collins, *The Second Vatican Council on Other Religions* (Oxford: Oxford University Press, 2013), 84–108.

[44] Paul VI's 1964 encyclical, *Ecclesiam Suam*, had already firmly encouraged such dialogue: AAS 56 (1964), 609–59, at 639–40.

[45] On some results and difficulties, see the following chapters in *Catholics and Interreligious Dialogue*, ed. James L. Heft (New York: Oxford University Press, 2012): Daniel A. Madigan, "Muslim-Christian Dialogue in Difficult Times," 57–87; Francis X. Clooney, "Learning Our Way: Some Reflections on Catholic-Hindu Encounter," 89–125; James L. Fredericks, "Off the Map: The Catholic Church in Its Dialogue with Buddhism," 127–68; Peter C. Phan, "Catholicism and Confucianism: An Intercultural and Interreligious Dialogue," 169–207.

[46] On GS, see O'Collins, *The Second Vatican Council on Other Religions*, 128–42.

Holy Spirit, all human beings can receive the gift of faith (GS 15), and can be united with the crucified and risen Christ (GS 22). Through the Holy Spirit, the risen Christ is at work in the hearts of human beings everywhere (GS 38). Second, from start to finish *Gaudium et Spes* endorses dialogue and collaboration with the religious "others" (GS 3, 28, 40, 84, and 92). This makes *Gaudium et Spes* a *rapprochement* manifesto par excellence. During the last session of Vatican II, the new attitude of *rapprochement* was also expressed by Paul VI visiting the United Nations headquarters on October 4, 1965 and pleading for world peace and an end to war.

Ressourcement and *Aggiornamento*

Faggioli writes of *Sacrosanctum Concilium* being "driven by the idea of *ressourcement*" and, by an idea that is "not less important," "*rapprochement*" (or what many prefer to call *aggiornamento*).[47] Let us see some details in the liturgical constitution that vindicate his judgment.

In pressing for the renewal or reform of the liturgy, *Sacrosanctum Concilium* prescribed a revision "according to the mind of healthy tradition," which might give the rites new vigour "for the sake of today's circumstances and needs" (no. 4). The twin principles recurred in a later article, which spoke of both "retaining healthy tradition" and "opening the way to legitimate progress" (no. 23). This was to set up two procedures: retrieving healthy tradition inherited from the past and discerning what present conditions call for. The two procedures, *ressourcement* and *aggiornamento*, featured right in the introduction (no. 4) to the first document promulgated by Vatican II.[48]

Far from "retrieval" and "updating" remaining opposed principles, recovering neglected teaching and practice both from the Scriptures and the great tradition serves the Church's adaptation in the present and progress into the future. The post–Vatican II liturgical changes show the two procedures working in tandem: for instance, the Second Eucharistic Prayer retrieved from the *Apostolic Tradition* of St. Hippolytus; the restoration of the ancient Rite of Christian Initiation of Adults

---

[47] Faggioli, "*Sacrosanctum Concilium* and the Meaning of Vatican II," 451, 452. On *aggiornamento*, see O'Malley, *What Happened at Vatican II*, 37–39, 299–300; on *ressourcement*, see ibid., 40–43, 300–305.

[48] On *ressourcement*, see Flynn and Murray, eds., *Ressourcement, passim*.

(SC 64); and the reintroduction of the "prayer of the faithful" (SC 53). "Retrieval" constitutes a major resource for renewal, whereas the task of *aggiornamento* may include "retrieval" but always involves discerning what should be changed and what should be introduced. Thus *ressourcement* and *aggiornamento* are different but complementary principles and procedures, with the former often, but not always, contributing to the latter.

These two principles can be translated in terms of inherited *tradition* and contemporary *experience*. The constitution prescribes taking into account "the general laws of the structure and intention" of the liturgy (which obviously derive from Christian tradition), and doing so in the light of "the experience coming from more recent liturgical renewal" (SC 23). The spirit of *ressourcement* encourages retrieving healthy traditions that have fallen into abeyance,[49] while the spirit of *aggiornamento* encourages discerning the contemporary experience of liturgy and other areas of Christian life and practice, so as to adopt whatever is found to be pastorally desirable.

When introducing norms for the renewal or reform of the liturgy and, in particular, what *aggiornamento* entailed, *Sacrosanctum Concilium* distinguished in the liturgy between (a) "a part that cannot be changed, inasmuch as it is divinely instituted" and (b) "parts that are subject to change." Apropos of (b), the constitution added at once that these parts ought to be changed, "if by chance there have crept into them things that might respond less well to the inner nature of the liturgy or that might have become less suitable [than they once were]." After dealing with elements that could be inappropriate or unsuitable, the document pressed ahead to express what it positively expected from the renewal of the rites. They should, in their revised form, "express more clearly the holy things that they signify," so that "the Christian people" can "understand [these things] easily and share in them through a community celebration that is full, active, and proper" (no. 21). In this way the constitution set out the norms governing the changes in the liturgy that a discerning *aggiornamento* calls for.

The document came back to these principles when treating in chapter 3 the sacraments (other than the Eucharist) and the sacramentals. It noted how "in the course of time, there have crept into the rites of

---

[49] Thus SC prescribed that valuable elements in the rites, which had been "lost" over the centuries "should be restored" (no. 50).

the sacraments and sacramentals certain things by which their nature and purpose have become less clear in our days." Hence "there is much more need to adapt certain things in them [the rites] to the needs of our age" (no. 62). With the aim of purging what is unsuitable and fails to communicate clearly and of adapting to the needs of our times, the constitution then enjoined that the rites of baptism, confirmation, penance, "the anointing of the sick" (the new name to replace "extreme unction"), ordination, marriage, and various sacramentals (e.g., the rites of burial) should be "revised" (nos. 66–82). Over and over again the reason given for such changes was to let significant elements at the heart of the rites "become clearer" (no. 67), to indicate them "more openly and more suitably" (no. 69), to express them "more clearly" (no. 72), and to "signify more clearly the grace of the sacrament" (no. 77). The desire for the rites to exercise more successfully their pedagogical function motivated and fashioned the far-reaching changes being mandated.

The liturgical constitution set going for the Council a whole program of "retrieval" and "updating." Thus the Decree on the Up-to-date Renewal of Religious Life, *Perfectae Caritatis* (promulgated on October 28, 1965), clearly endorsed these two principles for change. It emphasized that "an updated renewal of religious life comprises *both* a continual return to the sources of the whole Christian life and to the original inspiration of the institutes *and* their adaptation to the changed conditions of the times" (no. 2; emphasis added). The Declaration on Religious Freedom, *Dignitatis Humanae* (promulgated on December 7, 1965), acknowledged the widespread desire for "the free exercise of religion in society" and declared it to be "in conformity with truth and justice" (no. 1). Later the text observed not only that "people of today want to be able to profess their religion in public and in private," but also that "religious liberty is already declared a civil right in many constitutions and solemnly recognized in international documents" (no. 15). When *Dignitatis Humanae* disclosed its intention of catching up with the true and just concerns of contemporary humanity, the spirit of *aggiornamento* came into view. *Ressourcement* came into play when the decree declared that "this doctrine of [religious] freedom has roots in divine revelation" (no. 9). That meant appealing to the way Christ and his apostles always respected the religious freedom of human beings (nos. 9–15).

Unquestionably later documents promulgated by Vatican II practiced the twin principles of *ressourcement* and *aggiornamento*. But Faggioli is surely correct in naming *Sacrosanctum Concilium* as "the most radical instance of *ressourcement*," with its co-principle of *rapprochement* (or *aggiornamento*) matching its importance.[50]

Conclusions

This chapter has identified twelve ways in which the liturgy constitution prefigured and even set the agenda for what the later documents embodied. Sometimes (e.g., on priests, prophets, and kings) the subsequent texts massively developed what we read in *Sacrosanctum Concilium*. In other cases (e.g., on the centrality of the paschal mystery and, as we have just seen, on the procedures of *ressourcement* and *aggiornamento*), the liturgy constitution not only led the way but also had even more to offer. As Faggioli argues, *Sacrosanctum Concilium* proved "the most radical instance of *ressourcement*" at Vatican II.

Hence I agree with Faggioli in championing a hermeneutics of Vatican II based on *Sacrosanctum Concilium*. But I have argued (a) that we need to explain at least briefly the nature of our theory of interpretation, and (b) that the ecclesiology of the Council is better described as trinitarian rather than eucharistic. Moreover, one can enlarge the list of themes where *Sacrosanctum Concilium* prefigured and set the agenda for what was to come. Faggioli points us to seven themes: the centrality of the paschal mystery; the centrality of the Scripture; the collegiality of bishops; rites other than the Roman rite; adaptation; dialogue with others; *ressourcement* working with *aggiornamento*.

But further themes enter the trajectory initiated by the liturgy constitution: the sacramental nature of salvation and revelation; the (worshipping) people of God; a fuller appreciation of the Holy Spirit at work in the Church and beyond; priests, prophets, and kings; and the role of Christian hope. In this way, what I have proposed can support and enlarge Faggioli's thesis about the profound meaning of the liturgical constitution as "not only the chronological starting-point but also the theological starting-point" for the teaching and reforms of Vatican II.[51]

---

[50] Faggioli, "*Sacrosanctum Concilium* and the Meaning of Vatican II," 451, 452; id., *True Reform*, 17.

[51] Faggioli, *True Reform*, 10.

Chapter 4

Vatican II on the Liturgical Presence of Christ

The first document to be promulgated by the Second Vatican Council, the Constitution on the Sacred Liturgy (*Sacrosanctum Concilium* of December 4, 1963) contained a remarkable, if succinct, account of the active presence of the risen Christ in the liturgical celebrations of the Church (SC 7). In the following order, the Council listed five modes of that presence: Christ is present, first, "in the person of the minister"; second, "under the Eucharistic species"; third, in the celebration of all the sacraments (e.g., baptism); fourth, "in his word"; fifth, in the assembled community "when the Church prays and sings psalms [*psallit*]" together. As Josef Jungmann remarked, "the primary manner" of the risen Lord's being is his "continued existence . . . in his transfigured humanity in the glory of the Father." The Lord's primary manner of being "operates fully in all other modes of his presence, even though in different ways."[1] Let us look in more detail at these various modes of presence.

The Five Modes of Christ's Presence

1. The first mode of Christ's presence implicitly comments on the traditional teaching about ordained priests acting in the person of

---

[1] Josef A. Jungmann, "Constitution on the Sacred Liturgy," trans. L. Adolphus, in *Commentary on the Documents of Vatican II*, ed. Herbert Vorgrimler, vol. 1 (London: Burns & Oates, 1967), 1–88, at 13.

Christ.[2] They do so because the risen Christ is now offering himself through their eucharistic "ministry." It is not in his absence but in his dynamic presence that, either at the Eucharist or in the celebration of the other sacraments, they act "in the person of Christ" (SC 33).[3] They are visible signs of the invisible High Priest who continues to offer himself and constantly intercedes for human beings. This led St. Thomas Aquinas to state: "only Christ is the true priest, the others being only his ministers" (*Commentary on Hebrews*, 8.4). It is through these ministers that Christ is also present.

2. The constitution pointed to the special nature of the second mode of presence, in the consecrated species, by saying that Christ is present "supremely [*maxime*] under the eucharistic species." The eucharistic presence is the highest, the most intimate, and the most awesome mode of Christ's presence.

3. In *Sacrosanctum Concilium* (no. 7) the Council appropriately cited St. Augustine in support of the third mode of Christ's presence. Whenever baptism or any other sacrament is administered, Christ is personally and effectively present. In Augustine's words, "when Peter baptizes it is Christ who baptizes. When Paul baptizes, it is Christ who baptizes" (*Homilies on the Gospel of John*, 5.18; see 6.7).[4] Christ is present as the real, even if invisible, minister of all the sacraments. Every sacrament signifies and effects a presence of Christ: as High Priest (in the Eucharist); as reconciler (in the sacrament of penance); as healer (in the anointing of the sick); and so forth.

4. The Council expressed the fourth mode of Christ's presence as follows: "he is present in his word since it is he himself who speaks when the holy Scriptures are read in church" (SC 7). A later paragraph of *Sacrosanctum Concilium* taught that "in the Liturgy God speaks to his people, and Christ is still proclaiming the Gospel" (no. 33).

Yet the constitution went on to weaken a sense of Christ being present not only through the reading of the Scriptures *but also through*

---

[2] See Gerald O'Collins and Michael Keenan Jones, *Jesus Our Priest: A Christian Approach to the Priesthood of Christ* (Oxford: Oxford University Press, 2010), 114.

[3] See Bernard Dominique Marliangeas, "*In Persona Christi, In Persona Ecclesiae*: Note sur les origines et le développement de l'usage de ces expressions dans la théologie latine," in *La Liturgie après Vatican II: Bilan, Études, Prospective*, ed. Yves Congar and Jean-Pierre Jossua (Paris: Cerf, 1967), 283–88.

[4] SC 7 n. 21 refers to 6.7 of Augustine's *Homilies*; it could also have cited 5.18.

the word of preaching. It explained the purpose of the homily as draw-ing on "the sacred text" to "expound" the "mysteries of faith and the norms of Christian life" (SC 52). This was to understand the homily as an *instruction about* the Word rather than as an *encounter with* Christ, the living Word of God.

Later documents of Vatican II did better. According to the Dogmatic Constitution on the Church (*Lumen Gentium* of November 21, 1964), in the local churches "Christ is present" not only through the celebra-tion of the Eucharist but also through "the preaching of his Gospel" (LG 26). Apropos of the ministry of bishops, the same document had already pointed to the first mode of Christ's presence: "in the [person of] the bishops, whom the presbyters assist, the Lord Jesus Christ, the Supreme Pontiff, is present [*adest*] in the midst of the faithful." The same paragraph then drew attention, respectively, to the fifth, fourth, and third modes of Christ's presence: "while sitting at the right hand of God the Father, he is not absent [*non deest*] from the assembly of his pontiffs [fifth mode; see below], but it is above all through their excellent service that he *preaches the word of God* to all peoples [fourth mode] and continually administers to all the faithful the sacraments of faith [third mode]" (LG 21; emphasis added).

The Decree on the Church's Missionary Activity (*Ad Gentes* of December 7, 1965) recognized that "the word of preaching" makes "Christ, the author of salvation, present" (AG 9). This statement acknowledged, at least implicitly, how the revelatory ("the word of preaching") and salvific ("the author of salvation") dimensions of his presence are distinguishable but never separable. This teaching of *Lumen Gentium* and *Ad Gentes* also implied that, when preaching takes place, the "reality" that is proclaimed, the crucified and risen Christ, is made present for the preacher and the hearer alike, and is imparted to those who hear the preaching with faith.

5. The assembled community that "prays and sings psalms [*supplicat et psallit*]" forms the context for the fifth mode of his presence (SC 7).[5] Here the constitution appropriately cited the promise of Christ: "where two or three are gathered together in my name, I am there in the midst

---

[5] Karl Rahner, "The Presence of the Lord in the Christian Community at Wor-ship," in *Theological Investigations*, vol. 10, trans. David Bourke (New York: Seabury Press, 1977), 71–83.

of them" (Matt 18:20). His presence is realized in every assembly of his faithful, even in an assembly of only two or three.

A later chapter filled out what this involves. Christ is present and exercising his priestly office through and in the Church, not only when it gathers to celebrate the Eucharist but also in other ways: in particular, when his community performs the Divine Office. The constitution picked up the theme of *singing* together to acknowledge a worldwide presence of the incarnate and risen Christ: "Jesus Christ, the High Priest of the New and Eternal Covenant, when he assumed a human nature, introduced into this land of exile the hymn that in heaven is sung throughout all ages. He unites the whole community of humankind with himself and associates it with him in singing this divine canticle of praise" (SC 83). Earlier the constitution had taught that Christ is present "when the Church prays and sings psalms" to-gether.[6] Now it pictured this singing as one "divine canticle of praise," led by the incarnate Cantor himself, who gathers together the whole human race in singing the heavenly hymn he brought to earth.

This passage in *Sacrosanctum Concilium* strikingly portrayed the ac-tive, priestly presence of Christ in and with all human beings. The unity of the entire human race in him, which was foreseen in creation and actualized with the incarnation, must be understood to be strengthened through the resurrection. Finally, it will be perfected when human be-ings reach "the halls of heaven" and join the celestial choir.

St. Augustine of Hippo, whose influence shines through this passage, was second to none when he came to envisaging the final presence of Christ. He summoned Christians to their future life: "be [united] in him alone [Christ], be one reality alone, be one person alone [*in uno estote, unum estote, unus estote*]" (*Homilies on the Gospel of John*, 12.9). As Augustine expressed our future, that final communion of life will bring a chorus of praise in the divine presence: "there we shall praise; we shall all be one in the One [Christ], oriented towards the One [the Father]; for then, though many, we shall not be scattered [*ibi laudabimus, omnes unus in uno ad unum erimus; quia deinceps multi dispersi non erimus*]" (*Expositions of the Psalms*, 147.28).

---

[6] SC 33 puts this praying and singing into a dialogue: when God "speaks" and Christ "proclaims" the Gospel, "the people reply to God with both songs and prayer [*populus Dei respondet tum cantibus tum oratione*]."

The Reception of This Teaching on the Five Modes of Presence

What reception has this teaching on five modes of Christ's liturgical presence enjoyed in Roman Catholic teaching since Vatican II closed in 1965? In response let me look briefly at some works in sacramental theology. How much has the fivefold scheme of *Sacrosanctum Concilium* about the different modes of the risen Christ's presence impacted sacramental theology? Sad to say, post–Vatican II sacramental theology does not seem to have displayed much interest in the scheme of Christ's presence sketched by the liturgy constitution.

Let me mention four examples. Louis-Marie Chauvet, a creative French theologian, had a little to say about the eucharistic presence in his *Symbol and Sacrament* and then nothing about "presence" in *The Sacraments*.[7] Gifts and "presents" featured in David Power's *Sacrament*, but this work, despite its interest in the teaching of Vatican II, remained silent about "presence."[8] Herbert Vorgrimler, who had been a notable student and colleague of Karl Rahner, cited Rahner's article ("The Presence of the Lord in the Christian Community at Worship"), recalled the teaching of *Sacrosanctum Concilium* but dedicated less than two pages to "the presence of Jesus Christ in the liturgy."[9] A broad learning characterized Liam Walsh's *The Sacraments of Initiation*, but its main contribution to the theme of Christ's presence came in a reflection on his eucharistic presence.[10]

One can speculate about the reasons for this lack of interest in the Council's teaching on the manifold presence of the risen Christ. With the exception of Walsh, none of the theologians I have cited attend very much to Christ's resurrection and exaltation. That hardly leaves them predisposed to reflect on his risen and living presence in the Church's

---

[7] Louis-Marie Chauvet, *Symbol and Sacrament: A Sacramental Reinterpretation of Christian Existence*, trans. Patrick Madigan and Madeleine Beaumont (Collegeville, MN: Liturgical Press, 1995), 404–6; id., *The Sacraments*, (Collegeville, MN: Liturgical Press, 2001).

[8] David N. Power, *Sacrament: The Language of God's Giving* (New York: Crossroad, 1999).

[9] Herbert Vorgrimler, *Sacramental Theology*, trans. Linda M. Maloney (Collegeville, MN: Liturgical Press, 1992), 24–26.

[10] Liam G. Walsh, *The Sacraments of Initiation* (London: Geoffrey Chapman, 1988), 269–77.

liturgical life. Or is the neglect due to the general failure of theologians and philosophers to spend much time reflecting on "presence"? This widespread lack of interest shows up when major dictionaries of philosophy and theology fail to include an entry on "presence."[11] Whatever the reasons, one needs some analysis of "presence," if sacramental theology is going to receive and develop Vatican II's scheme of Christ's fivefold presence in the liturgy. Let me turn now to that task.

The Presence of Christ and the Sacraments

Before analyzing themes that presence involves and suggesting how they are manifested in Christ's presence in the sacraments, I wish to recall Karl Rahner's warning: presence "does not admit of any strict or precise definition." While recognizing what presence is, we will always find difficulty in expressing with anything like full clarity our experience of presence.[12] That said, let me suggest ten (overlapping) aspects of presence and apply each in turn to our experience of Christ's presence in the seven sacraments. Presence comes across as relational, mediated, personal, free, transformative, costly, bodily, multiform, feminine, and future-oriented. All of these items apply to the sacramental presence of the crucified and risen Christ.

Relational

Among the most obvious characteristics of presence is that it implies "presence to." Being present always means being present to someone or something. "I was present when Martin and Kate were married"; "I was present when my grandfather died"; "I was present when the Matisse exhibition opened." In other words, presence entails "being to" or "being in relation with," not simply "being in itself" or existence as such. Presence is not simply being but a relational mode of being.

[11] On the neglect of "presence," see Gerald O'Collins, *Christology: A Biblical, Historical, and Systematic Study of Jesus*, 2nd ed. (Oxford: Oxford University Press, 2009), 338–39. Martin Buber and Gabriel Marcel, however, attended to presence (ibid., 342 n. 6); see also, to some extent, John Macmurray, *Persons in Relation* (London: Faber, 1970), and George Steiner, *Real Presences* (London: Faber, 1989).

[12] Rahner, "The Presence of the Lord," 71.

Obviously, the presence of Christ in and through the sacraments is relational or a "presence to us." This may be a presence to us that initiates a lifelong relationship with him (baptism), a presence that relates us to his eternal sacrifice (the Eucharist), a presence that reconciles us or brings us back into relationship with him and his Church (the sacrament of penance), and so forth. Every sacrament signifies and effects a particular relationship between the risen Christ and ourselves—his presence to us and our presence to him.

Mediated

If presence involves a relationship between two entities that already are or are to become present to each other, there must be some common ground, unifying sphere or "mediation" that makes it possible for this mutual presence to be realized. A church ceremony formed the "common ground" for my presence at the wedding of two friends. Those who run a particular art gallery provided the conditions for my being present on the first day of the Matisse exhibition. A hospital and its administration functioned as the "medium" that allowed for being present at my grandfather's death. A famous image from the Book of Revelation pictures a meal (the messianic banquet) as the "unifying sphere" between the risen Christ and the Church of Laodicea: "I am standing at the door, knocking; if you hear my voice and open the door, I will come in to you and eat with you, and you with me" (Rev 3:20).

In the case of Christ's presence actualized through the seven sacraments (the third mode of presence), the Holy Spirit, as the "soul" or vital principle of the Church (1 Cor 6:19), mediates powerfully and personally the presence of Christ through the words and actions of all the sacraments. Baptism, for instance, means being born again of "water and the Spirit" (John 3:5), and it is administered "in the name of the Father, and of the Son, *and of the Holy Spirit.*" The Eucharist also illustrates strikingly the role of the Spirit in mediating Christ's presence. With the first eucharistic invocation (*epiclesis*) and the words of institution, the Spirit descends on the gifts to change them and bring about the most intense presence of Christ for the Church and the world (second mode of Christ's presence). Through a further *epiclesis* the Spirit is invoked to transform the members of the worshipping community and make them more Christ-like. This second *epiclesis*, intended to make believers more worthy members of the Church that is the Temple of the Holy Spirit, shows how the mediating work of the Holy Spirit is inseparably linked with the presence of Christ in the assembled community, the fifth mode of his presence cited by *Sacrosanctum Concilium*.

Furthermore, this mediating work of the Holy Spirit coincides with the fourth mode of Christ's presence listed by the Council: in his word. Christ is also made present when "the holy Scriptures are read in church" (see above), and the Spirit also mediates this presence. As St. Jerome insisted, the Sacred Scripture is to be read and interpreted in the same Spirit through whom it was written (*Commentary on Galatians*, 5.19–21; *Patrologia Latina*, 26.445A).[13] The Holy Spirit, who inspired the writing of the Scriptures, constantly proves inspiring by arousing through them a deeper experience of the risen Christ, present to those who hear the sacred texts with faith and devotion.

As we saw above, Christ's presence "in the word" includes the word of preaching. This presence also calls for the mediation of the Holy Spirit, as the Book of Acts repeatedly makes clear. When Peter witnesses at Pentecost to the living presence of the risen Jesus, he does so in the power of the Holy Spirit (Acts 2:32-33). In Acts, the speeches by Peter, Stephen, Paul, and others, which amount to nearly one third of the whole text, make Christ present in the word of preaching and do so through the power of the Holy Spirit (e.g., Stephen in Acts 7:55-56).

In spelling out the Holy Spirit's mediation of the risen Christ's presence, I have so far attended to the second, third, fourth, fifth modes of his presence that the Council listed. This mediation also applies to the first mode, the way in which ordained ministers who act "in the person of Christ" visibly manifest Christ's invisible presence. When the sacrament of holy orders is conferred, the rite repeatedly invokes the Holy Spirit and asks that the power of the Spirit descend on those being ordained. If they are to act "in the person of Christ," it is because they have been empowered by the Holy Spirit.

To sum up: the mediation of the Spirit belongs essentially to all five modes of Christ's presence. While distinct, the risen Christ and the Holy Spirit are inseparable "companions," with the Spirit providing the "medium" through and in which Christ is present to the

---

[13] Vatican II's Dogmatic Constitution on Divine Revelation (DV 12) refers to this passage in Jerome but inaccurately gives the reference as PL 26.417A.

world and, specifically, to those who encounter him in the Church's sacramental life.[14]

Personal

My first theme about presence concerned its relational character: presence happens in relationship. This was tantamount to naming presence as essentially personal. Only persons can, properly speaking, be present, even if one should admit that faithful dogs can imitate and supply some of the better features of human presence.

Many who reflect on personal existence argue that it should be primarily understood as being in relationship to other persons. The personal self can be a self only in relation to other selves.[15] Being personal means being relational, and we may add: being personal means being present to other persons. Being in relation and being present express what it is to be personal, and vice versa.

Thus "presence" picks up two essential aspects of being personal: the "togetherness" with or relationship to the other(s) and, at the same time, the distinction between each party. Without this distinction, presence would collapse into identity, and we would no longer have two or more persons present to each other. In brief, presence signifies "being personally with" but not "being identical with."

Clearly all the sacraments affect human beings inasmuch as they enjoy and grow in a personal relationship with Christ and his Holy Spirit. A classical theological slogan declared that "the sacraments [were instituted] for human beings [*sacramenta propter homines*]." We might adapt the slogan and say: "the sacraments [were instituted] for persons [*sacramenta propter personas*]." In and through the sacraments, human persons precisely as persons are involved with Christ and the Spirit. They become more "them-selves" by being present personally and sacramentally to the risen Christ in the Holy Spirit.

Free

As a (or rather the) form of self-bestowal, presence implies a free act, the exercise of our personal freedom. We are truly present to those

---

[14] See Théodore Strotmann, "Pneumatologie et liturgie," in *La Liturgie après Vatican II*, 289–314.

[15] On being a person-in-relation, see O'Collins, *Christology*, 242–47.

with whom we genuinely want to be present. In other words, we are and remain present to those toward whom we reach out in love. We are "there" because of our desire to give and receive love. Becoming and being present is always a free and loving act.

As regards the freedom exercised in the sacramental presence, the challenge was classically implied by the distinction between (a) *ex opere operato* ("on the basis of the act performed") and (b) *ex opere operantis* ("on the basis of the one acting"). According to (a), the objective efficacy and fruitfulness of sacraments do not primarily depend on the attitudes or merits of those receiving (or administering the sacraments). According to (b), the subjective dispositions for receiving a sacrament do not function as a cause but rather as a condition for the God-given grace to be fully effective. Personal language, which can and should replace this abstract terminology, puts this distinction in terms of loving freedom.

On his side (a), the risen Christ's free and loving initiative makes him unfailingly present when the sacraments are administered. Where his ministers, in and for the Church, perform the actions and words that belong to the sacramental rites, the faithful are united "in a hidden and real way" with the crucified and glorified Lord (LG 7). On their side (b), the more the faithful become freely attentive to the presence of the living Christ in all the sacramental rites, the more his redemptive work will transform them. At the Eucharist, this would involve, for instance, being lovingly attentive to the risen Christ present not only in the eucharistic elements but also in the assembled community, in the Scripture readings through which he speaks to us, and, hopefully, also in the homily which brings us his voice.

Transformative

The free self-giving that shapes interpersonal presence points to fresh possibilities and our being acted upon in ways that may profoundly transform our existence. Such presence can entail a new communion of life and love. The relationship of spouses to one another and that of parents to children (and vice versa) spring to mind as paradigm examples of transformative communion brought about by interpersonal presence. Such active presence and self-bestowal means disclosing oneself, sharing one's presence, and making others "at home" with an unconditional hospitality that gives, enhances, and transforms life.

It should go without saying that the vital presence of Christ in and through all seven sacraments acts upon the faithful in ways that aim at profoundly transforming their lives. This proves strikingly true not only of the sacraments of Christian initiation (baptism, confirmation, and Eucharist) but also of what are sometimes called "the sacraments in the service of communion": holy orders and matrimony. Let me say something about the transformative presence of Christ in and through the sacrament of matrimony.

In the Pastoral Constitution on the Church in the Modern World of December 7, 1965, the Second Vatican Council called married life "the first form of communion between persons," and an "intimate partnership of life and love" (GS 12, 48). The Council had already spoken of Christian spouses embodying "the unity and fruitful love that exists between Christ and the Church," and making their family into a kind of "domestic church" (LG 11). The Council articulated this fruitful, transformative interpersonal presence in the light of the risen Christ's ongoing impact on those who live out the sacrament of matrimony with one another and with their children: "The Christian family" that "springs from marriage" will "disclose to all people *the living presence of the Saviour* in the world" (GS 48; emphasis added). Within the family, this presence should prove deeply transformative and reveal itself "by the love of the spouses, [their] generous fruitfulness, unity, and fidelity, as well as by the loving way in which all members [of the family] cooperate [with each other]" (ibid.).

Where absence signifies lack of life and even death, presence signifies life and transformation. One might adapt John 10:10 and make it read: "I came that they may have my presence and have it abundantly." To enjoy, through the sacraments and in other ways, the Lord's bountiful presence, means being acted upon by him and receiving life in abundance. Whether they are aware of this or not, the life of all human beings can be seen as a longing for the transforming presence of Christ (with his Holy Spirit). Their history entails struggling for life in his presence, suffering from the experience of his apparent absence, and yearning for his definitive, face-to-face presence.

Costly

One should also recall the recurring "cost" of presence. Sheer physical distance may keep us apart from people, and means that making ourselves personally present to them (instead of merely phoning them or sending them e-mail messages) costs time and money. The psychological distance between ourselves and others, from whom we are separated by misunderstanding or worse, may call for a sharp sacrifice when we decide to seek them out and attempt to reestablish personal relations on a new footing. In our world of so much violence that is monstrously destructive, simply unjustified, and even senseless, becoming present to those in terrible need can be fraught with danger. In innumerable ways, presence can be "costly," even to the point of putting our lives at serious risk. Vulnerability shows itself to be a recurrent feature of personal presence.

Clearly, the gift of the sacraments resulted from Christ putting himself at mortal risk, being killed, and rising from the dead. Without the crucifixion, resurrection, and outpouring of the Holy Spirit, there would be no sacramental life. The sacraments and the death of Jesus remain inextricably intertwined. Paul presents baptism as sharing symbolically in the execution and burial of Jesus, so that we might then walk in newness of life (Rom 6:3-11). In the life of the baptized, the empowering presence of Christ is that of the One who, as Paul puts it, "loved me and gave himself for me" (Gal 2:20). Even more dramatically, the sacrament of the Eucharist shows itself to be an exceptionally costly gift. It was because Christ's body was broken and his blood poured out that his followers can share in the eucharistic sacrifice and meal.

Bodily

Various examples repeatedly offered above imply a seventh aspect of presence: it is charged with something physical and bodily. Since human beings are embodied spirits, the exercise of their freedom in making themselves present inevitably involves their bodies. Unquestionably, there is more to authentically human presence than mere bodily or spatial proximity. Nevertheless, we persistently and necessarily experience presence as involving our bodies and occurring in some particular place. The mutual presence of people involves their being close and within one another's "field of view."

In the context of any divine/human relationship, this aspect of presence raises the question: how can God, being purely spiritual and nonspatial, be present to human beings and so, in that sense, be located in space and time? One can and should respond that in all cases the beneficiaries of this divine presence, being human, supply the bodily, spatial "component." God is continuously related to these spatial-temporal creatures, even if not related in a spatial-temporal way. God is "beyond" space and time but continuously supports and interacts with human agents. On the side of the recipients, the presence of God proves to be bodily.

Furthermore, by personally assuming the human condition, the incarnate Son of God provided the bodily, spatial-temporal component on the divine side. Through the earthly body of his human history and then through his glorious, risen body, Christ has supplied, on the side of God, the bodily "requirement" for presence. Because of his incarnation, the Son of God assumed a "bodily place" in time and for all eternity. Thus the incarnation yielded a new way for a divine person to be bodily present somewhere and (through the transformation of his resurrection) everywhere.

These considerations about the bodily aspect of presence bear their obvious application to the sacraments and Christ's presence in the sacraments. All seven sacraments involve the human body and things done to the body. In baptism water is poured over a body; in confirmation hands are extended over our heads and our foreheads are anointed with chrism; and in the Eucharist Christ's body and blood are consumed. The bodily nature of the sacraments of initiation and of Christ's presence in them holds true of the other sacraments. For instance, the anointing of the sick, involving an imposition of hands and an anointing, recalls Christ's healing gestures and words when confronted with the bodies of sick, dying, or even dead persons.

To say all that almost inevitably raises the question about the mediation of the Holy Spirit in the administration of the sacraments. The Spirit has not taken on the bodily, human condition through an incarnation. Surely, unlike the visible mission of the Son, the mission of the Spirit must be called "invisible" and hence non-bodily and nonspatial? Yet to characterize the mission as simply invisible would not be appropriate, and that for two reasons. First, there is a certain visibility to this mission, inasmuch as the Spirit works at transforming bodily, human beings and transforming the material universe. The Spirit, Paul insists, produces visible effects "for the good of all" (1 Cor 12:7). Second, the Spirit's mission may be proper to the Spirit, but it is inseparably joined with the visible, bodily mission of the Son. This consideration also justifies recognizing some bodily visibility in the mission of the Spirit, which after all takes place in space and time.

Multiform

Presence exhibits very different forms, properties, and intensities. The relationships that constitute a presence between two or more entities seem endlessly various: interpersonal presences can always be closer, more intense, more freely chosen, and productive of an even richer communion of life. A seemingly infinite variety of properties and intensities characterizes the presences we experience. We never face a simple alternative: presence or absence. It is always a question of what kind of presence and what kind of absence, or how someone is present and how someone is absent. Every presence, short of the beatific vision or the final encounter with God, is always tinged with absence.

Given the stunning variety and qualitative differences that characterize human presence, we should be ready to acknowledge such variety and differences in the modes of sacramental presence exercised by the glorious Lord. Each sacrament signifies and effects a differing mode of his presence. Moreover, the concrete circumstances and devotion with which a particular sacrament is conferred will condition the impact of his sacramental presence. The primary manner of the risen Christ's being remains always the same, but there is huge variety in the given modes of his sacramental presence.

Feminine

Some find a feminine dimension to presence. Our first experience of presence was a maternal one, when we were umbilically bonded to our mother who enfolded, nurtured, and protected us. After birth, her presence continued to feed and shelter us. It is no wonder that there is a receptive, nurturing, and receptive feel to the presence of God, in whom "we live and move and have our being" (Acts 17:28). Inasmuch as it creates a quiet "space" in which to breathe and grow, human and divine presence wears a feminine face.

The notion of baptism as being "born again of water and the Spirit" (John 3:5; see Titus 3:5) encouraged Christians to picture the baptismal font or bath as a mother's womb from which the newly baptized were reborn. Then the blood and water that issued from the pierced side of Christ, already dead upon the cross (John 19:34), encouraged a motherly interpretation of the faithful being fed through the Eucharist. In his instructions to catechumens, St. John Chrysostom famously said: "have you seen with what kind of food he [Christ] feeds us all? It is by the same food that we have been formed and fed. As a woman feeds her child with her own blood and milk, so too Christ himself constantly feeds those whom he has begotten with his own blood" (*Catechesis*, 3.19).[16]

Thus two of the sacraments of initiation (baptism and the Eucharist) have been understood in a maternal way. Moreover, confirmation and the other sacraments, inasmuch as all seven sacraments involve the presence and mediation of the Holy Spirit, may also be understood in a feminine way. In a study of "The Motherhood of God and the Femininity of the Holy Spirit," Yves Congar draws on Syrian Christianity and other sources to illustrate how this long-standing conviction "works"—not least in the sacraments.[17] The feminine "face" of the Spirit underlies the feminine face of Christ's presence in all the sacraments.

Future-oriented

A tenth and final characteristic of presence is its future directedness. We live not only in virtue of what we already possess and enjoy but also in virtue of what is to come. Being open-ended projects, human beings are called to develop and grow in the various presences that shape their lives from cradle to grave. Nothing, not even the most wonderful and satisfying presence that we might enjoy, ever lasts but always proves fleeting. Relentlessly everything and the presence of every person pass away, as we move through life toward our final meeting with God, "the One who is, who was, and who is to come" (Rev 1:8). Every form of presence presses toward this future.

A future-orientation belongs essentially to all the sacramental modes of the risen Christ's presence. Famously an antiphon for the feast of Corpus Christi (now the feast of the Body and Blood of Christ)

---

[16] John Chrysostom, *Huit Catéchèses Baptismales Inédites*, ed. A. Wenger, *Sources Chrétiennes*, 50 (Paris: Cerf, 1957), 162.

[17] Yves Congar, *I Believe in the Holy Spirit*, vol. 3, trans. David Smith (London: Geoffrey Chapman, 1983), 155–64.

declared that in the "sacred banquet [*sacrum convivium*]" of the Eucharist "we receive a pledge of future glory [*futurae gloriae nobis pignus datur*]." But all the sacraments, in their different ways, "announce the death" and resurrection of the Lord, "until he comes" (1 Cor 11:26). That means that a future directedness characterizes every sacrament and the presence of the risen Lord in any liturgical action.

Conclusion

This chapter has set itself to articulate what the liturgical presence of Christ entails. It has argued that presence in general displays ten characteristics: as relational, mediated, personal, free, transformative, costly, bodily, multiform, feminine, and future-oriented. All these properties of presence can be applied to elucidate the presence of the risen Lord in the sacraments. Understood in this fuller fashion, the summary teaching of *Sacrosanctum Concilium* on the five modes of Christ's presence in the Church's liturgical celebrations can and should prove a rich lode of reflection for sacramental theology.

Chapter 5

Vatican II on Other Living Faiths

Building on what has already been said in chapters 1 and 2 above, this chapter critically evaluates what Vatican II taught about other living faiths in four documents: the Constitution on the Sacred Liturgy (*Sacrosanctum Concilium*, 1963), the Dogmatic Constitution on the Church (*Lumen Gentium*, 1964), the Declaration on the Relation of the Church to Non-Christian Religions (*Nostra Aetate*, 1965), and the Decree on the Church's Missionary Activity (*Ad Gentes*, 1965). Too often those who examine the Council's attention to other faiths consider only *Nostra Aetate*. Unquestionably, that declaration was central in importance and impact. Nevertheless, the three other documents just mentioned fill out Vatican II's integral teaching on the religious "others." The last and longest text from Vatican II, the Pastoral Constitution on the Church in the Modern World (*Gaudium et Spes*, 1965), also adds some significant teaching but will be considered here only in passing.[1]

It would be a mistake to limit the Second Vatican Council's teaching on other faiths to what was said explicitly. Right from the first document to be promulgated, the Council showed a mind-set that encompassed the whole of humanity.

Sacrosanctum Concilium

From the opening article of *Sacrosanctum Concilium*, Vatican II presented its renewal of the Church's liturgy within the context of

---

[1] For a full-scale treatment of Vatican II on other faiths, see Gerald O'Collins, *The Second Vatican Council on Other Religions* (Oxford: Oxford University Press, 2013).

the entire human race (SC 1).[2] The second article reflected a similar concern. Through the liturgy and especially through the Eucharist, "the faithful express and *manifest to others* the mystery of Christ and the genuine nature of the Church." As well as feeding their spiritual lives and bringing them to "the fullness of Christ," the Eucharist "strengthens their power to *preach Christ* and thus show forth *to those who are outside* the Church as a sign lifted up among the nations under which the scattered children of God may be gathered into one" (SC 2; emphasis added).[3] From the start, *Sacrosanctum Concilium* represented the Eucharist as *also* involving an open desire to "preach Christ" and "manifest his mystery" to the world.

Continuing in the same vein, *Sacrosanctum Concilium* quoted the classic New Testament text about God wanting "all human beings to be saved and come to the knowledge of the truth" (1 Tim 2:4). It referred then to Christ appearing as "the Mediator between God and human beings" (1 Tim 2:5), and summed up his work as "redeeming humankind and giving perfect glory to God" (SC 5). Over and over again the opening chapter of the liturgy constitution revealed the same encompassing vision and desire that "all human beings should know the one true God and Jesus Christ whom he had sent" (SC 6).

Given the world-encompassing mind-set of our document, it is not surprising that it mandated the restoration of the "prayer of the faithful," an old tradition which had never been given up in the East but which had disappeared in the Roman liturgy, except on Good Friday.[4] This prayer was to be restored "after the gospel and homily, especially on Sundays and holy days of obligation." Recalling in a footnote 1 Timothy 2:1-2 (which enjoins a similar form of prayer), *Sacrosanctum Concilium* explained: "by this prayer in which the people are to take part, intercessions are to be made for the holy Church, for those who lead us politically, for those weighed down by various needs, *for all human beings, and for the salvation of the entire world*" (SC 53; emphasis added).

---

[2] On SC, see Massimo Faggioli, *True Reform: Liturgy and Ecclesiology in Sacrosanctum Concilium* (Collegeville, MN: Liturgical Press, 2012).

[3] In fn. 6, SC refers to what John 11:52 announces about Jesus dying "not for the [Jewish] nation only but to gather into one the children of God who had been scattered."

[4] See Gerard Kelly, *Lord, Hear Our Prayer: Praying the General Intercessions* (Strathfield, NSW: St. Paul's Publications, 2008), 11–17.

This text encouraged Catholics to worship in solidarity with the entire world and become actively concerned about the salvation of all people.

Before leaving *Sacrosanctum Concilium*, we should note a text that has largely escaped even scholarly attention. Many experts on Christianity and other religions seem to have remained unaware that an image, with which the Council began its teaching on the Divine Office (chap. 4), is particularly significant for their area of specialization. The liturgy constitution opened that chapter by saying: "Jesus Christ, the High Priest of the New and Eternal Covenant, when he assumed a human nature, introduced into this land of exile the hymn that in heaven is sung throughout all ages. He unites the whole community of humankind with himself and associates it with him in singing the divine canticle of praise" (SC 83). Earlier the liturgy constitution had taught that the risen Christ is present "when the Church prays *and sings psalms*" (SC 7; emphasis added). Now the document speaks of singing one "divine canticle of praise," led by the incarnate Cantor himself, who gathers together the whole human race to share this heavenly hymn that he has brought to earth. Christ is pictured here as associating with himself not merely those who know and believe in him but also the entire human community. Together they all form a choir, of which he is the leader. The Cosmic Choirmaster unites with himself the baptized and non-baptized alike. Even those who have never heard his name are mysteriously but, through grace, truly in the hands of Christ the Choirmaster of the world.

As regards other living faiths, the teaching of *Sacrosanctum Concilium* remained largely implicit, and was not as dramatically challenging as what came two years later in the declaration on "Non-Christian Religions." Nevertheless, right from the first text promulgated by the Council, we can see how the salvation of all humanity shaped the vision and agenda of the bishops and their advisors at Vatican II.

Lumen Gentium

Before we come to the key articles in *Lumen Gentium* about the "religious others," we should pause to retrieve two items from its first chapter.[5] First, in richly biblical language that chapter emphasized the

[5] On LG, see Gérard Philips, *L'Église et son mystère au IIe Concile du Vatican: histoire, texte et commentaire de la Constitution "Lumen Gentium,"* 2 vols. (Paris: Desclée, 1967).

sacramental reality of the Church, from which "shines" the "light" of Christ and which is "the sign and instrument of intimate communion with God and of unity among the whole human race" (LG 1). The opening words were obviously meant to evoke the strikingly universal texts of Second and Third Isaiah (40–55 and 56–66, respectively) about foreign peoples to whom divine salvation is extended and who join themselves to Israel. It is in these terms that a poem pictures the glorious restoration of Jerusalem: "Arise, shine, for your light has come, and the glory of the Lord has risen upon you . . . Nations shall come to your light, and kings to the brightness of your dawn" (Isa 60:1, 3). With the two words that became its title ("The Light of the Nations"), *Lumen Gentium* signalled its universal outlook. The short, opening article pressed on to underline this mind-set by introducing five equivalent expressions for "the nations": "all human beings," "every creature," "the whole human race," "the whole world," and— once again—"all human beings." Chapter 7 will disclose the same all-encompassing mind-set; it looks forward to the whole human race, along, with the universe itself, being finally renewed in and through the risen Christ (LG 48).

Second, when interpreting the way of salvation for "the others," a distinction (but not a separation) between the Church and the kingdom of God is vital.[6] Speaking of "the people of God," the constitution recognized the purpose of the Church to be that of embodying "the Kingdom of God which God himself has begun on earth" and "will complete at the end of time" (LG 9). Here and in article 5, Vatican II distinguished (but did not separate) the Church from the kingdom of God, and so recognized how the kingdom forms the more encompassing reality and how the Church is there to serve the kingdom, and not vice versa.

The key responses in *Lumen Gentium* to questions about understanding "the religious others" in the light of Christian faith came with articles 16 and 17. An earlier article (LG 13) had framed the scope of what would be said there. Holding in faith that, through Christ's redeeming work, "all human beings are called to the new People of

---

[6] See Jacques Dupuis, *Christianity and the Religions: From Confrontation to Dialogue* (Maryknoll, NY: Orbis Books, 2003), 20–31, 195–217; id., *Toward a Christian Theology of Religious Pluralism* (Maryknoll, NY: Orbis Books, 1997), 330–57.

God," the Council reflected on how, "in different ways," they "belong [*pertinent*]" or "are ordered [*ordinantur*] to catholic unity." This is true, no matter whether "they are Catholic faithful, or others who believe in Christ, or lastly all human beings without exception [*omnes univer-saliter homines*], called by God's grace to salvation" (LG 16). Thomas Aquinas had prompted this language about all members of the human race being "ordered" variously to "catholic unity" under the universal headship of Christ.[7]

In considering how the final group, "those who have not yet received the Gospel," "are ordered to the People of God for different reasons," our document distinguishes between (a) Jews, (b) Muslims, (c) other believers in God, and (d) all those who, through no fault of their own, have not yet come to an explicit knowledge of God (LG 16).

For the first time in the history of Catholic Christianity, an ecumenical council spoke positively of Jews and Muslims. Meeting soon after the failure of the fifth and final (major) crusade, the Second Council of Lyons (1274) described "the Saracens" as "blasphemous," "faithless," and the "impious enemies of the Christian name."[8] Almost two centuries later in its notorious 1442 Decree for the Copts, the Council of Florence, adopting an extreme expression of the principle of "outside the Church no salvation," consigned to damnation "pagans," Jews, heretics, and schismatics. This Council presumed that those who did not accept and follow the message of Christ were guilty, and so excluded from eternal salvation.[9] The Second Vatican Council, however, not only avoided this presupposition but also avoided ever speaking of "pagans," "heretics," and "schismatics."

As regards (a) Jews, *Lumen Gentium* first selected some of the privileges listed by Romans 9:4-5 to speak of "the people to whom the covenants and promises were given and from whom Christ was born according to the flesh." Then it aligned itself with Paul in stating that "according to the [divine] election, they [the Jews] are a people most dear on account of the fathers; for the gifts and calling of God are without regret (Rom 11:28-29)" (LG 16). Before Vatican II, no ecumenical

---

[7] For details, see O'Collins, *The Second Vatican Council on Other Religions*, 30–31.

[8] See Norman P. Tanner, ed., *Decrees of Ecumenical Councils*, vol. 1 (London/Washington, DC: Sheed & Ward/Georgetown University Press, 1990), 309.

[9] For details, see O'Collins, *The Second Vatican Council on Other Religions*, 32–33.

council had either cited those two passages from Romans or spoken well of Jews. Now, prompted by John XXIII and other friends of the Jewish people and aiming to proscribe effectively any anti-Semitism, the Council found its scriptural warrant in the classical texts of Paul about God's irrevocable election of Israel.[10] In the longer treatment of the Jewish people that appeared a year later in *Nostra Aetate*, the Council once again quoted Romans 9:4-5 (NA 4) and in a reference to Romans 11:28-29 recalled the use of that verse in *Lumen Gentium* 16 (NA 4, fn. 11). Undoubtedly, what is said about Judaism in *Nostra Aetate* is longer and more significant—especially in view of the emerging Catholic-Jewish dialogue.[11] Nevertheless, the decisive step toward *rapprochement* had already been taken in *Lumen Gentium*.

Vatican II was likewise (b) the first Council of Catholic Christianity to offer some positive teaching on Muslims. It was a teaching that highlighted common ground: the divine "plan of salvation also embraces those who acknowledge the Creator, in the first place among whom are the Muslims. While describing Muslims as those "who profess to hold the faith of Abraham" rather than simply state that they hold the faith of Abraham, the Council agreed that they "acknowledge the Creator," "adore with us the one, merciful God," and also share with Christians the expectation of a general judgment "on the last day" (LG 16). A year later in its declaration on "Non-Christian Religions," Vatican II would fill out its positive view of Islam (NA 3). Nevertheless, *Lumen Gentium* had already taken a first step toward *rapprochement*.

After the Muslims, *Lumen Gentium* turned to (c) other believers in God: "nor is this God distant from others who in shadows and images seek the unknown God, since to all he gives life and breath and all things (see Acts 17:25-28) and [since] the Saviour wishes all human beings to be saved (see 1 Tim 2:4)." Because God is both the Creator who gives life to all human beings and the Savior who wishes all to be saved, Vatican II held that the divine presence also embraces all God-seekers, even if it is "in shadows and images" that they seek "the

[10] On these verses from Romans, see Brendan Byrne, *Romans* (Collegeville, MN: Liturgical Press, 1996), 285–87, 351–52, 356; Joseph A. Fitzmyer, *Romans* (New York: Doubleday, 1993), 545–47, 626; Douglas Moo, *The Epistle to the Romans* (Grand Rapids, MI: Eerdmans, 1996), 559–68, 729–32.

[11] On the results of postconciliar, interfaith dialogues, see James L. Heft, ed., *Catholicism and Interreligious Dialogue* (New York: Oxford University Press, 2012).

unknown God." Hence "those who through no fault [of their own] do not know Christ's Gospel and his Church and who, nevertheless, seek God with a sincere heart and under the influence of grace try in their actions to fulfil his will made known through the dictate of their conscience—these too may obtain eternal salvation" (LG 16).

We have come here to two key biblical passages, one firmly lodged in the tradition and the other making an appearance for the first time. The First Letter to Timothy 2:4, echoed in a remarkable letter by Pope Gregory VII to a Muslim king of Mauretania,[12] had been quoted by the First Vatican Council in chapter 3 of its constitution on faith, *Dei Filius*,[13] and then already quoted at Vatican II by *Sacrosanctum Concilium* (no. 5). After *Lumen Gentium*, it would be quoted by the Council's documents twice more and referenced three times more.[14] It was in *Lumen Gentium* 16 that Acts 17:25-28 was referenced for the first time by an ecumenical council. Paul's words about the search for the unknown God helped to shape the thinking of Vatican II about those who follow other faiths. In the last session of the Council, *Ad Gentes* 3 would cite Acts 17:27 and *Gaudium et Spes* 24 would cite Acts 17:26.

Finally, apropos of morally upright atheists (d), *Lumen Gentium* 16 added. "whatever good or true is found among them is considered by the Church to be a preparation for the Gospel, and given by him [the incarnate Word] who enlightens all human beings so that they may at length have life." A year later *Nostra Aetate* was to recognize "goodness and truth" and enlightenment by the Word among Hindus, Buddhists, and followers of other religions. *Lumen Gentium* 16 followed the example of Pope Paul VI. In article 107 of his first encyclical, *Ecclesiam Suam* (dated August 6, 1964), he had anticipated by a few months the positive teaching on Islam to come in *Lumen Gentium*. He wrote of Muslims "whom we do well to admire on account of those things that are true and commendable [*vera et probanda*] in their worship."[15] Here the "paired" blessings acknowledged by the pope may point toward

---

[12] See ND 1002; this letter, written in 1076, was referenced by NA 3 (n. 1).

[13] DzH 3014; ND 124.

[14] The First Letter to Timothy 2:4 is quoted by the Declaration on Religious Liberty, *Dignitatis Humanae* (no. 11), and by AG 7; the text is referenced by NA 1 (n. 2), by AG 42 (n. 21), and by the Decree on the Ministry and Life of Priests, *Presbyterorum Ordinis* 42 (n. 21).

[15] AAS 56 (1964), 609–59, at 654.

John's language about the Word being full of "grace and truth" that he has come to share (John 1:14, 17). Even more clearly *Lumen Gentium* picked up this "double-sided" terminology when speaking of Christ, who through the visible community of the Church, "communicates truth and grace to all [human beings]" (no. 8). In the same article the constitution seemed to press into service Johannine terminology when speaking of "the many elements of sanctification and truth" to be found among Christians not united with the Bishop of Rome.

When reflecting on the religious situation of "others" in terms of "whatever good or truth is found among them," the Council suggested two distinguishable but inseparable dimensions of the divine self-communication that has blessed them: salvation ("good") and revelation ("truth"). The Johannine language of revelation and salvation (in that order) followed at once when our passage in *Lumen Gentium* introduced "enlightening" (revelation) and "life" (salvation).

The following year the final documents of Vatican II were to include a similar double terminology inspired by the prologue to John, and did so in the order of revelation first and salvation second. In non-Christian religions the Council found elements of "what is true and holy" (NA 2). Six weeks later Vatican II followed the same order, while showing itself to be more critical of other religions. Missionary activity "purges of evil associations every element of truth and grace to be found among the peoples" (AG 9). Thus not only in *Lumen Gentium* but also in *Nostra Aetate* and *Ad Gentes*, John's language about "grace and truth" enjoyed some important echoes, when the Council spoke about "the religious others." In a christological context, *Ad Gentes* expressly quoted John 1:14 to describe Christ, "the new Adam," who is "the head of a renewed humanity" and "full of grace and truth" (no. 3).

Apropos of John 1:9 ("he was the true light that enlightens everyone coming into the world"), we saw above that *Lumen Gentium* 16, albeit without referencing this verse, stated that the incarnate Word "enlightens all human beings." The following year and once again without adding a reference, *Nostra Aetate* would also echo the verse when it said of the Church's attitude to other religions: "it is with sincere respect that she considers those ways of acting and living, those precepts and doctrines, which, although they differ in many respects from what she herself holds and proposes, nevertheless, *often reflect a ray of that Truth, which illuminates all human beings*" (NA 2; emphasis added). It was left to *Gaudium et Spes* to quote from John's gospel the words about "the true light that enlightens every human being" (no. 57).

All in all, not only in *Lumen Gentium* but also in three other documents (NA, AG, and GS) Vatican II effectively appealed to the language of "grace and truth" and "the true light enlightening every human being." No previous ecumenical council had quoted or referenced these words from John. Vatican II made these texts central when it applied the biblical witness to the religious situation of those who follow other faiths.

Nostra Aetate

Nostra Aetate, with only five articles, may be the shortest of all the sixteen documents promulgated by Vatican II. But half a century of postconciliar history has seen it grow both in theological significance and in pastoral importance for interfaith dialogue and collaboration. It was quickly recognized not only for its contribution to Catholic-Jewish dialogue but also for its fresh approach to relations between Roman Catholics and followers of other religions.[16]

As we have seen, some items in *Nostra Aetate* (e.g., its positive teaching about Jews and Muslims, as well as themes and language drawn from John's gospel) were anticipated by *Lumen Gentium*. Even when the declaration on other religions began by observing how "in our age" the "human race is day by day becoming more closely united" and "the obligations between different peoples are increasing" (NA 1), such a pronouncement on the state of global humanity had already been anticipated by similar remarks in *Lumen Gentium* (the closing words in both nos. 1 and 28). In *Lumen Gentium* and, even more clearly, in *Nostra Aetate,* such judgments went far beyond merely theoretical pronouncements and flagged serious commitments. *Nostra Aetate* spoke at once of the Church's "duty to foster unity and charity" between individuals and nations as belonging to its mission to serve the entire human race. This prompted the Council into showing (a) what human beings have in common, and (b) what "leads to mutual fellowship." *Nostra Aetate* produced a brief answer to (a) (NA 1). Then in what followed about "the various religions of the world" (NA 2–5),

---

[16] For some bibliography on NA, see chap. 2 above, n. 50.

the Council engaged with (b): that is to say, religion as a major cause of fellowship among human beings.

As regards (a), the declaration first named three basic reasons for acknowledging what all nations have in common, to the point of making them "one community": their origin in God, the divine providence that extends to all people, and their common, heavenly destiny. On the basis of the unity between human beings finding its deepest foundation in what God has done, is doing, and will do, *Nostra Aetate* turns next to the common self-questioning that also—but this time, on the human side—bonds everyone. Its eloquent exposé of seven radical questions that haunt human beings has no precedent in the teaching of earlier ecumenical councils (NA 1). The theme of ever-recurring human questions was to be taken up by *Gaudium et Spes* (nos. 4, 10, 18, 21), and then correlated with the answer(s) that come from the crucified and risen Christ (GS 22). But *Nostra Aetate* had already initiated this theme.

The seven questions open by probing the human condition: "What is the human being?" They end by asking: "What, finally, is that ultimate and ineffable mystery which enfolds our existence, from which we take our origin and towards which we move?" Making a broad statement about the present and the past, *Nostra Aetate* observes that people "expect from the various religions a response to the obscure enigmas of the human condition, which, today as in the past, intimately disturb the hearts of human beings" (NA 1). After its introductory article that climaxed with the *unity* of the human race, the declaration turns to the *manifold* answers offered by the religions of the world, which "in various ways attempt to engage with the restlessness of the human heart by proposing" three things: "doctrines," "precepts for life," and "sacred rites." This triple scheme, which encompasses belief systems, codes of conduct, and modes of worship, may be conventional, but it remains enduringly serviceable for analysing what particular religions set before their followers.

In the event the declaration attended only to Hinduism, Buddhism, Islam, and Judaism. It had nothing to say, for instance, about Confucianism, Shintoism, Sikhism, and Taoism, and, even more broadly, nothing to say about traditional religions to be found in Africa, Asia, Oceania, and the Americas. Both at the time of the Council and later, commentators have regretted the failure to address, even in passing, ethnic or tribal religion.

When it tackled specific religions, *Nostra Aetate* spoke about the religions themselves rather than about the followers of these or those religions. It concerned itself primarily with the systems they followed. Even then the declaration never attempted to describe fully the different religions.[17] It said nothing, for example, about various schools of Hinduism, or about any "negative" Buddhist understanding of salvation, or about differences between Sunni and Shi'a Muslims. While acknowledging such limitations, we should recognize that *Nostra Aetate* did something no ecumenical council had ever done before: it reflected explicitly and positively on some aspects of Hinduism and Buddhism, two religious ways of life that existed centuries before the coming of Christ himself. Vatican II was not "doing a theology of religions" but set itself to indicate only some key spiritual values that could set the basis for dialogue. The declaration never aimed at a complete treatment; yet lengthy descriptions were not needed to achieve the purpose of the document—to lay the ground for dialogue and collaboration.

By recognizing what is "true and holy" in other religions (no. 2), *Nostra Aetate*, as we have seen above, followed the lead of *Lumen Gentium* in using a Johannine, double-sided terminology that distinguishes (but does not separate) the two dimensions of the divine self-communication: revelation and salvation. What or rather who has given rise to "those things that are true and holy" in the other religions? The Council responded by pointing to the person of Christ.

Without condemning various "ways of acting and living," as well as various "precepts and doctrines" to be found in other religions but simply saying that they "differ" in many respects from what the Catholic Church teaches, *Nostra Aetate* then acknowledged something extraordinarily positive: the beliefs and practices of other religions "often reflect a ray of that Truth, which illuminates all human beings" (NA 2). Since what is "true" among the others reflects "the Truth" that is the Word of God, presumably what is "holy" among them also comes from the Word who is the life of humankind (John 1:4). If Christ is "the truth" for everyone, he is also "the life" for them. This article of *Nostra Aetate* does not expressly state that Christ is both universal Revealer and universal Savior, but what it says amounts to

---

[17] For all its limits, NA respected the irreducible particularity of these religions and what made them distinctive—a principle recently stressed by more and more specialists in comparative religion.

that. How can he "illuminate" all human beings without conveying to them something of God's self-revelation and hence also the offer of salvation?

The Council did not, however, attempt to identify precisely what shape the divine revelation has taken in other religious traditions. It is one thing to maintain the origin and common destiny of all people in God, along with the universal revealing and saving impact of the word of God. But it would be quite another to risk spelling out precisely what is "true and holy" in world religions and how that state of affairs has come about through the revealing and saving activity of God. As we will see below, the decree on missionary activity respected the mysterious ways in which the divine self-disclosure can call forth human faith.

On the basis of what the first article of *Nostra Aetate* observed about the growing unity of the human race and of what the second article observed about other religions, the declaration "exhorted" Catholics, while acting "with prudence and charity" and "witnessing to Christian faith and life," to take up "dialogue and collaboration with followers of other religions." Such dialogue and collaboration should involve Catholics in "recognizing, protecting, and promoting those spiritual and moral goods, as well as those socio-cultural values" found among the followers of other religions (NA 2).[18] In the aftermath of Vatican II, numerous official and unofficial initiatives, as well as the practice of John Paul II, showed the fruits of the interreligious dialogue and collaboration that emerged.

Nostra Aetate devoted an entire article to the Muslims (NA 3), first acknowledging major features in their doctrine of God: "they worship God, who is unique, living and subsistent, merciful and almighty, the Creator of heaven and earth, who has spoken [*allocutum*] to human beings." This involves them in "submitting themselves wholeheartedly to the hidden decrees" of God, "just as Abraham submitted himself to God." The declaration added at once that "Islamic faith willingly refers itself" to Abraham—primarily, one presumes to the faith of Abraham and Sarah.

While reluctant to state straight out that Muslims share the faith of Abraham and Sarah, *Nostra Aetate* clearly recognized how Muslims

---

[18] Paul VI's encyclical of 1964, *Ecclesiam Suam*, had already firmly encouraged such dialogue: AAS 56 (1964), 609–59, at 639–40.

want to share that faith by "willingly" referring their faith to Abraham. In any case the declaration had already indicated how Islamic faith responded to God's revelation. It was because God had "spoken [in some kind of personal self-revelation] to human beings" and, specifically, to Muslims that they had come to faith in God as "unique, living and subsistent, merciful and almighty, the Creator of heaven and earth." Hence they could truly "worship God," now revealed to them.[19] The divine self-disclosure had made possible not only their worship of the true God but also their submission to God's decrees. To be sure, *Nostra Aetate* characterized the decrees of God as "hidden." But, obviously, they cannot have remained totally and completely hidden. Otherwise how could Muslims have known what they should submit themselves to? God must have partially revealed the divine will to prompt such submission on their part.

The declaration on other religions built on what *Sacrosantum Concilium* and *Lumen Gentium* had already taught and then added some fresh themes of its own (e.g., the deep questions which all human beings share and the call to dialogue and collaboration with followers of other faiths). Something similar holds true for the Decree on the Church's Missionary Activity *Ad Gentes* shared common ground with *Sacrosanctum Concilium*, *Lumen Gentium*, and *Nostra Aetate*. But it also added at least one very significant consideration of its own.

Ad Gentes

Before examining one remarkable but relentlessly neglected advance made by *Ad Gentes* (as we shall see, a retrieval from St. Irenaeus) in thinking about the religious condition of all human beings, let me recall four areas in which the decree gave its own accent to themes already enunciated: the Trinitarian missions; the "seeds of the Word"; the presence of "truth and grace"; and dialogue and collaboration with "the religious others."[20]

---

[19] To say that God had "spoken [*allocutum*] to human beings" obviously evokes a traditional way of expressing divine revelation as *locutio Dei*, or God breaking silence to speak and address human beings. The verb *alloquor* corresponds to the noun *locutio*.

[20] On AG, see Heinrich S. Brechter, "Decree on the Church's Missionary Activity," in *Commentary on the Documents of Vatican II*, ed. H. Vorgrimler, vol. 4 (London:

While *Sacrosanctum Concilium* had little to say about the Holy Spirit (nos. 2, 5, and 6), *Lumen Gentium* gave its reflection on the Church a fully trinitarian face (e.g., LG 1–4 and 17). *Nostra Aetate* remained silent about the Holy Spirit. *Ad Gentes* more than made up for this neglect when founding the Church's missionary activity in the plan of God the Father, whose "love" and "goodness" gave rise to the mission of the Son and the mission of the Holy Spirit. Through these missions, God who "in his great and merciful kindness has freely created us [all human beings], graciously calls us to share in his life and glory" (AG 2).[21] This trinitarian vision of the origin of missionary activity leads naturally to three matching images of the goal of that activity, when the whole human race "form one people of God [the Father], come together into the one body of Christ, and are built up into the temple of the Holy Spirit." Then "all who share human nature, regenerated in Christ through the Holy Spirit," will be able to "gaze together on the glory of God [the Father]" (AG 7). Thus, in reflecting on the religious state of the entire human race, both Christians and non-Christians alike, *Ad Gentes* wishes to consider everyone in relationship with the Father, Son, and Holy Spirit.

Second, *Lumen Gentium* echoed the language of Justin Martyr and other early Christian writers when it said: "whatever good is found sown [*seminatum*] in the heart and mind of human beings or in the particular rites and cultures of peoples, so far from being lost, is healed, elevated and consummated" (LG 17). Yves Congar who had played his part in drafting that article[22] repeated those words in *Ad Gentes* when describing the passage to Christian faith, and indicated in a footnote their source in *Lumen Gentium*: "whatever good is found sown [*seminatum*] in the heart and mind of human beings or in the particular rites and cultures, so far from being lost, is healed, elevated, and consummated" (AG 9, and n. 52). Once again, while expressing the saving impact on those who move to faith in Christ (through this

---

Burns & Oates, 1969), 87–181; Yves Congar, "Principes doctrinaux (nos. 2 a 9)," in *L'activité missionaire de l'Église*, ed. Johannes Schütte (Paris: Cerf, 1967), 185–221; Peter Hünermann, "Theologischer Kommentar zum Dekret über die Missionstätigkeit der Kirche: *Ad Gentes*," in *Herders Theologischer Kommentar*, 4:219–336.

[21] On grounding the Church's mission in the mystery of the Trinity, see James B. Anderson, *A Vatican II Pneumatology of the Paschal Mystery: The Historical-Doctrinal Genesis of "Ad Gentes" 1.2–5* (Rome: Gregorian University Press, 1988).

[22] See Yves Congar, *My Journal of the Council*, trans. Mary John Ronayne and Mary Cecily Boulding (Collegeville, MN: Liturgical Press, 2012), 871.

"healing, elevating, and consummating"), the passage in *Ad Gentes* recognized the good already "sown in the mind and heart of human beings" and in "their rites and cultures." Presumably we deal here with a "divine passive" or a sowing that had been carried out by God, and hence with the divine presence in them of a measure of divine self-communication. Even before accepting the gospel, these "others" already enjoy some elements of revelation and salvation. The process of "healing," "elevating," and "consummating" embodies a degree of continuity between what God had already blessed them with and what they become as Christians.

Ad Gentes went on to talk expressly of "the seeds of the Word" that are "hidden" in "the national and religious traditions" of various peoples and that need to be "gladly and reverently uncovered." The decree then characterized these "seeds of the Word" as "the riches which the bountiful God has distributed to the nations." The disciples of Christ should "try to illuminate these riches with the light of the Gospel, to set them free, and to bring them back to the dominion of God the Saviour" (AG 11). Thus the move to Christian faith involves both a revealing and enlightening process (riches being illuminated "with the light of the Gospel") and a saving liberation (riches being "set free"). But this happens to people who have already been richly blessed by the grace of God and enjoy some measure of the presence of the Word. Talking of (a) "the seeds of the Word" that have already been sown by God in "the religious traditions" of various peoples and of (b) "riches distributed" by "the bountiful God" prioritizes the divine initiative rather than any human search. To be sure, the language about these riches being "illuminated" and "set free" obviously suggests that, before the gospel is accepted, the religious situation is not yet as complete and perfect as it could be. Nevertheless, *Ad Gentes* envisages what God has already done in the "religious traditions" of different nations by "sowing" in them the seeds of the Word and by "distributing" to them "the riches" of divine grace.

A later article of the missionary decree takes up again "the seeds of the Word" by stating that "the Holy Spirit calls all human beings to Christ through the seeds of the Word and the preaching of the Gospel" (AG 15). This is to picture the process of moving to Christian faith happening by the word of preaching being addressed to people who, through "the seeds of the Word," *already* enjoy through the Holy Spirit, albeit mysteriously, the hidden presence of Christ.

Finally, with an eye on Buddhist, Hindu, and Muslim prayer life and asceticism, *Ad Gentes* encourages Roman Catholic religious who work in missionary situations to "consider attentively how traditions of asceticism and contemplation, the *seeds* of which have been sometimes planted by God in ancient cultures, could be taken up into Christian religious life" (AG 18). This last appeal of the missionary decree to the theological theme of "the seeds of the Word" clarifies what has hitherto taken the form of a "divine passive": it is God the Holy Spirit who sows and plants these seeds. The passage also specifies one form of the "good" that has been sown and "the riches" that have been distributed by God: the ascetic and contemplative traditions that could be incorporated into the lives of Christian religious institutes. This clarification and specification complete the development that *Ad Gentes* gave to what *Lumen Gentium* had retrieved (very briefly) from Justin and other early Church writers, the theme of "the seeds of the Word."

Third, *Ad Gentes*, when characterizing the religious situation of those who have not or have not yet accepted faith in Christ, picks up the "double" terminology we already saw in *Lumen Gentium* and *Nostra Aetate* but in this case follows precisely the Johannine language (see John 1:14, 17). When "the word of preaching and the celebration of the sacraments" make "Christ, the author of salvation present," whatever elements of "truth and grace," which are "already found among the nations," are, "as it were, a secret presence of God." This may sound like setting "the presence of God" over against the presence of Christ. But the decree at once makes it clear that Christ, "the author of salvation," is also "the author" of these elements of "truth and grace" already found among the nations before they hear the word of Christian preaching (AG 9). The "secret presence of God" is equivalently the secret presence of Christ. As the giver of the gifts of truth and grace, Christ comes with the gifts.

"Truth and grace" define what "the seeds of the Word" bring. It is a matter of the (a) revealing and (b) saving presence and activity of Christ, with "truth" pointing to (a) and "grace" to (b).

A fourth item to be retrieved from *Ad Gentes* is the call to dialogue and collaboration which we already saw in *Nostra Aetate*. In lyric language, *Ad Gentes* describes "the sincere and patient dialogue" with the religious others to be expected from Christians engaged in missionary activity. Thus the disciples of Jesus, "profoundly imbued by" his Spirit, will be able to "learn what riches the bountiful God has distributed to the nations," so that they might "try to illuminate these riches with the light of the Gospel, to set them free, and bring them back to the dominion of God the Saviour" (AG 11).

This "fraternal dialogue" should lead Christians to "collaborate with all others," both Christians and non-Christians, "in the right ordering of economic and social affairs." Another lyric passage spells out the collaboration needed in the areas of education, health care, and the work for "better living conditions" and "peace" (AG 12). Such collaboration should also include "members of international organizations" (AG 41).

In the early twenty-first century, interreligious dialogue and collaboration may appear an obvious obligation to be embraced by Catholics and other Christian believers. But such interfaith consciousness took centuries to emerge. No previous ecumenical councils of Catholic Christianity ever imagined, let alone encouraged, the dialogue and collaboration with "religious others" inculcated by *Nostra Aetate*, *Ad Gentes*, and, one should add, *Gaudium et Spes*. These official conciliar texts have shaped the story of Roman Catholicism in a way from which there is no turning back.

We have looked at four areas in which *Ad Gentes* developed reflections which concerned those of other living faiths and which had been taught by three documents already promulgated at the Second Vatican Council (SC, LG, and NA). The most striking developments involved the second and fourth areas ("the seeds of the Word," and a practical dialogue with others). On one key theme, the universality of revelation and faith, *Ad Gentes* broke new ground.

To explain "the preparation for the Gospel" (AG 3), the missionary decree quotes, in the corresponding footnote 2, two passages from Irenaeus: "the Word existing with God, through whom all things were made . . . was always present to the human race." Hence, "from the beginning the Son, being present in his creation, reveals [*revelat*] the Father to all whom the Father desires, at the time and in the manner desired by the Father" (*Adversus Haereses*, 3.18.1; 4.6.7). Here *Ad Gentes* draws on Irenaeus to acknowledge (a) the Word of God as the agent in creating all things (see John 1:1-3, 10; 1 Cor 8:6; Heb 1:2). Consequently the Word has always been present to the entire human race and not merely to certain groups or nations. Granted the Christological origin and character of creation, (b) right from the start of human history the Son has been *revealing* the Father to human beings. In all its sixteen documents it is only here that Vatican II explicitly applies the verb "reveal" to the knowledge and experience of God mediated through the created world and its history. Obviously this revelation of God through creation and human history allows for endless variety, as "the Son reveals the Father to all whom the Father desires [and] at the time and in the manner desired by the Father."

The two quotations from Irenaeus highlight the universal divine activity by which the Word/Son of God prepares people for the coming of the gospel. Using the term "reveal" for the divine activity implies the counterpart of human faith. It is with true faith that human beings, whoever they are, respond to the initiative of the Son of God, who, being present in and through creation, reveals God to them. The decree expressly acknowledges a faith-response to the personal divine revelation made to the non-evangelized: "in ways known to himself" God can lead "those who, through no fault of their own, are ignorant of the Gospel to that faith without which it is impossible to please him (Heb 11:6)" (AG 7).

Recognizing explicitly that the divine activity of revelation and the human response of faith also take place among those who follow other religions or none at all occurs briefly in *Ad Gentes*. But the decree stands apart in being the first text from any ecumenical council to acknowledge expressly that (a) God's self-revelation reaches all people and (b) that human beings, no matter who they are, can and should respond with faith.

Conclusions

What conclusions might we draw from this examination of Vatican II's teaching on the religious situation of those who follow other living faiths (or none at all)? Six conclusions suggest themselves.

First, from the first document it promulgated, the liturgy constitution, the Council showed a universal mind-set, concerned with the divine self-communication reaching all people. *Sacrosanctum Concilium* manifested this mind-set by, for instance, mandating the restoration of the "prayer of the faithful," which includes praying for "the salvation of the entire world."

Second, through its striking picture of the High Priest heading a choir that includes all human beings, *Sacrosanctum Concilium* led the way in putting on the conciliar agenda the cosmic presence of Jesus

Christ. This involved *Lumen Gentium* (very briefly) and *Ad Gentes* (more elaborately) in retrieving the patristic doctrine of "the seeds of the Word." Far beyond Lumen Gentium 17, the missionary decree developed the theme of "the seeds of the Word," sown everywhere by God and "hidden" everywhere, in particular, in "religious traditions" (AG 9, 11, 15, 18). The "secretly present" Christ is "the author" of elements of "truth and grace" found "among the nations" (AG 9), the "Truth" that illuminates all human beings (NA 2).

Third, *Ad Gentes* taught, most importantly, that the Son, "present in creation" reveals the Father universally (AG 3 n. 2), and human beings can respond with saving faith (AG 7).

Fourth, most emphatically in *Ad Gentes* the Council presented the divine plan for human salvation in terms of the Trinity and the Trinitarian missions.

Fifth, Vatican II set itself to reflect on the situation of all human beings, the beneficiaries of God's saving love. *Nostra Aetate* innovated by reflecting on the human condition in the light of seven deep questions that affect all men and women.

Sixth, we can list further innovations introduced by the Council. It was the first ecumenical council to retrieve teaching from John's gospel that illuminates the religious situation of all human beings, as well as being the first council to allow its teaching on Jews to be shaped by two classical texts from Paul's Letter to the Romans. Unlike any earlier council, Vatican II offered positive teaching on Judaism, Islam, Hinduism, and Buddhism; this helped to prepare the way for groundbreaking initiatives in interfaith dialogue and collaboration.

Even though I have not included considerations drawn from the final document from Vatican II, the Pastoral Constitution on the Church in the Modern World, four earlier texts yield rich themes for anyone wanting to reflect on the religious situation of the "religious others." It is at our peril that we limit our reading in this area to the Declaration on the Relation of the Church to Non-Christian Religions.

Chapter 6

Implementing *Nostra Aetate*

The Second Vatican Council's Declaration on the Relation of the Church to Non-Christian Religions, *Nostra Aetate* ("of our age"), promulgated on October 28, 1965, was quickly recognized for its fresh approach to relations between Roman Catholics and followers of other living faiths.[1] Yet some of that development did nothing else than retrieve teaching from the early centuries of Christianity—notably what Justin Martyr and others wrote in the second century about the universally present "seeds of the Word."[2]

Even pre–Vatican II ecumenical councils recognized by Catholic Christianity had not totally ignored the doctrines, ways of life, and sacred rituals of "the others." Citing a classic passage from the prophet Malachi,[3] the Council of Trent acknowledged "the clean oblation of-

---

[1] See Roman A. Siebenrock, "Theologischer Kommentar zur Erklärung über die Haltung der Kirche zu den nichtchristlichen Religionen *Nostra Aetate*," in *Herders Theologischer Kommentar zum Zweiten Vatikanischen Konzil*, ed. Peter Hünermann and Bernd Jochen Hilberath, vol. 3 (Freiburg im Breisgau: Herder, 2005), 591–691.

[2] See Gerald O'Collins, *The Second Vatican Council on Other Religions* (Oxford: Oxford University Press, 2013), 16–18.

[3] "The Lord says: 'From the rising of the sun to its setting my name is great among the nations, and in every place incense is offered to my name; and a pure offering for my name is great among the nations'" (Mal 1:11; see 1:6–2:9; 3:3-4). In his historical context the prophet contrasts the corrupt practices of the Jewish priests who serve in the temple with the pure worship offered among the Gentiles (or just possibly with the worship offered by Jews in the Diaspora). Trent followed a long-standing Christian tradition and understood the contrast to be drawn between the Jewish worship in the temple and the worship of Gentiles in

fered in all places" to the name of the Lord, and understood the sacrifice of the Mass to be "prefigured by various types of sacrifices" not
only in the Old Testament but also "under the regime of nature." The
eucharistic sacrifice "includes all the good that was signified by those
former sacrifices; it is their fulfilment and perfection" (DzH 1742;
ND 1547). This teaching from Trent (that belonged to a defense of
the sacrificial character of the Mass) allowed for much which was
deemed good in the sacrificial rituals of other religions and which was
fulfilled and perfected by Christ's sacrifice. Sadly, this teaching was
normally ignored by Catholics who in later centuries wrote about the
world's religions.

But in *Nostra Aetate*, by dedicating a whole document to a positive reflection on other living faiths (in particular, Hinduism, Buddhism, Islam, and Judaism—in that order), Vatican II broke much
new ground. This teaching on "the others" had been preceded by
some teaching in the Constitution on the Sacred Liturgy (*Sacrosanctum
Concilium*) and two articles in *Lumen Gentium* (nos. 16 and 17), and
had been followed up by important passages in two documents promulgated on the final day of the Council: the Decree on the Church's
Missionary Activity (*Ad Gentes*) and the Pastoral Constitution on the
Church in the Modern World (*Gaudium et Spes*).[4]

There are many fruitful approaches to *Nostra Aetate*. In this chapter
I want to do three things: reflect on seven ways its teaching was creatively implemented by Pope John Paul II,[5] explore three issues which
the text of the declaration raises and which have not received adequate
attention, and then briefly indicate how further documents from the
Second Vatican Council fill out what *Nostra Aetate* encouraged Catholics
to accept about other religions.

"the regime of nature." On the passage from Malachi and Trent's use of it, see
Gerald O'Collins, *Salvation for All: God's Other Peoples* (Oxford: Oxford University
Press, 2008), 49–53; Gerald O'Collins and Michael Keenan Jones, *Jesus Our Priest:
A Christian Approach to the Priesthood of Christ* (Oxford: Oxford University Press,
2010), 171–73.

[4] See O'Collins, *The Second Vatican Council on Other Religions*: on SC (60–68), on
LG (68–83), on NA (85–108), on AG (109–27), and on GS (128–42).

[5] See ibid., 168–80.

John Paul II Develops *Nostra Aetate*

1. Like some sections of *Gaudium et Spes* (e.g., 10), *Nostra Aetate* adopts the method of correlation: the religions offer answers to the "unresolved riddles of human existence." People of all times and places question themselves about the meaning and purpose of life, asking: "What is upright behavior, and what is sinful? Where does suffering originate and what end does it serve? How can genuine happiness be found? What happens at death?" And, finally, "What is the ultimate mystery from which we take our origin and towards which we tend?" (NA 1). Such an account of the human condition privileges the notion and reality of *homo interrogans* (the human being as questioner).

Rather than correlating human questions and divine answers, John Paul II in his first encyclical *Redemptor Hominis* correlated two "mysteries," that of Christ and that of human beings (e.g., nos. 8 and 10).[6] Here the pope followed another theme, also found in *Gaudium et Spes*, that of Christ, "the last Adam" revealing not only the mystery of God but also the mystery of human beings (no. 22).[7] The language of "mystery" permeated *Redemptor Hominis*, with a special accent on the way in which "the mystery of the redemption" reveals the nature and destiny of human beings (e.g., nos. 13 and 18). In and through Christ two "mysteries" meet: that of the Redeemer himself and that of those he has come to redeem.

John Paul II published *Redemptor Hominis* in 1979. As he moved further into his papacy, and especially after the attempt on his life in May 1981, he dwelt more on the human mystery as a mystery of suffering, the painful struggle caused by suffering, and the meaning and power that suffering can draw from the mystery of Christ's crucifixion and resurrection. In his 1984 apostolic letter *Salvifici Doloris* and later texts, John Paul II shared a vision of the mystery of human suffering that Christ's passion, death, and resurrection can illuminate. *Nostra Aetate*, as we saw earlier, had included such questions as: "Where does

[6] As stated before, there are numerous editions and translations of such encyclicals and other papal documents; they are all to be found in English on the Vatican website.

[7] For John Paul II on GS 22, see Hans-Joachim Sander, "Theologischer Kommentar zur Pastoralkonstitution über die Kirche in der Welt von heute *Gaudium et Spes*," in *Herders Theologischer Kommentar*, 4:581–886, at 859–61.

suffering originate, and what end does it serve?" The pope came to privilege this approach to the mystery of the human condition, and offered more teaching on suffering than any previous pope or council had ever done.[8]

2. *Nostra Aetate*, while concerned with other "religions," appreciates the intimate link in human history between religions and cultures; they are distinguishable but hardly separable. Hence, before summarizing what it values in Hinduism and Buddhism, the declaration remarks: "the religions connected with the progress of *culture* attempt by way of more refined concepts and a more elaborate language to answer these questions [about the nature, origin, and destiny of human beings]" (no. 2; emphasis added). The same paragraph ends by exhorting Christian believers, while "witnessing to their faith and way of life," to "acknowledge, preserve, and encourage the spiritual, moral goods, as well as the *socio-cultural* values to be found" among others (emphasis added).

On a number of occasions John Paul II took up the deep link between religion and culture, not least in his 1990 encyclical letter *Redemptoris Missio* and its teaching on the universal activity of the Holy Spirit: "the Spirit's presence and activity affect not only individuals but also society and history, people, *cultures and religions.*" The pope then linked this activity with the hidden presence of Christ, "the seeds of the word" that Christian writers from the second century acknowledged to be everywhere: "it is the Spirit who sows 'the seeds of the Word' present in the various *customs and cultures*, preparing them for full maturity in Christ" (no. 28; emphasis added).[9]

3. This notion of the Holy Spirit sowing "the seeds of the Word," while drawing on a tradition that goes back to the second century, went beyond Justin and later writers by attributing the activity of "sowing"

---

[8] See e.g., his address to the sick and staff in a hospital in Rome (April 1, 1990), in *Osservatore Romano*, English edition, April 30, 1990; his address at the Coliseum (May 7, 2000), in AAS 92 (2000), 677–79, and *Origins* 30, no. 1 (2000): 4–5.

[9] This passage echoes Vatican II's account of the Church's activity, empowered by the Holy Spirit, in helping those who hear the gospel message and are baptized "to grow up through charity into *full maturity in Christ*," by bringing to perfection "whatever good is found *sown* in the heart and mind of human beings or in *rites and cultures* proper to various peoples" (LG 17; emphasis added; these words are repeated in AG 9); speaking of "full maturity in Christ" echoes, of course, Eph 4:13.

to the Spirit.[10] The papal teaching about the role of the Holy Spirit also went beyond what *Nostra Aetate* explicitly stated. That declaration first mentioned God the Father in passing (no. 2) and then dedicated an entire article to the heavenly Father and the practical implications of the divine fatherhood (no. 6). The Holy Spirit, however, did not appear in the text of *Nostra Aetate*.[11] One must look elsewhere in the conciliar documents for a fully trinitarian view of God's loving activity for the entire human race—above all in *Ad Gentes* 1–4.

From his first encyclical *Redemptor Hominis* (no. 6), John Paul II attended to the universal action of the Holy Spirit, expressing it even more strongly in the 1996 encyclical *Dominum et Vivificantem* (no. 53) and in his 1999 apostolic exhortation *Ecclesia in Asia* (nos. 16 and 18). He persistently affirmed the active presence of the Spirit of God not only in religious traditions but also in the religious life of individual non-Christians. As he stated in an address to the members of the Roman Curia on December 22, 1986, "every authentic prayer is called forth by the Holy Spirit who is mysteriously present in the heart of every person." Thus the pope saw the Spirit active everywhere, both for religious groups and for individuals.

4. *Nostra Aetate* has proved an enduringly important document in the history of Jewish-Catholic relations. Half of its text is dedicated to the Jewish people (the long no. 4). It follows *Lumen Gentium* (no. 16) and, ultimately, St. Paul (Rom 11:28-29) in holding that God has never taken back the gifts he bestowed [on the chosen people] or the choice he made [of them]" (NA 4). There is a straight line from this conciliar theme to the way John Paul II insisted that the special covenant made through Moses with God's chosen people has never been revoked.[12] It has not been rendered obsolete or inoperative by the covenant inaugurated by Christ's passion, death, and resurrection.

---

[10] AG 15 speaks of the Holy Spirit "arousing in [human] hearts the submission of faith by the seed of the Word and the preaching of the gospel," but does not expressly say that the Spirit had already sown the seed of the Word in human hearts.

[11] Originally intended to be part of the document on ecumenism (eventually UR), NA was then moved to being an appendix to LG and, finally, became a self-standing document. The absence of any reference to the Holy Spirit in the final text of NA may (at least partly) be explained by its being removed from its original setting in UR and LG; both of these texts have much to say about the Spirit.

[12] See the pope's speech on November 17, 1980 to a Jewish audience in Mainz: AAS 73 (1981), 78–82, at 80.

By his actions and gestures, John Paul II constantly endorsed friendship with the Jewish people and total rejection of any anti-Semitism (see NA 4 and 5). In April 1986 he visited the main synagogue in Rome; he was probably the first pope to visit and pray in a synagogue since the early days of Christianity. In April 1994 he hosted a Holocaust memorial concert in the Paul VI Audience Hall of the Vatican. The Royal Philharmonic Orchestra came from London and was conducted by a Brooklyn-born Jew, Gilbert Levine. John Paul II sat with the chief rabbi of Rome, Elio Toaff, who had brought with him his congregation. The concert was part of the Pope's personal mission to keep alive the memory of the Holocaust at the centre of the Catholic world. On that occasion he also arranged for the Kaddish, the traditional Jewish prayer for the dead, to be recited.

One could pile up many further examples, not least those from the celebration of the Jubilee Year 2000. On March 12, John Paul II presided over a special penitential service in St. Peter's Basilica, aimed at asking God's forgiveness for the past and present sins of "the sons and daughters of the church." One of the seven requests for pardon concerned "sins against the People of Israel," and the pope offered the following prayer: "God of our Fathers, you chose Abraham and his descendants to bring your name to the nations. We are deeply saddened by the behaviour of those who in the course of history have caused these children of yours to suffer. And asking for forgiveness, we wish to commit ourselves to genuine brotherhood with the people of the covenant." Two weeks later during a visit to Israel, John Paul II stood before the Western Wall of the temple, also known as the Wailing Wall. After praying in silence, the pope placed in the wall a personally signed copy of the prayer. There was a firm line between (a) his teaching and practice, and (b) what *Nostra Aetate* said about the special relationship between Christians and Jews.

5. In completing what it had to say about Islam, *Nostra Aetate* urged Muslims and Christians to join forces "for the benefit of all people, in defending and promoting together social justice, moral goods, peace and freedom" (no. 3). Less than six weeks after the promulgation of *Nostra Aetate*, the last and longest document of Vatican II, *Gaudium et Spes*, spelled out in detail what was involved in true human development and justice in the affairs of the world, particularly for the poor and oppressed. It ended by expressing a deep desire to work together

with all human beings in order "to build up the world in a spirit of genuine peace" (no. 92).

During his long pontificate, John Paul II kept encouraging solidarity and collaboration between those of different religions in their common responsibility for human welfare. In a letter dated September 10, 1992, endorsing a day of prayer for world peace, he stressed the need for believers of all faiths to remedy the situation of extreme economic and social differences between rich and poor countries.[13] His 1995 encyclical on the value and inviolability of human life, *Evangelium Vitae*, called for the concerted efforts of "all those who believe in the value of life." They must defend and promote human life as "everyone's task and responsibility," a common service shared alike by Christians and "followers of other religions" (no. 91). This sense of a common cause for all religious believers, "men and women without distinction" who strive together to build "a civilization of love founded upon the universal values of peace, justice, solidarity, and freedom," introduced the chapter on "the service of human promotion" in *Ecclesia in Asia* (nos. 39–41). In working to bring about this "civilization of love," John Paul II exhorted Catholics in Asia and elsewhere to make common cause with all believers everywhere.

As regards the common action of Christians and Muslims in promoting "social justice, moral goods, peace and freedom" (NA 4), there is much to cite from the speeches and gestures of John Paul II. Many would highlight here what he did in August 1985. At the invitation of King Hassan II of Morocco, he spoke in Casablanca to over one hundred thousand young Muslims on the religious and moral values common to Islam and Christianity. In his speech the pope called not only for a common witness to God but also for common action in the service of human dignity and a more humane world.[14] Since the days when Muhammad founded Islam, no pope had ever been invited to address such a large group of Muslims. But what I want to underscore here is the clear continuity between (a) the encouragement *Nostra*

---

[13] The letter, written in French and addressed to Cardinal Edward Cassidy on the sixth anniversary of a 1986 day of prayer for peace at Assisi, is found on the Vatican website.

[14] For the text of this speech, see AAS 78 (1986), 95–104; and Gerald O'Collins, Daniel Kendall, and Jeffrey LaBelle, eds., *John Paul II: A Reader* (Mahwah, NJ: Paulist Press, 2007), 148–58.

Aetate gave to collaboration between Christians and Muslims in the cause of peace, justice, freedom, and other moral values, and (b) what John Paul II did in August 1985—not to mention on other occasions.[15]

6. In normal editions and translations, *Nostra Aetate* runs to less than five pages. But, despite its brevity, it still manages to state the eschatological or future-oriented nature of the human condition. In, under, and through God, human beings share "one final end." Using imagery from the closing chapters of the Book of Revelation, the declaration speaks of "the elect" who "will be gathered together in the Holy City which the glory of God will illuminate and in which the people will walk in his light" (no. 1). A year earlier *Lumen Gentium* dedicated a lyric chapter to "the pilgrim people of God," the Church on her way toward the final glory of heaven (nos. 48–51). But *Nostra Aetate* addresses the hopes of all humankind, whether or not people consciously and frequently entertain these hopes.

The eschatological dimension of the human condition turned up repeatedly in the teaching of John Paul II. Let me limit myself to two examples from 1998: the apostolic letter *Dies Domini* and the encyclical *Fides et Ratio*. The first text attended to "the pilgrim and eschatological character of the People of God," who move "towards the final Lord's Day, that Sunday which knows no end." The letter invoked the language of Revelation by picturing the assembled Christian community going "forward to the unending Sunday of the heavenly Jerusalem, which 'has no need of the sun or moon to shine upon it, for the glory of God is its light and its lamp is the Lamb'" (nos. 37 and 84; see Rev 21:23). *Fides et Ratio* envisages the present and future situation of all human beings. It recalls the duty of believers to proclaim the truth of revelation, albeit with a sense that for each human being "every truth attained is but a step towards that fullness of truth which will appear with the final revelation of God. 'For now we see in a mirror dimly but then face to face. Now I know in part; then I shall understand fully' (1 Cor 13:12)" (no. 2). As regards the happiness of future

---

[15] See further Gerald O'Collins, "John Paul II on Christ, the Holy Spirit, and World Religions," *Irish Theological Quarterly* 72 (2007): 323–37; "Muslim Responses," in *John Paul II and Interreligious Dialogue*, ed. Byron L. Sherwin and Harold Kasimow (Maryknoll, NY: Orbis, 1999), 169–204. On the full scope of John Paul II's teaching on other religions, see Aleksander Majur, *L'insegnamento di Giovanni Paolo II sulle altre religioni* (Rome: Gregorian University Press, 2004).

glory (*Dies Domini*) and the future thrust of human knowledge (*Fides et Ratio*), John Paul II maintained the future-directed nature of the human condition.

7. *Nostra Aetate*, with reference to the Jewish people, speaks of "the saving mystery [singular] of God" (no. 4). This preference for the singular reflects a pervasive tendency of the Vatican II documents in highlighting *the mystery* of the tripersonal God revealed through Christ and inviting human beings to share in a new and final communion of love. This linguistic preference is based on the Pauline letters and their message of "the revelation of the mystery" or the great truth of salvation for all, now made known through Christ (Rom 16:25-26; see Eph 1:9; 3:4, 9). In the next chapter we will see this preference enshrined in the Dogmatic Constitution on Divine Revelation. The same preference also shows up in other texts from Vatican II: the sixteen documents use "mystery" in the singular 106 times and "mysteries" in the plural only twenty-two times.

Right from his first encyclical John Paul II exemplified the same tendency. *Redemptor Hominis* referred fifty-nine times to "the mystery of redemption," "the mystery of Christ," "the paschal mystery," "the mystery of the divine economy," and so forth, without every using the term "mystery" in the plural.[16] In his 1980 encyclical *Dives in Misericordia*, he used "mystery" thirty-nine times and "mysteries" only twice. Like *Nostra Aetate*, the pope envisaged a single design of universal salvation uniquely mediated through Christ (with the Holy Spirit)—a mystery that remains inseparably one, even if we can and should distinguish within it various stages and dimensions: for instance, the participated forms of mediation (of different kinds and degrees) of which John Paul II wrote in *Redemptoris Missio* (no. 5).

Three Further Themes of *Nostra Aetate*

In his very first encyclical John Paul II recalled the teaching of *Nostra Aetate* and made it his own (*Redemptor Hominis* 11). We have examined seven aspects of this continuity, a continuity that was creative—for instance, in the way in which the pope developed his teaching

---

[16] In *Redemptor Hominis* (no. 6), the pope wrote of "the truths [plural] revealed by God and proclaimed by the church."

on the universal presence and activity of the Holy Spirit. Yet, brief and all as it is, the declaration on other religions contains at least three further points which should be retrieved and developed: a Johannine use of "truth and grace," "truth and goodness," or similar "doublets"; the revelatory dimension of Christ's saving mission; and Christ's role as Wisdom. The first point was developed in the last chapter but deserves repetition, not least because it serves as a platform for the second and third points.

1. In his first encyclical, *Ecclesiam Suam* (August 1964), Paul VI wrote of what is "true and good" in the Muslim worship of God.[17] Within a few months similar language surfaced in *Lumen Gentium*: "The one Mediator, Christ, established and ever sustains here on earth his holy Church . . . as a visible organization through which he communicates *truth and grace* to all human beings" (no. 8; emphasis added). Eight paragraphs later, the same constitution applied some parallel pairs of terms, this time not to what the Church communicates but to what she finds among those "who, without any fault of their own, have not yet arrived at an explicit knowledge of God and who, not without grace, strive to lead a good life." "Whatever is *good or true* to be found among them," the constitution declared, "is considered by the Church to be a preparation for the gospel and given by him who *enlightens* all human beings that they may at length have *life*" (no. 16; italics mine). Here the Johannine language of revelation and salvation ("enlightens" and "life") (John 1:4, 9) alternated with the recognition of elements of salvation and revelation ("whatever is good and true"; see John 1:14, 17) to be recognized among upright nonbelievers.

Nostra Aetate and another document also promulgated during the fourth and final session of the Council (*Ad Gentes*) included similar "double" terminology. Implying that other religions, even often, can exhibit elements of truth and holiness, *Nostra Aetate* declared: "The Catholic Church rejects nothing of what is *true and holy* in these religions. She has a high regard for the manner of life and conduct, the precepts and doctrines which, although differing in many ways from her own teaching, nevertheless often reflect *a ray of that Truth [Veritas] that enlightens all human beings*" (no. 2). Once again echoing John's gospel, the Council combined here the terms in the order of revelation and salvation ("true

---

[17] AAS 56 (1964), 609–59, at 654.

and holy"). Six weeks later it followed the same order, while being more critical in the way it thought about other religions: "missionary activity . . . purges of evil associations every element of *truth and grace* which are found among peoples" (AG 9; emphasis added).

In their different ways *Nostra Aetate* and *Ad Gentes* depend on two articles of *Lumen Gentium* (nos. 16 and 17), which deploy a variety of terms to indicate the *revelatory* and *salvific* dimensions of the divine self-communication. This double-sided terminology of *Nostra Aetate* and the other two texts enjoys two important implications. First, we may not raise the question of salvation without raising that of revelation, and vice versa. When reflecting on anyone's or any group's situation before God, we need to recall the two inseparable dimensions of the one divine self-communication. Second, the terminology adopted by *Nostra Aetate* and the other two conciliar documents bears witness to the way in which Christ's mediation entails his being universal Revealer as well as universal Savior. He cannot be accepted as Savior for all without also being accepted as Revealer for all, "the true Light that enlightens everyone coming into the world" (John 1:9). In Johannine terms, he is both the Light of the world and the Life of the world.

2. In their official teaching, public liturgy, and mainline theology, Catholics and other Christians have normally attended much more to the saving role of Christ's mission. A eucharistic prayer from the ancient *Apostolic Tradition* of St. Hippolytus spoke of Christ as "the Saviour" and "Redeemer" sent "in the last times."[18] Theologians usually raise the question of Christ's unique and universal role in terms of salvation. As one example among many, one can cite here the 1971 study by Kurien Kunnumpuram, *Ways of Salvation: The Salvific Meaning of Non-Christian Religions according to the Teaching of Vatican II.*[19] In its 1997 document on "Christianity and the Religions," the International Theological Commission concluded that the followers of the world's religions could reach salvation by following the ways proposed to them: "Because of such explicit recognition of the presence of Christ's Spirit in the religions [*Redemptoris Missio* 90], one cannot exclude the possibility that these [religions] as such exercise a certain salvific function"

---

[18] Hippolytus of Rome, *La Tradition apostolique*, ed. Bernard Botte, 2nd ed. (Paris: Cerf, 1984), 48–49.

[19] Pune: Pontificium Athenaeum, 1971.

(no. 84). Normally official documents, liturgical texts, and theologians do not talk about Christ "the Revealer," "ways of revelation," or the religions exercising a certain "revelatory function." A striking exception to this normal practice came in John Paul II's encyclical *Fides et Ratio*; it dedicated a chapter to Christ's work as "Revealer" (nos. 7–15).

Vatican II, almost everywhere, limited the explicit language of "revelation" to the divine self-manifestation communicated through the history of the Jewish people (NA 4) and then reaching its decisive fullness with Jesus' life, death, and resurrection, together with the coming of the Holy Spirit (DV 2 and 4). A remarkable exception to this terminological choice came, as we saw in the last chapter, with footnote 8 to *Ad Gentes*, which cited some words from the *Adversus Haereses* of Irenaeus (4.6.7) about the universal revealing activity of the Word or Son of God: "from the beginning the Son, being present in his creation, reveals [*revelat*] the Father to all whom the Father desires, at the time and in the manner desired by the Father." This footnote can prompt us to look anew at the language of *Nostra Aetate* about "that Truth who enlightens all human beings [*omnes homines*]" (no. 2), as well as at the earlier text from *Lumen Gentium* about the Son of God "who enlightens all human beings [*omnes homines*] that they may at length have life" (no. 16). One can and should understand this Johannine language to mean that the Son of God brings revelation to everyone. Texts may convey such a claim, even if they do not use the explicit language of "revelation."

The Gospel of John never expressly gives Christ the title of "Revealer," but it conveys a clear sense of this role through equivalent terms: "Word," "Light," Christ as the One who "witnesses to the truth" and is "the Truth," the "I am" sayings, and so forth. The language of the Fourth Gospel is heavily and persistently revelational,[20] and quite explicitly so when it adopts the verb "Φανερόω" (John 1:31; 2:11; 3:21; 7:4; 9:3; 17:6: 21:1, 14). Their use of Johannine language supports reading the passages just cited from *Nostra Aetate* and *Lumen Gentium* in terms of a revelatory activity that Christ exercises everywhere and for everyone.

---

[20] See Ignace de la Potterie, *La Vérité dans Saint Jean*, 2 vols. (Rome: Biblical Institute Press, 1977).

Since Christ pursues such a universal revelatory activity, it follows that in some way or another he calls all people to *faith*. Revelation and faith, as we shall see in the next chapter, are reciprocal realities. The divine offer of revelation does not, so to speak, hang in the air; it aims at summoning forth human faith. Interestingly, *Ad Gentes*, which began by quoting St. Irenaeus on the universal character of revelation, went on to affirm that the divine activity of revelation, can initiate "faith" through many "ways" known to God (no. 7). The document is concerned here with the need for faith if human beings are to be saved, a need supported by the Letter to the Hebrews: "without faith it is impossible to please God" (11:6).[21] Significantly Hebrews is cited to illuminate the situation of those who "through no fault of their own do not know the gospel" (no. 7).[22] Millions of people in such a situation have followed and do follow various religions. Revelation reaches them, and hence they can respond with faith, "please God," and so receive salvation. To argue otherwise hardly seems compatible with the teaching of *Lumen Gentium* and *Nostra Aetate*.

3. *Nostra Aetate*, when describing the universal revelatory activity of Christ, called him "the Truth" who enlightens everyone. Vatican II also retrieved the patristic language about "the seeds of the Word" (e.g., AG 11). Without belittling the value of such language about "the Truth" and "the Word," we might be encouraged by *Fides et Ratio* to develop the image of Wisdom to convey Christ's revealing (and saving) activity on behalf of all people. In that encyclical John Paul II dedicated a chapter to the scriptural theme of wisdom, which reached its climax with the personal divine Wisdom revealed as Jesus Christ (nos. 16–23).

An obvious advantage to interpreting Christ's role as universal Revealer (and Savior) through the image of wisdom comes from the fact that the Jewish-Christian Scriptures and religion do not have a monopoly on wisdom. In one form or another, at least some wise teachings and ways of life turn up in all cultures and religions. As John Paul II put matters, "every people has its own native and seminal

[21] On this verse see O'Collins, *Salvation for All*, 254–57.

[22] Here AG echoes what LG had said a year earlier about the situation of non-Christians, including those "who, through no fault of their own, have not yet arrived at an explicit knowledge of God and who, not without grace, strive to lead an upright life" (art. 16). AG, however, thinks rather of those who, through no fault of their own, do not know the gospel and yet can be brought to faith by God.

wisdom," which is "a true cultural treasure" (*Fides et Ratio* 3). He wrote also of "the treasures of human wisdom and religion" (ibid., 31). Being found everywhere, sapiential modes of thought and life make an obvious bridge between Christians and those of other religions. Christian faith can see in all genuine wisdom the revealing and saving presence of Christ: *"ubi sapientia ibi Christus* [where there is wisdom there is Christ]."

To recognize in Christ the full revelation of God (and the Savior of all) is not then to deny to other religions any true revelation of God and mediation of salvation. The unique and normative role of Christ in the history of revelation and salvation extends to the numerous and various ways he works as divine Wisdom in the lives of people who follow other religions and receive salvation through them.

The Move to Christian Faith

Given its scope, *Nostra Aetate* did not and could not reflect on the situation of those "others" who come to embrace Christian faith. Here both *Lumen Gentium* and *Ad Gentes* fill out the picture by opening a window on how the Council evaluated those who make such a move.

Those who accept the gospel undergo a revelatory and saving process by being, respectively, "enlightened and corrected" (AG 3). For their part, Christ's disciples, while acknowledging "the riches which a generous God has distributed among the nations," should "try to illuminate these riches with the *light* of the Gospel, *set them free,* and bring them once more under the dominion of God *the Saviour*" (AG 11; emphasis added). Despite the cultural and religious "riches" already distributed to them by a "generous" God, non-Christians need the illumination of complete revelation and the liberation of salvation in all its full scope.

Lumen Gentium uses three schemes to interpret the change in those who accept the good news. They move from an implicit to an "explicit knowledge," from "shadows and images" to light, and from a state of "preparation for the Gospel" to "full maturity" (nos. 16–17; see AG 3). In all cases there is no question of starting from zero. Implicit knowledge, while not yet a "full and conscious" acceptance of Christianity (AG 7), is still a form of knowledge; shadows and images rise above mere formless darkness; a preparation always sets someone in movement toward a goal.

Three verbs help to express the conciliar vision of those who do not yet accept the good news. Their condition somehow leaves them wounded, at a lower level, and imperfect. The effect of the Church's missionary work is that "whatever good is found sown in the human heart and mind in the rites and cultures of peoples, so far from being lost, is *healed, raised to a higher level, and perfected* for the glory of God" (LG 17; emphasis added). The key verbs in this passage (*sanare, elevare,* and *consummare*) were to be repeated a year later in *Ad Gentes:* "every element of goodness found present in the human heart and mind or in the particular customs and cultures of peoples, so far from being lost, is *healed, raised to a higher level* and *perfected* for the glory of God" (AG 9; emphasis added).

These two passages from *Lumen Gentium* and *Ad Gentes*, respectively, emphasize the saving impact of conversion to Christianity. But the reference to the *goodness* already found in "the human *mind*" can be understood as referring to the divine revelation already communicated and known prior to the acceptance of the gospel. Those who become Christians bring with them elements of revelation (and salvation). All is not lost or discarded. The process of healing, elevating, and perfecting obviously bespeaks some measure of continuity. Furthermore, by referring to the "rites and cultures of the peoples" (LG), or "the particular customs and cultures of peoples" (AG), the two documents suggest that the community, even more than the individual, is the primary partner of God's revelatory and salvific self-communication.

To conclude, *Nostra Aetate* was a dramatic milestone in the history of the Church's relations with the followers of other living faiths. It was reflected and developed in the teaching that came from John Paul II during the more than twenty-six years of his pontificate. In particular, he moved official teaching forward by his vision of the universal presence and activity of the Holy Spirit. Brief and all as it was, *Nostra Aetate* contains some items that have been insufficiently acknowledged, in particular the *revelatory* (as well as salvific) implications of its Johannine terminology. Christ exercises everywhere and for everyone his role as universal Revealer. At the same time, it could be worth going beyond the declaration's language of Christ as the Truth to that of his being the divine Wisdom present everywhere.

To establish the full picture of Vatican II's teaching on Christ and the world's religions, we should acknowledge not only *Nostra Aetate* but also other conciliar texts, in particular *Lumen Gentium* and *Ad Gentes*. The language and images they adopt when commenting on what happens when people embrace Christianity help us to appreciate the elements of revelation and salvation already found among "the others."

Yet much more remains to be done in two areas. First, *Gaudium et Spes* adds to *Nostra Aetate* some remarkable and relevant passages: for instance, about the universal activity of the Holy Spirit in mediating revelation and salvation.[23] Second, dealing fully with the reception and implementation of *Nostra Aetate* would involve examining the history and results coming from postconciliar dialogues with, for instance, Jews, Muslims, Hindus, and Buddhists.[24]

[23] See O'Collins, *The Second Vatican Council on Other Religions*, 109–42; for what the liturgy constitution, SC, contributes to teaching on other religions, see ibid., 60–68.

[24] See James L. Heft, ed., *Catholicism and Interreligious Dialogue* (New York: Oxford University Press, 2012).

Chapter 7

Dei Verbum and Revelation

The 1985 Extraordinary Synod of Bishops met in Rome (November 24 to December 8) to celebrate the Second Vatican Council (which had ended twenty years earlier on December 8, 1965), to evaluate the Council's role in the postconciliar Church, and to develop some principles for the further reception of its teaching.[1] The final report of the synod produced six principles for interpreting the sixteen conciliar texts.[2]

Avery Dulles paraphrased the first principle as follows: "Each passage and document of the Council must be interpreted in the context of all the others, so that the integral meaning of the Council may be rightly grasped."[3] Presupposing that meaning and truth are to be found in the whole, this principle recalled approaches to the Scriptures that interpret the texts in the light of the final, canonical form of the entire Bible.[4] Yet the synod's report added at once a second principle that brought to mind another scriptural approach: namely, those interpretations which in various ways presuppose a "canon within the canon."[5] "The four major constitutions of the Council," the report states, "are

[1] See Giuseppe Alberigo and James Provost, eds., *Synod 1985: An Evaluation* (Edinburgh: T. & T. Clark, 1986).

[2] *The Final Report of the 1985 Extraordinary Synod* (Washington, DC: National Conference of Catholic Bishops, 1986).

[3] Avery Dulles, "The Reception of Vatican II at the Extraordinary Synod of 1985," in *The Reception of Vatican II*, ed. Giuseppe Alberigo, Jean-Pierre Jossua, and Joseph A. Komonchak (Washington, DC: Catholic University of America Press, 1987), 349–63, at 350.

[4] See The Pontifical Biblical Commission, *The Interpretation of the Bible in the Church* (Vatican City: Libreria Editrice Vaticana, 1993), 50–53, 93–94.

[5] DV itself adopts a version of the "canon within the canon," when it endorses the special place of the four gospels ("they are deservedly pre-eminent") within all the books of the Bible (no. 18).

the hermeneutical key for the other decrees and declarations."[6] These constitutions are, in chronological order of their promulgation, The Constitution on the Sacred Liturgy (*Sacrosanctum Concilium*), the Dogmatic Constitution on the Church (*Lumen Gentium*), the Dogmatic Constitution on Divine Revelation (*Dei Verbum*), and the Pastoral Constitution on the Church in the Modern World (*Gaudium et Spes*).

If these four constitutions provide such a "hermeneutical key," does one of them, as a kind of "*primus inter pares*," enjoy a certain "primacy" over the other three when we set ourselves to interpret Vatican II and its teaching? Many scholars and others have assigned this primacy to *Lumen Gentium*, but, given the priority of divine revelation over the doctrine of the Church (which is derived from revelation), it might be preferable to name *Dei Verbum* in first place. Jared Wicks commented on certain editions of the conciliar documents: "Some editions place *Lumen Gentium* at the head of the Vatican II constitutions, but would not the conciliar ecclesiology be better contextualized if it were placed *after* the council text starting with 'hearing the word of God reverently and proclaiming it confidently . . .' and ending with 'the word of God . . . stands forever,' as does *Dei Verbum*?"[7] Wicks, Christoph Theobald, and others make a strong case for the primacy of *Dei Verbum* when interpreting the conciliar teaching.

Naming *Dei Verbum* "the Dogmatic Constitution on Divine Revelation" implies that the self-revelation of God, even if explicitly addressed only by the first chapter, takes precedence over what follows on tradition (chap. 2) and the inspired Scriptures (chaps. 3–6). All of this suggests how supremely important it is to present correctly chapter 1 of *Dei Verbum*, along with what can be gleaned about divine revelation from other passages in the conciliar documents. Let me take up this task in three stages and set out what the constitution clearly develops about revelation, what it barely touches on, and what needs to be added from some of the other fifteen conciliar texts.

---

[6] Dulles, "Reception of Vatican II," 350.

[7] Jared Wicks, "Vatican II on Revelation—From Behind the Scenes," *Theological Studies* 71 (2010): 637–50, at 639. In various publications, Christoph Theobald has also assigned a pivotal role to *Dei Verbum* for interpreting the sixteen conciliar texts; see Massimo Faggioli, *Vatican II: The Battle for Meaning* (Mahwah, NJ: Paulist Press, 2012), 127–28, 181.

Chapter 1 of this book initiated a discussion of *Dei Verbum*, high-lighting some aspects of its genesis and its place in the story of *ressource-ment* theologians overcoming the manualist tradition. Here we attend rather to the content of the constitution's teaching on revelation.

Six Clear Themes from *Dei Verbum*

At least six themes about God's revelation emerge as clearly developed by *Dei Verbum*.[8]

First, right from the beginning *Dei Verbum* presents revelation as primarily being God's self-disclosure. After quoting 1 John 1:2-3 about the Word, who is divine Life and Light in person, "appearing to us" (no. 1), the constitution states firmly: "it pleased God, in his goodness and wisdom, to reveal himself and to make known the sacrament [*sacramentum*] of his will (see Eph 1:9)" (no. 2). The tripersonal God took the initiative to enter freely into a dialogue of love with human beings, so that through responding with integral faith they may receive salvation. Along with 1 John 1:2-3 and Ephesians 1:9, the opening chapter of *Dei Verbum* (no. 4) cites a third, classical New Testament text that also indicates the personal character of the divine self-revelation: "after God spoke in many places and numerous ways in the prophets, lastly in these days he has spoken to us in [his] Son" (Heb 1:1-2).

The opening chapter of *Dei Verbum* makes it repeatedly clear that revelation *primarily* means the self-revelation of God or of Truth (in uppercase) itself. *Secondarily*, of course, the divine revelation discloses something about God and human beings. The interpersonal "dialogue," which is God's self-communication, says and communicates information. Through encountering the divine Truth in person, human beings know new truths.

Hence the second chapter of *Dei Verbum* opens as follows: "God most kindly [*benignissime*] arranged that *the things which he had revealed* for the salvation of all peoples should remain integrally throughout time, and be transmitted to all generations" (DV 7; emphasis added). Since it deals with the transmission of revelation, that same chapter

---

[8] On the making of DV, see Riccardo Burigana, *La Bibbia nel Concilio: La redazi-one della costituzione Dei Verbum* (Bologna: Il Mulino, 1998); Jared Wicks, "Pieter Smulders and *Dei Verbum*," *Gregorianum* 82 (2001): 241–77, 559–93; 83 (2002): 225–67; 85 (2004): 242–77; 86 (2005): 92–134.

naturally speaks of "all revealed things" (no. 9) and uses a classic term for the content of the revelation communicated through Christ and his apostles: "all that it [the official magisterium] proposes to be believed as being divinely revealed it draws from this one *deposit of faith*" (no. 10; emphasis added). At the end, *Dei Verbum* talks of "the treasure of revelation entrusted to the Church" (no. 26), which she should faithfully preserve and proclaim.

The distinction *Dei Verbum* makes between the primary and secondary sense of revelation is expressed in an appropriate style of language. It highlights *the* mystery (singular) of the tripersonal God revealed through Christ in the history of salvation and inviting human beings to share in a new communion of love. This choice of the "singular" follows not only the verse cited from Ephesians 1:9 (see above) but also other passages from the Pauline letters (e.g., Rom 16:25-26; Eph 3:4, 9; 6:19; Col 1:27; 4:3). Revelation primarily means meeting the Mystery of God in person and only secondarily knowing the divine mysteries (plural and in lowercase). Talk of "the mystery" forms a leitmotif in *Dei Verbum*; five times the constitution speaks of "mystery" in the singular (nos. 2, 15, 17, 24, and 26) and never of "the mysteries" in the plural. The same tendency shows up, as we saw in the last chapter, in other texts promulgated by Vatican II. Right from his first encyclical John Paul II, as we also saw in the last chapter, exemplified the same tendency.

Over the primary and secondary sense of revelation, Vatican II differs from Vatican I. In its constitution on divine faith (*Dei Filius* of 1870), the First Vatican Council, while once talking of God "revealing himself" (DzH 3004; ND 113), in general understood divine revelation to be primarily God communicating the divine truths (plural), which otherwise would be inaccessible to human reason or at best known only with difficulty. This entailed presenting human faith as submitting to the divine "authority" and believing to be true "that which God has revealed" (DzH 3008; ND 118); it also entailed speaking of "the mysteries" (plural) "contained in divine revelation" (DzH 3041; ND 137; see DzH 3016–17; ND 132–33). After Vatican I, a development of doctrine intervenes when Vatican II presents divine revelation as being primarily the self-disclosure of God and not primarily the manifestation of divine truths which would otherwise not be known. There has been a shift from emphasizing "knowing about God" to "knowing God" personally.

A second theme, which we have already glimpsed in chapter 3 above, concerns the nature of revelation as *salvific* and *sacramental*. Right from its prologue *Dei Verbum* indicates how God's self-revelation and the offer of salvation coincide. Vatican II wanted "the whole world" to hear "the summons to salvation" (no. 1). The plan or "economy of revelation" is, more or less, synonymous with "the history of salvation" (no. 2). Repeatedly and without hesitation the constitution passes from the language of revelation to that of salvation, and then back to revelation (e.g., nos. 3, 4, 6, 7, 14, 15, 17, and 21). Thus it recognizes that we deal with two inseparable, if distinguishable, realities. God's revealing word necessarily offers salvation. In Johannine terms, since Jesus is *the* Truth in person, he is also *the* Life in person.

When enunciating the Easter mystery, *Dei Verbum* deftly links revelation and salvation: through his life, death, and resurrection (along with the sending of the Holy Spirit), Christ revealed that "God is with us, to deliver us from the darkness of sin and death, and to raise us up to eternal life" (no. 4). The self-revelation of God and redemptive deliverance of human beings go hand in hand.

As something which applies equally to the "economy of revelation" and "the history of salvation," *Dei Verbum* puts on display sacramental language. When administrating the sacraments, the words and actions of persons interact to communicate God's revelation and salvation: thus "this economy of revelation takes place [*fit*] by deeds and words, which are intrinsically connected with each other. As a result, the works performed by God in the history of salvation manifest and bear out the doctrine and realities signified by the words; while the words proclaim the works and bring to light the mystery they contain" (no. 2; see 4 and 14). It is above all in the case of Jesus himself that the words and deeds of a person convey the saving self-revelation of God: "Christ established on earth the Kingdom of God [and] revealed [*manifestavit*] his Father and himself by deeds and words" (no. 17). It is worth noting how a year earlier *Lumen Gentium* had said something very similar, using "shines forth [*elucescit*]": "this kingdom [of God] shines forth before human beings in the word, works, and presence of Christ" (no. 5).

Some have interpreted this "sacramental" way of presenting God's saving and revealing self-communication as having an ecumenical origin. Was it a Catholic way of welcoming and joining together themes favoured by two different schools of Protestant theologians? Did *Dei*

Verbum combine the language of (a) such word-of-God theologians as Karl Barth and Rudolf Bultmann with (b) that favored by Oscar Cullmann, George Ernest Wright, and Wolfhart Pannenberg about God's revealing and saving acts in history? Without discounting completely this explanation, one should recall how from November 1962 Pieter Smulders began to be involved in preparing what would become *Dei Verbum*; in passages that he helped to draft one finds the language of divine revelation being mediated through "words" and "deeds."[9] A world-class expert on St. Hilary of Poitiers, Smulders was familiar with his use of that language. In the opening article of *Tractatus Mysteriorum*, Hilary wrote of the biblical "words [*dicta*]" and "facts [*facta*]" that "announce [*nuntiare*]" and "express/reveal [*exprimere*]" the coming of Christ.[10] A few days before Smulders was co-opted into the work toward elaborating the constitution on revelation, Bishop Emile Guano had proposed at a plenary session of Vatican II that the "exordium" of the new "schema" on revelation should state that "God speaks to human beings through . . . his Word made flesh." Christ "speaks to human beings, to begin with through his words [*dicta*] but also . . . through his works (*facta*) and deeds (*gesta*), indeed through his very person."[11] One should also recall how the language of "words" and "works" also turned up in a paper ("On Revelation and the Word of God") that Jean Daniélou prepared in November 1962 for Cardinal

[9] On Smulders's role in the preparation of *Dei Verbum*, see Gerald O'Collins, *Retrieving Fundamental Theology: Three Styles of Fundamental Theology* (Mahwah, NJ: Paulist Press, 1993), 57–62, 160–64. One should also add what Smulders communicated several months earlier to Archbishop Giuseppe Beltrami, the papal nuncio in The Hague: revelation embraces not only the *"locutio Dei"* (the revelatory word) but also the *"magnalia Dei"* (the great deeds of God). On this see Wicks, "Vatican II on Revelation," 637–50, at 643–45; this excellent article also draws attention to (a) the role of Daniélou, Rahner, Ratzinger, and other *periti* in elaborating the text of *Dei Verbum*, and provides references to (b) an outstanding series of articles by Wicks on the contribution to the Council that came from Ratzinger and Smulders (see fn. 8 above), and to (c) relevant dissertations on the Council produced by Wicks's own doctoral students.

[10] *Traité des mystères*, 1.1, ed. Jean-Paul Brisson, *Sources Chrétiennes* 19, 2nd ed. (Paris: Cerf, 2005), 71.

[11] *Acta Synodalia S. Concilii Oecumenici Vaticani II*, I/111 (Vatican City: Typis Polyglottis Vaticanis, 1971), 260. In combining word and deed, Bishop Guano did not suggest that he was intending to blend two (Protestant) views about the mediation of revelation and salvation.

Gabriel Garrone, a member of the joint commission charged with revising the "schema" on "the Sources of Revelation."[12]

In the event, the final text of *Dei Verbum* four times described revelation as communicated "by deeds and words" (nos. 2, 4, 14, and 15). As terms which suggest somewhat better the personal nature of revelation, *"gesta"* (twice) and *"opera"* (twice) rather than *"facta"* (only once) were used in the definitive version of the constitution. Finally, one should not overlook the way in which earlier Catholic theology had already taken up the language about revelation being mediated through "words and deeds." Back in 1900, Herman Schell wrote of the divine revelation as follows: "the supernatural revelation of God means the free self-communication of God *through word and deed* to a personal and real community of life with the created spirit."[13] In short, a "Catholic" combination of two Protestant schools of thought (the word of God and the saving divine acts in history) may have contributed to the sacramental language that *Dei Verbum* used in presenting revelation. But there were other sources for this language—and not least, one must add, *Sacrosanctum Concilium*, as we provisionally indicated in chapter 3 above.

Promulgated in December 1963, the constitution on the liturgy spoke not only of the eucharistic "mystery of faith" involving both "sacred action" and "instruction by God's word" (no. 48) but also of the act of "celebration" and the "words" that constitute the other sacraments (no. 59). Being what Massimo Faggioli has happily called "a theological starting point" for Vatican II,[14] *Sacrosanctum Concilium* prepared the way for the sacramental language of *Dei Verbum*. This liturgical constitution also encouraged holding together "the economy of revelation" with "the history of salvation" through rehabilitating "the table of God's word" (no. 51) alongside "the table of the Lord's Body" (no. 48). The revealing word belongs inseparably with the saving sacrament of the Eucharist. To sum up: *Dei Verbum*'s stress on the salvific and sacramental nature of divine self-revelation applies to the

---

[12] For details, see Wicks, "Vatican II on Revelation," 647–50.

[13] Herman Schell, *Katholische Dogmatik*, ed. Josef Hasenfuss, Heinrich Petri, and Paul-Werner Scheele, vol. 1 (Munich: Schöningh, 1968), 28 n. 1; trans. and emphasis mine.

[14] Faggioli, *Vatican II: The Battle for Meaning*, 103.

broader reality of revelation what *Sacrosanctum Concilium* had already enunciated about the liturgy.

A third major theme, perhaps better a major "term," embodied in chapter 1 of *Dei Verbum* is that of the divine *self-communication*: "by divine revelation God wished to manifest and *communicate himself* and the eternal decrees of his will concerning the salvation of human beings" (no. 6).[15] The special value of this term comes from the way in which it holds together God's self-revelation and self-giving through saving grace. The divine communication is not merely "informative" but also constitutes a real self-communication of God, which both makes salvation known and brings it in person.

Smulders had some role in the language of divine "self-communication" entering the final text of *Dei Verbum*.[16] After the Council, this term moved further ahead in official Catholic teaching. John Paul II used it in a 1980 encyclical *Dives in Misericordia* (no. 7) and then repeatedly in a 1986 encyclical on the Holy Spirit, *Dominum et Vivificantem* (nos. 13 [twice], 14, 23, 50 [four times], 51 [twice], and 58 [twice]). We saw above how Herman Schell had written in 1900 of "the free self-communication of God," and we find the term in the works of Karl Barth, Rudolf Bultmann, Romano Guardini, Karl Rahner, and F. D. E. Schleiermacher. But that language had already enjoyed its place in the long history of theology. In the third part of his *Summa Theologiae*, St. Thomas Aquinas endorsed a principle from Pseudo-Dionysius the Areopagite ("good diffuses itself") to expound the incarnation as the supreme act of God's self-communication: "it belongs to the scheme [*rationem*] of goodness to communicate itself to others as Dionysius shows. Hence it belongs to the scheme of the highest good to communicate itself to the creature in the highest way" (3a.1.1 resp., trans. mine).

In a fourth major theme *Dei Verbum* recognizes the paschal mystery as the high point of divine self-revelation: "Jesus Christ . . . completed

---

[15] This passage echoes Vatican I and the only passage where it spoke of revelation as God's self-revelation: "it pleased his [God's] wisdom and goodness to reveal himself and his eternal decrees" (DzH 3004; ND 113). Where Vatican I's constitution on faith (*Dei Filius*) spoke of God's "revealing himself," *Dei Verbum* doubled the verb to speak of God's "manifesting and *communicating himself*" (emphasis added).

[16] O'Collins, *Retrieving Fundamental Theology*, 52–53.

and perfected revelation and confirmed it with the divine witness. [He did this] by the total presence of himself and [self-manifestation]—by words and works, signs and miracles, but especially by his death and glorious resurrection from the dead, and finally by sending the Spirit of truth." As we noted above, this article linked the climax of revelation with its saving point and purpose: Christ revealed that "God is with us, to deliver us from the darkness of sin and death, and to raise us up to eternal life" (no. 4).[17]

Once again *Sacrosanctum Concilium* had prepared the ground for such teaching by highlighting Easter as that "supremely solemn" of all feasts (no. 102), as well as every Sunday, when the Church celebrates "the paschal mystery" being "the foundation and kernel of the whole liturgical year" (no. 106). The highpoint in liturgical celebration, the resurrection of the crucified Jesus, came to be acknowledged as the highpoint of his redemptive revelation. The liturgy indicated the priority of Easter for the doctrine of revelation.[18]

A fifth significant, and still sometimes contentious, teaching of *Dei Verbum* concerns the way it sets out the divine self-disclosure as being past, present, and future. Here, once again, the constitution follows the lead of *Sacrosanctum Concilium* (see chap. 3 above).

We have just quoted the text of *Dei Verbum* about the *past* completing and perfecting of revelation at the resurrection of the crucified Jesus and the outpouring of the Spirit at the first Pentecost. Nevertheless, the constitution also portrays revelation as a *present* event that invites human faith: "'The obedience of faith' (Rom 16:26) must be shown to God as he reveals" himself (no. 5). *Dei Verbum* associates revelation as it happened then and as it happens now in the Church: "God, who spoke in the past, uninterruptedly speaks to the spouse of his beloved Son" (no. 8). In its closing chapter the constitution cites St. Ambrose of Milan to picture what happens when personal prayer accompanies the reading of sacred Scripture and "a dialogue" takes place between God and human

---

[17] See Raúl Biord Castillo, *La Resurrección de Cristo como Plenitud de la Revelación. Análisis del tema en la teología fundamental a partir de la Dei Verbum* (Rome: Gregorian University Press, 1998).

[18] The language of *Dei Verbum* about "the total presence of Christ" enjoys a prior "intimation" in what SC taught about the pluriform presence of Christ in the liturgy (no. 7); see chap. 4 above.

beings: "we address him when we pray; we listen to him when we read the divine oracles" (no. 25). Besides being completed in the past and repeatedly actualized in the present, revelation is also to be expected in the future at "the glorious manifestation of our Lord, Jesus Christ" (no. 4).

Faced with this scheme of revelation as past, *present*, and future, some are still tempted to allege that present revelation is not revelation in the proper sense but only a growth in the collective understanding of biblical revelation completed and "closed" once and for all with Christ and his apostles. Undoubtedly such a growth of understanding can and does take place. *Dei Verbum* takes up this theme: "the tradition that comes from the apostles makes progress in the Church, with the help of the Holy Spirit. There is growth in knowledge of the realities and words that are passed on . . . . [Thus,] as the centuries go by, the Church is constantly moving towards the fullness of divine truth" (no. 8). Nevertheless, we would not do justice to tradition if we credited it only with the development in understanding of a closed and past revelation but denied that it actualizes the revelation of God. *Dei Verbum* offers no such "low" version of tradition. The constitution interprets in the following terms the results of tradition as guided by the Holy Spirit: "Through the same tradition . . . the Sacred Scriptures themselves are more deeply understood and ceaselessly actualized. Thus God, who spoke in the past, speaks uninterruptedly with the spouse of his beloved Son. And the Holy Spirit, through whom the living voice of the gospel rings out in the Church—and through her in the world—leads believers into all truth, and makes the word of Christ dwell abundantly in them" (no. 8). Here the Council expresses its conviction that, through the force of tradition, the divine self-revelation recorded in the Scriptures is not only "more deeply understood" but also "actualized." God continues to speak, and through the Spirit "the living voice of the gospel" never ceases to ring out.

To deny present revelation is to doubt the active power here and now of the Holy Spirit as guiding tradition and mediating the presence of the risen Christ. In effect this also means reducing faith to the acceptance of some revealed truths coming from the past rather than taking faith in its integral sense—as the full obedience personally given to God revealed here and now through the living voice of the gospel. In short to deny the revelation of God as happening also in the present is to *sell short its human correlative, faith.*

Of course, if one persists in thinking that revelation *primarily* means the communication of revealed truths, it becomes easier to relegate revelation to the past. As soon as the whole set of revealed truths is complete, revelation ends or is "closed." For this way of thinking later believers cannot immediately and directly experience divine revelation. All they can do is remember, interpret, and apply truths revealed long ago to the apostolic Church.

Dei Verbum and other conciliar and postconciliar documents describe revelation as something which reached its full completion in the past—through "the total presence" of Christ and his self-manifestation" (no. 4). There was content to this personal revelation, so that the constitution could refer to "the things that he [God] revealed for the salvation of all peoples" (no. 7), "the divinely revealed realities [*divinitus revelata*]" (no. 11), and "the deposit of faith" entrusted to the apostolic Church and to be maintained faithfully through the tradition (no. 10). Nevertheless, *Dei Verbum* does not hesitate to speak of "hearing the Word of God" here and now (no. 1), of the obedience of faith being given to God who reveals himself in the present (no. 5), of God "continuing to converse" with the whole Church, and of the Holy Spirit ensuring that "the living voice of the Gospel" rings out in the present (no. 8). In representing the divine self-revelation in Christ as not only a matter of the past and the future but also a present reality, *Dei Verbum* once again follows what the liturgical constitution stated.

Christ, *Sacrosanctum Concilium* explains, is actively present in the eucharistic celebration. "It is he himself," for example, who "speaks when the holy Scriptures are read" (no. 7). A later article adds that in the sacred liturgy "God speaks to his people and Christ is still proclaiming his Gospel" (no. 33); this is to recognize how the faithful encounter the living Word of God. To express the full scope of this personal encounter (through the past and the future, as well as in the present), the liturgical constitution cites the antiphon for the Second Vespers on the Feast of Corpus Christi (now the Feast of the Body and Blood of Christ) and calls the Eucharist "a paschal banquet in which Christ is consumed, the mind is filled with grace, and a pledge of future glory is given to us" (no. 47). The complete antiphon reads: "O sacred banquet in which Christ is consumed, his suffering is remembered [from the past], the mind is filled with grace [in the present], and a pledge of future glory is given to us [*O sacrum convivium, in quo Christus sumitur, recolitur memoria passionis eius; mens impletur gratia; et futurae gloriae nobis pignus datur*]." When quoting the antiphon, *Sacrosanctum Concilium* does not include "his suffering is remembered," since the same article has just spoken of the Eucharist as "a memorial of his [Christ's] Death and Resurrection." The passage from the constitution naturally highlights salvation and, specifically, the grace and glory communicated by the Eucharist. Nevertheless, it also points to revelation as past (remembering Christ's death and resurrection), as present ("the mind" being "filled with grace"), and as future (the vision of God in "future glory"). One might adapt the antiphon and say: "O sacred revelation, in which Christ is encountered: a revelation fully conveyed through his life, death, and resurrection (along with the sending of the Spirit) which we remember; a revelation which can here and now fill our minds through the grace of his self-disclosure; and a revelation which promises us his glorious self-manifestation to come."

One could sum up *Dei Verbum*'s teaching on revelation by saying that, through Christ, it has been fully communicated in the past, that it will be consummated at the future end of history, and that it happens here and now. Revelation as present actualizes the living event of the divine self-manifestation but does not "enlarge" the essential "content" of what was completely revealed through Christ's life, death, resurrection, and the sending of the Holy Spirit. Revelation continues to be an actual encounter with the self-manifesting God, but this personal dialogue adds nothing to "the divinely revealed realities" (which essentially amount to Jesus Christ crucified, risen from the dead, and to come one day in glory, together with all that these events effect and imply). We might express the three "moments" of revelation by distinguishing between, but not separating, "foundational" (past) revelation, present or "dependent" revelation (which essentially depends upon foundational revelation), and future (or eschatological) revelation.[19]

A sixth and final theme on revelation to be gleaned from *Dei Verbum* touches the human response to the present self-disclosure of God: the obedience of faith (no. 5) or submission to God of the whole human person. Revelation is a reciprocal event and is not truly "there" until human beings respond with faith. In the words of the constitution, "by revelation" "the invisible God" "addresses human beings as his

---

[19] On these distinctions, see Gerald O'Collins, *Rethinking Fundamental Theology: Toward a New Fundamental Theology* (Oxford: Oxford University Press, 2011), 128–35.

friends . . . and moves among them, in order to invite and receive them into his own company" (no. 2). In short, revelation reaches its goal when believing hearts and minds open themselves to the divine self-communication and share the life and "company" of God.

At the third session of the Council, Cardinal Julius Döpfner expressed the reception of faith (in a summary offered by Jared Wicks): "faith is primarily God's work in humans to make his word of revelation effective, so that, in faith, revelation's essence completes itself. Beyond a dialogue, faith is *participative* of and in what God reveals."[20] Together with the cardinal's reflections, one should also cite a similar position on revelation's essential link with faith developed by a notable Vatican II *peritus*, Joseph Ratzinger. Now that the complete edition of Ratzinger's *Habilitationsschrift* has been published, we can see how he followed St. Bonaventure. Revelation is realized only when the action of God reaches its "term" or intended outcome: namely faith.[21] Divine revelation exists in living subjects, those who respond with faith. In a lecture given in 1963, Ratzinger insisted that "revelation always and only becomes a reality where there is faith . . . revelation to some degree includes its recipient, without whom it does not exist."[22]

Human Experience and Divine Revelation

Thus far we have seen how *Dei Verbum* has yielded six clear items of teaching on revelation: it is primarily God's self-manifestation and secondarily the disclosure of new truths; it is essentially salvific and sacramental; it can be happily expressed as God's "self-communication"; it reached its highpoint with Christ's death and resurrection; as foundational, dependent, and eschatological, it spans past, present, and future, respectively; it reaches its intended outcome in the response of human faith. The constitution has more to say (or imply) about such themes as the complex relation between revelation and tradition, and

---

[20] Wicks, "Vatican II on Revelation," 640 n. 7; see also Gianluca Montaldi, *In fide ipsa essentia revelationis completur: Il tema della fede nell'evolversi del Concilio Vaticano II; La genesi di DV 5–6* (Rome: Gregorian University Press, 2005), at 355–60.

[21] For details see Wicks, "Vatican II on Revelation," 642 n. 12.

[22] Joseph Ratzinger, "Revelation and Tradition," in Karl Rahner and Joseph Ratzinger, *Revelation and Tradition*, trans. W. J. O'Hara (London: Burns & Oates, 1966), 26–49, at 36.

the equally complex relation between revelation and Scripture.[23] But let me limit myself to raising some pressing questions about human experience, the context in which the self-revelation of God takes place and yet a theme that barely makes an appearance in the constitution on revelation (nos. 8, 14) and was introduced in chapter 1 above.

The Gospel of John, the letters of St. Paul, the *Confessions* of St. Augustine, and other classical works established and encouraged an experiential approach to understanding and interpreting the divine-human relationship. A long line of spiritual and mystical authorities examined this relationship in the key of experience. William of Saint-Thierry (1085–1148) proved one of many Christian men and women who explored in depth our spiritual experience. Nevertheless, two modern documents of the Catholic magisterium, *Dei Filius* (from Vatican I in 1870) and *Pascendi* (from Pope Pius X in 1907), warned against denying that external signs could lend credibility to divine revelation, against appealing only to the internal experience of individuals (DzH 3033; ND 127), and against making faith in God depend on the "private experience" of individuals and maintaining that interior, immediate experience of God prevails over rational arguments (DzH 3484). This justified opposition to one-sided versions of religious experience unfortunately encouraged the delusion that somehow we could encounter the divine self-revelation "outside" human experience.

The Second Vatican Council, in general, introduced sparingly the terminology of "experience." The conciliar documents reflected some unease about this language. One can ascribe that inhibition to the long shadows cast by the condemnation of "Modernism" in the decree *Lamentabili* and the encyclical *Pascendi* (both of 1907). In condemning "modernists," St. Pius X and his collaborators showed a certain blindness to historical developments in Christianity but were right on other scores. Some "modernists" went astray in one-sidedly emphasising religious experience. Misuse of this category should not, however, have led to ruling it out or downplaying its centrality. Yet for much of the twentieth century that was the case in the Catholic circles of many countries. Seminarians, in particular, were trained to be suspicious of "experience," as if it were merely private, emotional, and dangerously subjective.

[23] See O'Collins, *Rethinking Fundamental Theology*, 190–233.

In 1965, *Dei Verbum* cautiously began setting the record straight at the level of official teaching. Through their special history of revelation and salvation, the Israelites "experienced the ways of God with human beings" (no. 14). In the post–New Testament life of the Church, their "experience" of "spiritual realities" has helped believers contribute to the progress of tradition (no. 8). Then followed *Gaudium et Spes*, which proved nothing less than a profound reflection on the experience of the whole human family in the light of the crucified and risen Christ. Through Christ's revelation "the sublime calling and profound misery, which human beings experience, find their final meaning" (no. 13). Here and elsewhere the constitution set itself to correlate "the light of revelation" with human experience (e.g., no. 33). But it was left to a pope to feed the theme of experience directly into the bloodstream of official Catholic teaching.

With his background in the phenomenology of Edmund Husserl, Max Scheler, and others of a philosophical school that aims at describing the way things, as they actually are, manifest themselves, John Paul II had no aversion to "experience" and the language of "experience." In his first encyclical, *Redemptor Hominis* of 1979, he introduced the noun "experience" four times and the verb "experience" twice. A year later in *Dives in Misericordia*, he appealed to collective and individual experience (no. 4), and went on to use "experience" thirteen times as a noun and six times as a verb. One can readily justify the pope's choice of terminology. If the divine self-revelation does not enter our experience (to arouse faith or strengthen an already existing faith), it simply does not happen as far as we are concerned. Non-experienced revelation makes no sense.[24]

Four Further Themes Left Untouched

Thus far we have examined six themes found in the teaching of *Dei Verbum* on revelation and one theme (experience) that hardly comes into view in that constitution. The first principle from the final report of the 1985 Extraordinary Synod (see above) prompts me into recall-

---

[24] See further Gerald O'Collins, "John Paul II and the Development of Doctrine," in *The Legacy of John Paul II*, ed. Gerald O'Collins and Michael A. Hayes (London: Continuum, 2008), 1–16. On experience and religious experience, see O'Collins, *Rethinking Fundamental Theology*, 42–55.

ing briefly what other documents of Vatican II offer, so that we might grasp the "integral" conciliar doctrine on God's self-revelation. Four themes suggest themselves: the human condition, the credibility of revelation, divine revelation reaching those who are not Christians, and "the signs of the times."

(1) The brief opening chapter of *Dei Verbum* did not respond to the question: who are the human beings addressed by God's self-disclosure? Nevertheless, from the opening sentence of the constitution, one can glean that they are (potential) hearers of the divine word (art. 1). They are endowed with "reason" (no. 6) but need to be delivered from "the darkness of sin and death" (no. 4). For a fuller account of the human condition, we must look elsewhere: to the Declaration on the Relation of the Church to Non-Christian Religions (*Nostra Aetate*) and, much more to *Gaudium et Spes*. *Nostra Aetate* presents religious faith as an answer to the fundamental questions which belong to human existence and which human beings must sooner or later face (NA 1–2). *Gaudium et Spes* dedicates its introduction to the human situation (nos. 4–10) and its opening chapter to the dignity of human persons (nos. 12–22). Here the constitution has much to say about human beings as created in the image of God, sinful yet free, and faced with the mystery of death. Elsewhere *Gaudium et Spes* has more to say about the condition of human beings who need and receive the revealing and redemptive self-communication of God.

(2) Apropos of reasons for accepting this revelation—what we might call the "credibility" of revelation—*Dei Verbum* has little or nothing to offer, apart from the coherent clarity of its six chapters, which resulted from debates and discussions that continued through the four sessions and three intersessions of the Council. While *Gaudium et Spes* never set itself directly to establish the credibility of God's revelation in Christ, the constitution over and over again vividly proclaims Christ as the One who answers the deepest questions and yearnings of human beings (e.g., nos. 22, 38, and 45). Second, it presents attractively the Church as the community founded by Christ and offering to the whole world the light and life of his message (e.g., nos. 40–43, 92–93). To this we should add that the unfolding story of the Council, convoked and opened by John XXIII and brought to a conclusion by Paul VI, caught the attention of the world and did not leave untouched many people who hungered for religious meaning and nourishment. In that sense, the whole "event" of Vatican II provided reasons for finding a

believable creed in what the Christian Church proclaims about the divine self-revelation in Christ.

(3) A third crucial issue, left untouched in *Dei Verbum*, enquires about divine revelation reaching the religious "others," those who have not heard the Christian message or have not yet found reasons for accepting it. The final article of its chapter on revelation briefly repeats the teaching of Vatican I about the knowledge of God being available through the created world (no. 6) but does not develop what this might mean for the many millions who follow "other" religious faiths. Here four documents of Vatican II step in to provide new, official teaching about the possibility of responding in faith to the divine self-revelation: *Lumen Gentium* (nos. 16 and 17); *Nostra Aetate*; the Decree on the Church's Missionary Activity (*Ad Gentes*) (esp. chap. 1); and *Gaudium et Spes* (various articles). Once again we find the first document approved by the Council, *Sacrosanctum Concilium,* leading the way. It initiated this concern for "the religious others" and displayed a mind-set open to the salvation of the world.[25]

(4) Finally, *Gaudium et Spes* proposed that "the signs of the times" (Matt 16:3) and "the voices of our age" (no. 44) can convey God's intentions. Discerning the signs of the times belongs with the call to open oneself to the full scope of the present, "dependent" divine revelation, which also reaches us through the Church's liturgy and Scriptures, through public and private prayer, and through many other experiences, both individual and collective.[26] John XXIII had introduced the theme of "the signs of the times" in his 1962 "bull" convoking Vatican II, *Humanae Salutis*, and a year later in the encyclical *Pacem in Terris* (nos. 126–29). *Gaudium et Spes* picked up this theme: "the Church carries the responsibility of scrutinizing the signs of the times and interpreting them in the light of the Gospel" (no. 4). It is the whole "people of God," led "by the Spirit of the Lord who fills the whole world," who try "to discern" "in the events, the needs, and the longings that it shares with other human beings of our age," what "may be true signs of the presence or of the purpose of God" (no. 11).

---

[25] For details on what these five conciliar texts say about "the religious others," see my *The Second Vatican Council on Other Religions* (Oxford: Oxford University Press, 2013), as well as chaps. 5–6 above.

[26] On discerning the signs of the times, see Gerald O'Collins, *Fundamental Theology*, 2nd ed. (Mahwah, NJ: Paulist Press, 1986), 102–7.

To conclude, *Dei Verbum* merits a place at the head of the four constitutions promulgated by the Second Vatican Council. In particular, its doctrine of the divine self-revelation in Christ offers a key for understanding all the conciliar documents. Nevertheless, it is only by interpreting this constitution in the context of the other fifteen documents that will make us grasp the integral teaching of the Council on the self-manifestation of the Word of God.

Chapter 8

Vatican II
and Fundamental Theology

One might describe Fundamental Theology (hereafter FT) as the discipline that, in the light of faith, studies such foundations of theology and basic theological issues as (1) the self-revelation of the tripersonal God which unfolded in the history of Israel and Jesus Christ; (2) the conditions that open human beings up to this self-communication of God; (3) the credibility of God's revelation which makes Christian faith a reasonable option; and (4) the transmission and interpretation (through the tradition and inspired Scriptures) of the experience of God's self-communication. The teaching of Vatican II and, specifically, the Constitution on Divine Revelation (*Dei Verbum*) have proved fruitful for those engaged with the four issues that provide FT with its essential identity.

But before taking up these issues in the light of Vatican II, let me introduce three preliminary observations. First, FT is to be distinguished from the philosophy of religion, a discipline that studies religious beliefs, conduct, and cult in the light of reason alone. As such, the philosophy of religion claims to examine matters "from the outside," without endorsing any particular confessional or believing stance. FT, however, is a genuinely theological discipline that does its work "from the inside," as an exercise of Christian faith seeking to understand divine revelation, to promote justice, and to assist worship. The requirements of reason, justice, and worship, respectively, may be primary in shaping the activity of theologians. Yet they all carry out their enterprise as "insiders," members of the community whom they wish to serve through their gifts.[1]

Second, its basic interests distinguish (but do not separate) FT from dogmatic or systematic theology. Of course, over some points dogmatic theology raises fundamental questions. Sacramental theology, for instance, must examine the basic nature of signs and symbols before going on to consider the individual sacraments. But in general the various areas of dogmatic theology dedicate most attention to specific issues and particular truths drawn from the history of revelation (such as various models for interpreting the Trinity, the union of two natures in the one person of Christ, and the life of grace as divine indwelling). FT characteristically takes up general or basic questions, such as the essential nature of revelation, without examining in depth particular revealed truths.

Third, while recognizing how the roots of FT reach back to the Christian apologists in the second and third century, I want to explore the teaching of the Second Vatican Council as a starting point for considering the tasks of contemporary FT.[2] While never using the term "fundamental theology," the Council provided guidelines for FT not only through the teaching on revelation, tradition, Scripture, and theology provided by *Dei Verbum* but also through other documents: for instance, the Constitution on the Church in the Modern World (*Gaudium et Spes*) and the Declaration on the Relation of the Church to Non-Christian Religions (*Nostra Aetate*).[3] An adequate reception of Vatican II's teaching on revelation and other themes that belong to FT, as we saw in the last chapter, involves drawing not only on *Dei Verbum* but also on further conciliar texts. At times they add new and

---

[1] On these three "styles" of theology, see Gerald O'Collins, *Rethinking Fundamental Theology: Toward a New Fundamental Theology* (Oxford: Oxford University Press, 2011), 323–31.

[2] For important examples of FT, see Walter Kern, Hermann J. Pottmeyer, and Max Seckler, eds., *Handbuch der Fundamentaltheologie*, 4 vols. (Freiburg im Breisgau: Herder, 1985–88); René Latourelle and Rino Fisichella, eds,, *Dictionary of Fundamental Theology* (New York: Crossroad, 1994).

[3] See René Latourelle, "Absence and Presence of Fundamental Theology at Vatican II," in *Vatican II: Assessment and Perspectives*, ed. René Latourelle, vol. 3 (New York: Paulist Press, 1989), 378–415.

important points that go beyond *Dei Verbum*.[4] Let us first identify five ways in which thinking about the divine self-revelation developed.

The Divine Self-Revelation

1. In its dense opening chapter, *Dei Verbum* presented revelation as primarily the self-revelation of the tripersonal God, a revelation that is inseparable from salvation and that enjoys a "sacramental" character, since it takes place through an interplay of "words" and "actions." In the past this divine revelation reached its high point and fullness with the life, death, and resurrection of Jesus Christ, together with the outpouring of the Holy Spirit. But revelation remains a living, actual reality (DV 8, 25), and will be consummated through the glorious manifestation of Christ at the end of world history (DV 4).[5]

In the aftermath of Vatican II, John Paul II (pope, 1978–2005) insisted on the present and future dimensions of the divine self-communication in Christ. First, in his 1979 apostolic exhortation *Catechesi Tradendae* (nos. 35–36) and then in his most significant teaching on revelation, the 1980 encyclical *Dives in Misericordia* (nos. 6, 7, 9, and 15), he showed that revelation is a present force, repeatedly active here and now as it calls forth human faith. Second, drawing on the language of 1 Corinthians 13:12 about believers in this life perceiving only dimly the divine reality, *Catechesi Tradendae* presented faith as a journey toward "things not yet in our possession" (no. 60). The same text from St. Paul turned up in the pope's 1998 encyclical *Fides et Ratio* and supported the theme that "the fullness of truth will appear" only "with the final revelation of God" (no. 2). In other words, any theology of revelation must respect the fact that the definitively full revelation of God has not yet taken place.[6]

2. The decades after the close of Vatican II in 1965 saw further progress in the theology of revelation: for instance, the theme developed by Avery Dulles and others that revelation is a *symbolic* communication

---

[4] See the last chapter, and Gerald O'Collins, *Retrieving Fundamental Theology* (Mahwah, NJ: Paulist Press, 1993), 63–78.

[5] On revelation as past, present, and future, see O'Collins, *Rethinking Fundamental Theology*, 128–35.

[6] The full texts of these papal documents are available on the Vatican website, as well as in different published versions.

of God.[7] This approach built on the teaching of *Dei Verbum* about the sacramental nature of revelation.

In a largely unnoticed phrase, *Dei Verbum* observed that "by divine revelation God wished to manifest and *communicate himself* and the eternal decrees of his will for the salvation of human kind" (no. 6). This theme of the divine self-communication or symbolic self-communication would emerge more fully in official teaching and theology. In his 1986 encyclical *Dominum et Vivificantem*, John Paul II twelve times called the Holy Spirit the self-communication of God. When examining the divine offer of revelation and salvation, Karl Rahner dedicated pages to the idea of God's "free and forgiving self-communication."[8] It is certainly productive to interpret God's revealing and saving activity as the divine self-communication, adding that this self-communication takes place through symbolic events, words, persons, and things, which human beings experience.[9]

3. A further development after the Second Vatican Council concerned the language and reality of *experience*. As we saw in the last chapter, *Dei Verbum* introduced the verb or noun "experience" only sparingly (nos. 8 and 14). This and other documents of Vatican II still reflected a residual unease about the language of "experience." But, as we also saw in the last chapter, with his philosophical background in phenomenology John Paul II had no such aversion to this language. Since his doctoral studies drew on St. John of the Cross, the future pope was also able to appropriate the experience of love expounded by the mystics. In his 1980 encyclical *Dives in Misericordia*, John Paul II appealed with ease to "experience," both collective and individual, when spelling out "the revelation of the mystery of the Father and his love" (no. 1).

John Paul II went beyond Vatican II by using freely the language of experience in *Dives in Misericordia* and other documents and thus

---

[7] See Avery Dulles, *Models of Revelation* (Maryknoll, NY: Orbis Books, 1992), 131–54; O'Collins, *Retrieving Fundamental Theology*, 98–107, 167–68. In an essay originally published in 1959, Karl Rahner developed some seminal ideas on symbol: "The Theology of the Symbol," *Theological Investigations*, vol. 4, trans. Kevin Smyth (London: Darton, Longman & Todd, 1966), 221–52.

[8] Karl Rahner, *Foundations of Christian Faith: An Introduction to the Idea of Christianity*, trans. William V. Dych (New York: Seabury, 1978), 116–33.

[9] O'Collins, *Retrieving Fundamental Theology*, 98–119.

helped to show how divine revelation engages human experience. By repeatedly making the Spiritual Exercises of St. Ignatius Loyola, Karl Rahner and some other Jesuit theologians (including myself) were also prepared to be comfortable about employing the language of experience when expounding the nature of God's self-revelation that feeds our life of faith.[10] These "Exercises" prescribe a program of prayer and reflection that allows God's active presence to be experienced, discerned, interpreted, and acted upon.

4. The last two paragraphs have introduced the theme of human faith, since our faith and God's revelation belong together. The initiative always comes from the self-revealing God, but revelation achieves its goal when human beings respond in faith. But FT cannot avoid the question: is there a God to be experienced by us? Or are the supposed personal encounters between human beings and the self-revealing God merely acts of self-deception? Since they deny existence to God, atheists would write off as delusion any alleged experiences of God. Vatican II devoted several paragraphs both to atheism and its causes and to "remedies" for atheism (GS 19–21). After the Council closed in 1965, militant atheism in such forms as European Communism has largely disappeared. It was left to Richard Dawkins and other non-Communist writers to keep the cause alive.

Apologists of various Christian backgrounds have argued that modern science and evolutionary theory have not made belief in God obsolete. Faith in God is not irrational and morally destructive. The presence of horrendous evil does not rule out the existence of an all-powerful, all-loving God.[11]

---

[10] See ibid., 108–19, 168–69.

[11] John Cottingham, *Why Believe?* (London: Continuum, 2009); Richard Dawkins, *The God Delusion* (London: Bantam, 2006); David Fergusson, *Faith and Its Critics: A Conversation* (Oxford: Oxford University Press, 2009); Anthony C. Grayling, *Life, Sex and Ideas: The Good Life without God* (New York: Oxford University Press, 2003); id., *Six Polemics on Religion and an Essay on Kindness* (London: Oberon Press, 2007). See also such responses to Dawkins and his allies as Tina Beattie, *The New Atheists: The Twilight of Reason and the War on Religion* (Maryknoll, NY: Orbis Books, 2007); John C. Lennox, *God's Undertaker: Has Science Buried God?* (Oxford: Lion Publications, 2007); Alister E. McGrath, *Dawkins' God: Genes, Memes, and the Meaning of Life* (Oxford: Blackwell, 2005); id., *The Dawkins Delusion: Atheist Fundamentalism and the Denial of the Divine* (London: SPCK, 2007); id., *A Fine-Tuned Universe: The Quest for God in Science and Theology* (Louisville, KY: Westminster John

If it were to reconvene in these early years of the third millennium, Vatican II might be inclined to address a movement that was born in the seventeenth and eighteenth centuries and that has returned today, at least in the Western world: deism. We deal here with an "umbrella" term, since deism can take various forms. Yet deists normally agree that God exists but reject in principle all special divine actions. Thus deists rule out any revelation of God that is distinct from the "normal" intentions and power which God manifests in creating and conserving the universe. At most, deism allows for what has been called "general" revelation: that is to say, the manifestation of God and the divine attributes coming through the created world and its natural workings. Deists exclude any divine revelation mediated through special persons (e.g., the prophets and, above all, Jesus himself), special events (e.g., his miracles and resurrection), and special words (e.g., the texts written under the inspiration of the Holy Spirit that form the Bible). Hence those who disagree with deists and maintain a special history of divine self-revelation that reached its highpoint with the life, death, and resurrection of Jesus (along with the coming of the Holy Spirit) need to make their case for the possibility of knowing that God has acted in special ways and has communicated some special truth above and beyond what might be gleaned from God's normal activity in conserving and guiding the created universe. This task belongs squarely to contemporary FT.[12]

Human Beings Open to Revelation

This exercise in mapping the tasks of FT in the light of Vatican II has examined some features of the divine self-revelation. It brings us next to the conditions for the possibility of men and women being open to the self-communication of God. What makes then for potential hearers of the

---

Knox, 2009); Mary Midgley, *The Solitary Self: Darwin and the Selfish Gene* (Durham: Acumen, 2010); Thomas Nagel, *Mind and Cosmos: Why the Materialist Neo-Darwinian Conception of Nature Is Almost Certainly False* (Oxford: Oxford University Press, 2012); Robert B. Stewart, ed., *The Future of Atheism: Alister McGrath and Daniel Dennett in Dialogue* (Minneapolis: Fortress Press, 2008); Eleonore Stump, *Wandering in Darkness: Narrative and the Problem of Suffering* (Oxford: Clarendon Press, 2010).

[12] On special divine activity, see O'Collins, *Rethinking Fundamental Theology*, 23–29 (select bibliography provided).

word of revelation and believers in the message of salvation? Vatican II, above all in *Gaudium et Spes*, developed a scheme of questions/answers, a correlation between basic human questioning and the divine reply. Revelation corresponds with the self-questioning and deepest desires of the human hearts. The divine self-manifestation in Christ illuminates the human existence, created and sustained in existence by God. The deep questions raised by the human condition find their answers provided by Christ the Revealer. It is the revelation of the mystery of Christ that interprets and clarifies the mystery of the human person (GS 10, 21–22, 41). In this connection it was only to be expected that the Council would quote the opening words of Augustine's *Confessions* about the self-questioning of the human heart that can find a satisfying answer and peace in the message of Christ: "Lord, you have made us for yourself and our hearts will not rest until they rest in you" (quoted GS 21).

The Council spoke of an interior "call" and "offer" coming to all human beings, when, through the Holy Spirit, they are invited to share in the life of the risen Christ (GS 22). Both before and after Vatican II, Rahner developed the notion of "the supernatural existential" to account for the way human beings are preconditioned to accept this offer of God's self-communication. Even before they freely accept this offer, they have been positively determined to encounter in faith the holy mystery of God.[13]

In his first encyclical, published in 1979, John Paul II took the conciliar teaching further by speaking not merely of an offer or a call but of a reality: from the first moment of their conception, all human beings actually share in the "mystery" of Christ (*Redemptor Hominis* 13). Years before coming to "the age of reason," they all already participate in some way in the self-communication of God. What the pope then wrote in the 1990 encyclical, *Redemptoris Missio*, paralleled Rahner's language of an "existential" but gave this language a personal ring by introducing the Holy Spirit. John Paul II understood the Holy Spirit to operate "at the very source" of each person's "religious questioning." As the pope put it, "the Spirit is at the very source of human beings' existential and religious questioning, a questioning which is occasioned not only by contingent situations but [also] by the very structure of their being" (no. 28). Where *Gaudium et Spes* (no. 10) and

---

[13] See Rahner, *Foundations of Christian Faith*, 126–33.

Nostra Aetate (no. 1) spell out the basic questions that arise for human beings, they do so without attributing this profound questioning to the presence and activity of the Spirit. The theme of the Holy Spirit at work in the deepest human questions belongs to the development of doctrine about the Spirit that is a major element in the legacy of John Paul II.[14] It is also a theme that merits its place when FT reflects on the human openness to divine revelation and salvation.

The Credibility of Revelation

We noted above how challenges to revelation may have relocated but have certainly not gone away. Is faith in the God preached by Jesus Christ compatible with modern science? Has Charles Darwin made religion obsolete? Did Jesus really rise from the dead? How much do we know about his life and activity? Books, articles, and lectures—not to mention television programmes and feature articles in Sunday papers—constantly thrust these and further questions at those who accept the message of the New Testament.

From second-century apologists such as St. Justin Martyr (d. around 165) down to Blessed John Henry Newman, C. S. Lewis, G. K. Chesterton, Dorothy Sayers, and other modern writers, a case has been developed for accepting faith in God, the following of Jesus Christ, and membership in his Church. In the context of their world and the cultivated reason of their day, they aimed to justify Christian faith. But where have all the apologists gone? Is there anyone out there responding to objections raised by agnostic or atheist critics and establishing the credentials of such central beliefs as the existence of a personal God, the divine self-revelation in Jesus Christ, and his resurrection from the dead? Are there still writers who have set themselves to make basic Christian doctrines intelligible and acceptable and so "give an account of their hope" (1 Pet 3:15)? Has the Second Vatican Council and the FT which it encouraged contributed anything toward defending and commending faith and hope?[15]

---

[14] See Michael A. Hayes and Gerald O'Collins, eds., *The Legacy of John Paul II* (London; Continuum, 2008).

[15] On the history and nature of Christian apologetics, see Avery Dulles, *A History of Apologetics* (orig. ed. 1971; San Francisco: Ignatius Press, 2005); Dulles and René

When responding to the call of John XXIII to update and renew Catholic Christianity, Vatican II faced some long-standing objections: for instance, the claim that science and religious faith are incompatible (GS 36; see 57, 62). The Council probed the causes of atheism and, specifically, the notion that belief in God threatens the proper autonomy of human beings and their commitment to earthly affairs (GS 19–20).

The Constitution on Divine Revelation appropriated the widely accepted scheme of three stages in the transmission of testimony to Jesus' words and deeds: (a) the initial stage in his earthly life when his disciples and others listened to him, saw him in action, spoke about him, repeated to others his teaching, and began interpreting his identity and mission; (b) the handing on by word of mouth or in writing of testimony to him after his death and resurrection; and (c) the authorial work of the four evangelists later in the first century. Through the gospels, readers have access to the Jesus of history (DV 19). In general this constitution, by deftly relating revelation to its transmission through tradition and the inspired Scriptures produced a coherent and credible account of the foundations of faith

The two constitutions on the Church (LG and GS), the former by retrieving biblical testimony and interpretation and the latter by engaging in dialogue with the contemporary world, fashioned a more attractive and believable image of the Church. By rejecting anti-Semitism and, more broadly, by its positive and respectful teaching on Judaism, Islam, Hinduism, Buddhism, and other living faiths (LG 16; NA 1–5)—a teaching that led to interfaith dialogue at the international and national level—Vatican II returned to the authentic and appealing attitudes of early Christianity (see also AG 11, 12). Likewise, repudiating the polemics that for centuries distorted relations with other Christians and initiating dialogue and collaboration with their Churches and ecclesial communities, the Council firmly endorsed a credible and more truly Christian reversal of attitudes (LG 8, 15; UR *passim*; GS 92).

The Second Vatican Council endorsed and embodied teaching that opened the way to furthering an essential task of FT, establishing the basic credibility of Christianity. In particular, the Council encouraged

---

Latourelle, "Apologetics," in Latourelle and Fisichella, *Dictionary of Fundamental Theology*, 28–39.

developments toward producing a reasonable case for believing in God, following the crucified and risen Jesus, and belonging to the Church he founded. It launched trajectories for papal teaching and theological work from the closing decades of the twentieth century.

John Paul II, in particular, pressed the need for collaboration between technical-scientific culture and religious faith.[16] He constantly encouraged a dialogue between science and theology that would be mutually enriching.[17] In his 1998 encyclical *Fides et Ratio* he set himself to show how faith and reason enjoy their distinct but never separate functions.[18] Cultivated reason pursues not merely philosophical and historical studies but also a wide range of natural sciences and new human sciences like psychology and sociology that have their own distinct characteristics and procedures. No matter what discipline they are engaged with and no matter whether they are aware of this or not, the practitioners do not pursue their discipline in isolation from the "big picture," or the ultimate nature and destiny of human beings and the holy mystery of God that surrounds us.

At the practical level, John Paul II encouraged conferences and further joint work involving scholars and scientists of other Christian Churches or of no particular faith. One response (among many) was a collaborative discussion between distinguished scientists and theologians over belief in bodily resurrection.[19] The Templeton Foundation has been even more outstanding in promoting, at an ecumenical level, interaction between science and faith.[20]

---

[16] See e.g., John Paul II's address to scientists in Cologne on November 15, 1980; the full text is found in the *Osservatore Romano* (English edition) for November 24, 1980, 6–7; key extracts are found in ND 67–70.

[17] John Paul II, "Letter to the Director of the Vatican Observatory" of June 1, 1988; the full text is found in *Origins* 18 (1988–89): 375–78; key extracts are found in ND 74–77.

[18] This encyclical is found on the Vatican website, as well as in numerous print editions; key extracts are found in ND 89–94.

[19] Ted Peters, Robert J. Russell, and Michael Welker, eds., *Resurrection: Theological and Scientific Assessments* (Grand Rapids, MI: Eerdmans, 2002).

[20] See e.g., Gerald O'Collins and Mary Ann Meyers, eds., *Light from Light: Scientists and Theologians in Dialogue* (Grand Rapids, MI: Eerdmans, 2012); to evaluate scientific and theological understanding of light, the Templeton Foundation's Humble Approach Initiative brought together seven scientists and seven theologians for two conferences (held in Istanbul and Oxford, respectively) that produced this book.

Where John Paul II was concerned to show that science should not be conceived as hostile to belief in God, the Pontifical Biblical Commission has taken up various issues concerned with scriptural sources and, in particular, the methods and approaches which can find in the gospels a reliable access to the person and work of Jesus.[21] The Commission's work continues the trajectory emerging from Vatican II's biblical teaching found in the Constitution on Divine Revelation (see above). So too did the writing of Raymond Brown on the birth and death of Jesus, the magisterial volumes from John Meier, and the contributions of others.[22] This trajectory has flourished through ecumenical "allies", other Christian scholars who have helped in putting the case for a reliable knowledge of Jesus' life, death, and resurrection, a knowledge that plays its essential role for Christian faith.[23]

In the aftermath of the Council, fully deployed contributions to the apologetic task that FT prescribes have come from a variety of scholars—some Catholics and inspired by Vatican II and some (e.g., Alister McGrath; see above) who belong to other Christian Churches. Let me mention four such scholars: Avery Dulles, René Latourelle, Karl Rahner, and Wolfhart Pannenberg.

After his *Apologetics and the Biblical Christ* (1983), Dulles offered a credible account of divine self-revelation (*Models of Revelation*, 1983), the human response of faith (*The Assurance of Things Hoped For: A Theology of Christian Faith*, 1993), and the Church founded by Christ through his apostles (*Models of the Church*, 1978, and *A Church to Believe In: Discipleship and the Dynamics of Freedom*, 1982). An apologetical dimension and intent that belongs to FT continued to characterize many of the

---

[21] Pontifical Biblical Commission, *The Interpretation of the Bible in the Church* (Vatican City: Libreria Editrice Vaticana, 1993). For a full-scale and persuasive treatment of the historicity question, see Paul Rhodes Eddy and Gregory A. Boyd, *The Jesus Legend: A Case for the Historical Reliability of the Synoptic Jesus Tradition* (Grand Rapids, MI: Baker Academic, 2007).

[22] Raymond E. Brown, *The Birth of the Messiah*, rev. ed. (London: Geoffrey Chapman, 1993); id., *The Death of the Messiah*, 2 vols. (New York: Doubleday, 1994); John P. Meier, *The Marginal Jew: Rethinking the Historical Jesus*, vols. 1–3 (New York: Doubleday, 1991–2001) and vol. 4 (New Haven: Yale University Press, 2009).

[23] See Richard Bauckham, *Jesus and the Eyewitnesses: The Gospels as Eyewitness Testimony* (Grand Rapids, MI: Eerdmans, 2006); James D. G. Dunn, *Christianity in the Making*, vol. 1, *Jesus Remembered* (Grand Rapids, MI: Eerdmans, 2003); N. T. Wright, *The Resurrection of the Son of God* (London: SPCK, 2003).

lectures and articles coming from Cardinal Dulles up to his death in December 2008.

A similar apologetic scope qualified the work produced after Vatican II by Latourelle (b. 1918). A towering figure in modern FT, he was driven by one desire and one desire only—to show the credibility of Christian claims. After his best-selling *The Theology of Revelation* (1966), he put the case for Jesus and his Church (*Christ and the Church: Signs of Salvation*, 1972), for access to the historical Jesus (*Finding Jesus through the Gospels*, 1979), for the authenticity and meaning of his miracles (*The Miracles of Jesus and the Theology of Miracles*, 1988), and for the correlation between the basic human quest for meaning and the person and message of Jesus (*Man and His Problems in the Light of Christ*, 1981). In these and other books Latourelle developed an *apologia* for the basics of Christian faith and integrated the apologetical task into the broader scope of FT. For the *Dictionary of Fundamental Theology* (1994), which he co-edited, he joined Dulles in writing the entry "apologetics."

The crowning theological work by Rahner (1904–84), *Foundations of Christian Faith* (1978), draws together his answers to the fundamental issues with which he grappled for a lifetime: What is Christian faith? How can one justify it and live with intellectual honesty? Does faith cohere with the basic dynamism of the human spirit? Rahner's classic volume forms a holistic apology for God's answer to the universal questions of human beings. This apology uses contemporary human understanding to validate the divine self-communication provided by Christ and the Church he founded. Throughout the book, Rahner argues not only "ad intra" or from the internal coherence of the lived experience of Christian faith but also "ad extra" or from external testimony. When, for example, he puts the case for Jesus' resurrection from the dead, he may characteristically refrain from citing biblical passages. Yet every claim he makes could be supported by Easter witness coming from St. Paul and the gospels.[24]

Over many years Pannenberg (b. 1928) argued for Christian doctrines on philosophical and anthropological grounds, as well as defending them as reasonable conclusions from "historical facts" construed in revelatory terms. Thus, in dialogue with modern, scientific reason he maintained that God's historical revelation, Jesus' resurrection

---

[24] Rahner, *Foundations of Christian Faith*, 264–85.

from the dead, his divine identity, and further pillars of Christian faith are reasonable and credible. Pannenberg's publications culminated in the three volumes of his *Systematic Theology*. This outstanding work differed from normal systematic or dogmatic theology through its persistent appeal to critical rationality. He wanted to confirm the truth of revelation while unfolding its content. In a sophisticated apologetical manner, he argued for the true significance of Christian teaching. Pannenberg is a Lutheran Christian. But, given the way he had long addressed some of the central concerns of FT, it was no wonder that the Catholic editors of the four-volume *Handbuch der Fundamentaltheologie* (1985–88) invited him to be one of their contributors.

Before leaving the task of FT in establishing the credibility of Christian faith, I should note first, that, without reference to FT, Christians of various denominations practice apologetics. It is an ecumenical enterprise more than ever, a task that belongs squarely to FT, whether they know this or not. Second, the best contemporary apologetics is learned, modest, and good-humored. Without supposing that those who fail to agree are either knaves or fools, it deals with objections to faith and makes a reasonable case for the central claims of Christianity. It does not ignore the indispensable role of the Holy Spirit in bringing people to faith but wishes to point to reasons that support these claims. Third, various writers may refrain from introducing the term "apologetics." But what they do in "fundamental" or "foundational" theology, in "natural" theology, in "philosophical" theology, in "systematic" theology, or in biblical studies belongs to a long tradition of Christian apologetics.

Fourth and finally, the apologetics with which the third section of this chapter has been concerned offers an intellectual justification of basic beliefs. But in our world what often defends and commends Christian faith more effectively is the witness of loving service to those in desperate need, as well as steady commitment to public worship and private prayer. Such "lived" apologetics counts as much or even more than the brilliant writing of Newman, Chesterton, Lewis, Sayers, and their contemporary successors.

The Transmission of Revelation

A fourth way in which the Second Vatican Council fed into FT came through its teaching on tradition (found notably but, far from exclusively, in chap. 2 of DV). Once again, while achieving certain goals (in particular, on the vexed question of the relationship between tradition and the Scriptures), the Council signalled a starting point for further developments: notably, the notion of tradition as collective memory.[25]

The Constitution on Divine Revelation spoke of tradition as both (a) process (*traditio*) and (b) content (*traditum*). This pointed to the distinguishable but inseparable *act* of handing on and the *content* of what is handed on.

(a) With the Holy Spirit as the invisible carrier of tradition (DV 8, 9, 10), all members of the Church, and not merely the official teachers who make up the magisterium, are involved in the process of tradition: "the [whole] Church, in her doctrine, life, and worship perpetuates and transmits to every generation all that she herself is, all that she believes" (DV 8).[26] As a process in which the whole Church takes part, Christian tradition remains inseparably *connected* with the Scriptures in their past origin, present function, and future goal: "they flow out from the same divine well-spring [= revelation], come together [*co-alescunt*] in some fashion, and move towards the same goal" (DV 9).

Far from thinking of any "dead hand of tradition," DV emphasizes life and speaks of "the living Tradition of the whole Church" (no. 12). The picture of tradition, flowing out from the same divine spring (*scaturigo*) as the Scriptures and uniting with the Scriptures as they move toward the same goal, suggests a living stream. The Council speaks of a "life-giving [*vivificam*] presence" of tradition, "whose riches are poured out [*transfunduntur*] into the practice and life of the believing and praying Church" (DV 8).[27] In particular, tradition acts by effectively making known "the integral canon" of the Sacred Scriptures, making them "more deeply understood [*penitius intelliguntur*]" and constantly "making them actual [*actuosae redduntur*]" (DV 8).

Besides speaking of tradition in such a personal way (as a process of making known, understood, and actualized), the Council also pictures

---

[25] See David Braithwaite, "Vatican II on Tradition," *Heythrop Journal* 53 (2012): 915–28.

[26] The active role of all the baptized in transmitting tradition includes the way they hand on the good news by actively participating in the liturgy—a "right" and "duty" emphasized by SC (see chap. 3 above on "Priests, Prophets, and Kings").

[27] Talking of "the believing and praying Church" echoes, of course, the axiom from St. Prosper of Aquitaine (d. around 463): "let the law of prayer establish the law of belief [*legem credendi lex statuat supplicandi*]."

tradition, along with the Bible, as a "mirror" in which the Church "contemplates God" (DV 7), as her "supreme rule of faith" (DV 21), and as her "permanent foundation" (DV 24). Obviously mirrors, rules, and foundations are less directly personal; yet it is human beings who look into mirrors, follow rules, and build on foundations.

To present the whole Church as handing on "all that she herself is, all that she believes" (see above) points toward tradition as (b) content or "object [*traditum*]." To describe tradition as "object," the Council adopts a classical term, "deposit" or "deposit of faith" (DV 10), but also introduces a more vital term, "treasure of Revelation" (DV 26). "Deposit" can suggest something inert (e.g., an alluvial deposit), even if a "bank deposit" can increase through a good rate of interest. "Treasure" enjoys better biblical overtones. Jesus urges us to build up our "treasure in heaven"; he points out that "where your treasure is, there will your heart be also" (Matt 6:19-21). DV comes close to suggesting that we should treasure and love the tradition we have received.

Other documents from Vatican II have much to add about tradition as "object." If we wish to present the Council's integral teaching, we should recall what *Sacrosanctum Concilium*, *Unitatis Redintegratio*, and further conciliar texts add.[28] Thus *Sacrosanctum Concilium* recalls the "musical tradition" of Christianity (nos. 112, 119); *Unitatis Redintegratio* pays tribute to "the fullness of Christian tradition" to be found in the spiritual riches inherited from the Eastern fathers (no. 15); *Presbyterorum Ordinis* exhorts priests to read and meditate on "the monuments of traditions," the works of the fathers and doctors of the Church (no. 19). Seminarians should learn what both the Eastern and Western fathers of the Church have contributed to "the faithful transmission of revealed truths" (DV 16). In bringing about the renewal of religious life, attention should be paid to "the sound traditions" of institutes (PC 2).

At the third session of Vatican II, Cardinal Albert Meyer, when commenting on what was to become the final text of *Dei Verbum*, pointed out the "limits" and "defects" that show up in the history of Christian traditions. He wanted the document to recognize the existence of such faulty and even corrupt traditions and the way to correct

[28] On the integral meaning of the Council's teaching, see the opening remarks of chap. 7 above.

them.[29] The 1963 Faith and Order Conference held in Montreal had raised the same issue: "Do all traditions which claim to be Christian contain the Tradition? How can we distinguish between traditions embodying the true Tradition and merely human tradition? Where do we find the genuine Tradition, and where impoverished tradition or even distortion of tradition?"[30]

While Meyer's proposal was not incorporated in the final version of *Dei Verbum*, in fact ways toward identifying and dealing with misleading and even corrupt traditions showed up in several other documents of Vatican II. Three of these texts (SC, PC, and DH) specifically embodied clear principles for reform and renewal (see chap. 2 above). Thus an integral reading of Vatican II discloses ways for discerning the Tradition (uppercase) within the particular traditions (lowercase), which may prove to be "sound" or otherwise.

Such an integral reading also helps us if we notice that *Dei Verbum* itself had nothing to say about the human reality of tradition. Let me explain. Human life is simply unthinkable without tradition—something regularly ignored by those who write about tradition in a theological context. Tradition shapes the cultural existence of human beings everywhere. "Tradition" is almost synonymous with a society's whole way of life or, in a word, with its culture. Tradition fashions a community's identity, unity, and continuity.[31] Hence one might say that the "grace" of Christian tradition "builds on" the "nature" of human tradition in general. While *Dei Verbum* remains silent about *human* tradition as such, *Sacrosanctum Concilium* attends to the traditions of different peoples (nos. 37–40), with particular attention to their marriage (no. 77) and funeral (no. 81) traditions. *Ad Gentes*

[29] Cardinal Albert Meyer, *Acta Synodalia Sacrosancti Oecumenici Vaticani II*, III/III (Vatican City: Typis Polyglottis Vaticanis, 1974), 180–81.

[30] Patrick C. Rodger and Lukas Vischer, eds., *The Fourth World Conference on Faith and Order, Montreal 1963* (London: SCM Press, 1964), 51. The text adopts here the distinction (not separation) between the Tradition (uppercase and in the singular) and the particular traditions (lowercase and in the plural) in which the Tradition or essential, revealed message is actualized and experienced. See Yves Congar, *Tradition and Traditions: An Historical and Theological Essay*, trans. Michael Naseby and Thomas Rainborough (London: Burns & Oates, 1966); the original French version appeared in two vols., 1960 and 1963.

[31] On the human reality of tradition, see O'Collins, *Rethinking Fundamental Theology*, 192–94.

likewise attends to "local" traditions and cultures (no. 22). Much of what *Gaudium et Spes* says about "culture" implicitly deals with human tradition (nos. 53–62).

While Christian and, in particular, Catholic theologians often do not attend to the human reality of tradition, some have introduced a theme that relates to it by speaking of tradition as "collective memory." In a work that appeared during the Council, Yves Congar wrote: "tradition is memory and memory enriches experience."[32] Joseph Ratzinger cited "the memory of the Church" and called it the "seat of all faith" and "the locus that gives unity to the content of faith."[33] Jean-Marie-Roger Tillard argued that "as the memory of the Church, Tradition represents the permanence of a word that is always alive."[34] George Tavard agreed: "One could analyse tradition from the standpoint of memory and define it as the Church's memory."[35]

A biblical theme about the Holy Spirit "reminding" Jesus' disciples of "all that I have said to you" (John 14:26) obviously played its part in encouraging a theology that explained tradition as collective memory. The 1994 *Catechism of the Catholic Church* could state firmly that "the Holy Spirit is the Church's living memory" (no. 1099).[36] In at least three documents, John Paul II introduced the theme of tradition as collective memory: *Catechesi Tradendae* of 1979 (no. 22); *Orientale Lumen* of 1995 (no. 8); and *Ecclesia in Europa* (nos. 7–8). But in this promising and widely shared interpretation of tradition as memory, one misses two developments.

First, how can we move from the consciousness and memory of an individual to the collective consciousness and memory of Christians? An individual human being exercises an individual memory. What then is being claimed when we extend language and attribute consciousness and memory to a collective subject such as the Roman Catholic

---

[32] Yves Congar, *Tradition and the Life of the Church*, trans. A. N. Woodrow (London: Burns & Oates, 1964; French orig. 1963), 8, see 77.

[33] Joseph Ratzinger, *Principles of Catholic Theology: Building Stones for a Fundamental Theology*, trans. Frances McCarthy (San Francisco: Ignatius Press, 1987), 23–24.

[34] J.-M.-R. Tillard, *Church of Churches: The Ecclesiology of Communion*, trans. R. C. De Peaux (Collegeville, MN: Liturgical Press, 1992), 141.

[35] George H. Tavard, "Tradition in Theology: A Problematic Approach," in *Perspectives on Scripture and Tradition*, ed. Joseph F. Kelly (Notre Dame, IN: Fides, 1976), 62. I wish to thank David Braithwaite for his help in research on tradition as collective memory.

[36] Vatican City: Libreria Editrice Vaticana, 1994.

Church? The notion of "tradition as memory" necessarily involves talk of "collective and conscious memory." Is it the group who consciously exercises that memory? Or, in the issue we are probing, should we think of the "collective memory" being, in fact, exercised by only one individual, the Holy Spirit? Such questions need to be addressed and answered, if the thesis of tradition as (collective) memory is going to prove genuinely fruitful.

Such probing will also affect the interpretation of the relationship between tradition and Scripture. Since the Bible has been heard over and over again in the public worship of all Christians, how has the scriptural word shaped their collective memory? The *Wirkungsgeschichte* of the Scriptures or their "history of effects" essentially includes their impact on the Church's collective memory and needs to be thoroughly investigated.

Second, since the close of the Second Vatican Council in 1965, there has been a boom of memory studies in history, sociology, and other disciplines.[37] Some biblical research and writing have successfully drawn on such memory studies.[38] But, with hardly an exception,[39] theologians have not taken advantage of the very useful insights on

[37] See Edward Casey, *Remembering: A Phenomenological Study* (Bloomington: Indiana University Press, 2000); Lewis A. Closer, ed., *On Collective Memory* (Chicago: University of Chicago Press, 1992); Paul Connerton, *How Societies Remember* (Cambridge: Cambridge University Press, 1989); id., *How Modernity Forgets* (Cambridge: Cambridge University Press, 2009); Astrid Erll et al., eds., *Cultural Memory Studies: An International and Interdisciplinary Handbook* (Berlin: William de Gruyter, 2008); Danièle Hervieu-Legér, *Religion as a Chain of Memory* (New Brunswick, NJ: Rutgers University Press, 2000); Wulf Kansteiner, "Finding Meaning in Memory: A Methodological Critique of Collective Memory Studies," *History and Theory* 41 (2000): 179–97; Barbara A. Misztal, *Theories of Social Remembering* (Philadelphia: Open University Press, 2003); Pierre Nora, ed., *Realms of Memory* (New York: Columbia University Press, 1983); Jay Winter, "The Generation of Memory: Reflections on the Memory Book in Contemporary Historical Studies," *Bulletin of the German Historical Institute* 27 (2000): 69–92.

[38] See, e.g., Rafael Rodriguez, *Structuring Early Christian Memory: Jesus in Tradition, Performance, and Text* (London: T. & T. Clark, 2010); Loren T. Stuckenbruck et al., *Memory in the Bible and Antiquity: The Fifth Durham-Tübingen Research Symposium* (Tübingen: Mohr Siebeck, 2007); Tom Thatcher, *Why John Wrote a Gospel: Jesus, Memory, History* (Louisville, KY: Westminister John Knox Press, 2006).

[39] See Joseph G. Mueller, "Forgetting as a Principle of Continuity in Tradition," *Theological Studies* 70 (2009): 751–81; Paul Ricoeur, *Memory, History, Forgetting*, trans. Kathleen Blamey and David Pellauer (Chicago: University of Chicago Press, 2004).

memory and forgetting coming from other disciplines. If the notion of tradition as "collective memory" is to be developed further, theology needs to engage in much interdisciplinary dialogue.

Reflecting on collective memory implies examining both positive and negative questions. On the "positive" side, the Eucharist involves a special remembering in which the community participates. On the "negative" side, we face such issues as the community's traumatic, guilty, and distorted memories. What is to be made of such themes as a collective neglect of memory and memories that have been manipulated and even erased? Should we make room for the notion and reality of collective forgetting? In tackling such questions, theologians obviously should draw on modern experts in memory studies—something that has scarcely happened so far.

Conclusion

This chapter has investigated the impact of Vatican II on FT's four tasks in expounding (1) the self-revelation of God, (2) the openness of human beings to revelation, (3) the credibility of claims about revelation, and (4) the tradition that transmits the message of revelation. We noted the "ecumenical" nature of these four tasks. In particular, Christians of various allegiances have pursued the work of showing the reasonable case that can be made for belief in God, Christ, and his Church. Without necessarily understanding themselves to be engaged in FT or even in apologetics, they have contributed massively to the task discussed under (3).

For some theological disciplines the Second Vatican Council offered teaching that directly concerned those disciplines. Thus *Sacrosanctum Concilium* became a magna carta for liturgical studies; the two constitutions on the Church (LG and GS) impacted directly on ecclesiology; *Unitatis Redintegratio* proved relevant for ecumenical studies and dialogue; *Nostra Aetate* provided a platform for interfaith dialogues. The Council never mentioned FT by name, yet offered teaching on revelation, anthropology, the credibility of the gospel, and tradition that could and did feed into that theological discipline. But, all in all, instead of a "reception," let alone a straightforward reception, of Vatican II, the picture is rather that of a trajectory emerging from the Council, which left four tasks to be continued by Christian leaders (in particular, Catholic bishops) and theologians in the four areas treated in this chapter.

Chapter 9

Was the Teaching of Vatican II Nourished and Ruled by the Word of God?

At the General Congregations of the Second Vatican Council, all held in St. Peter's Basilica, the Book of the Gospels was enthroned each day right through the four sessions.[1] Symbolizing the presence of Christ, the book put on display from October 1962 what the Dogmatic Constitution on Divine Revelation, *Dei Verbum*, was to announce three years later about the bishops' teaching office: "The magisterium is not above the word of God, but serves it" (DV 10). That document began by describing the Council as "religiously hearing the Word of God and faithfully proclaiming it [*Dei Verbum religiose audiens et fidenter proclamans*]" (DV 1). With an eye on the transmission of divine revelation, the same constitution said that the magisterium "devotedly hears, reverently guards, and faithfully expounds [*pie audit, sancte custodit et fideliter exponit*]" the word of God (DV 10). This set the stage for the final chapter of DV to state that the Church "has always treated and treats them [the divine Scriptures], together with Sacred Tradition, as the supreme rule of her faith [*eas una cum Sacra Traditione semper ut supremam fidei suae regulam habuit et habet*]." Hence "the entire preaching of the church, like the Christian religion itself, should be nourished and ruled by Sacred Scripture [*omnis praedicatio ecclesiastica, sicut ipsa religio Christiana, Sacra Scriptura nutriatur et regatur oportet*]" (DV 21).

[1] See Romeo de Maio, *The Book of the Gospels at the Oecumenical Councils* (Vatican City: Biblioteca Apostolica Vaticana, 1963).

The enthroned Book of the Gospels showed how the Second Vatican Council clearly embraced a program of devotedly hearing and serving the word of God by faithfully expounding and proclaiming it. But in practice, how far were the sixteen distinct texts that delivered the Council's teaching "nourished and ruled" by the Scriptures? In shaping an answer, this chapter largely limits itself to examining the first two (of the four) constitutions that Vatican II elaborated: the Constitution on the Sacred Liturgy, *Sacrosanctum Concilium*, promulgated on December 4, 1963, and the Dogmatic Constitution on the Church, *Lumen Gentium*, promulgated on November 21, 1964.

We can also gather evidence about the Council's biblical mindset from other texts. In *Dei Verbum*, for example, Vatican II described the task of theology and did so through the images of foundational, strengthening, and rejuvenating functions: "it [theology] rests upon the written Word of God, together with Sacred Tradition, as on a permanent foundation, and is most firmly strengthened, and is always rejuvenated by it [the Word of God]." Hence "the study of the Sacred Page should be, as it were, the soul [*anima*] of Sacred Theology" (DV 24).[2] As we saw in chapter 1 above, Vatican II drew this description of the role of the Scriptures from the 1893 encyclical of Pope Leo XIII, *Providentissimus Deus*—a description which the Council had already introduced a few weeks earlier in its Decree on the Training of Priests, *Optatam Totius*, promulgated on October 28, 1965: "the study of Sacred Scripture . . . ought to be, as it were, the soul of the whole of theology" (OT 16). Even if Vatican II did not call the "study of the Scriptures" the "soul" of the magisterium, its appeal to biblical texts implies the foundational, strengthening, and nourishing contribution that the "Sacred Page" can make to the proper exercise of the official teaching office of bishops.

While *Optatam Totius* anticipated the language of *Dei Verbum* about the study of the Bible as the "soul" of theology, it also specified one object of this study: "the greatest themes of divine revelation," which should be taught along with "an accurate initiation into exegetical method" (OT 16). In particular, those who teach dogmatic theology

---

[2] Like 1 Pet 2:4-7, Vatican II imagines the foundation of a living house, a foundation stone that gives rise to "living stones" and provides them with nourishment and youthful energy.

should "first" attend to "biblical themes" before they expound the teaching of the fathers of the Church, the dogmatic teaching coming from councils and popes, and the implications drawn from the liturgical life (OT 16). We will see how the work of the Council went beyond an appeal to single scriptural texts and also involved attention to major biblical themes. Before Vatican II opened, the widely used dictionaries edited by Jean Giblet and Xavier Léon-Dufour had espoused this cause and drawn attention to biblical themes of theological and, specifically, ecclesial, relevance.[3]

Sacrosanctum Concilium

The liturgical constitution consists of an introduction, seven chapters, and an appendix (on the revision of the calendar).[4] The introduction and chapter 1, which include forty-six out of the 130 articles and so make up more than a third of the text, quote the Sacred Scripture ten times and refer to it thirty times. Then chapters 2, 4, and 6 contain only three biblical quotations and three biblical references. Finally, chapters 3, 5, and 7, together with the brief appendix do not contain either biblical quotations or references. In all, the constitution includes thirteen quotations from the Bible and thirty-three references to it. The heavy appeal to the Scriptures in the introduction and chapter 1 is, to some extent, due to their dealing with basic principles, while some of the other chapters contain more "practical" instructions: for instance, chapter 7 offers teaching on sacred art and furnishings.

The Pauline corpus (including the Pastorals but excluding Hebrews) accounts for six quotations and seventeen references. All in all, *Sacrosanctum Concilium* evokes the life of the early Church and its worship by introducing not only the Pauline corpus but also the Acts of the Apostles (two quotations and one reference), Hebrews (one quotation and two references), 1 Peter (two quotations and one reference),

---

[3] Jean Giblet, ed., *Grands thèmes bibliques* (Paris: Feu Nouveau, 1959); Xavier Léon-Dufour et al., eds., *Vocabulaire de théologie biblique* (Paris: Cerf, 1961).

[4] For a bibliography on SC, see Massimo Faggioli, *True Reform: Liturgy and Ecclesiology in* Sacrosanctum Concilium (Collegeville, MN: Liturgical Press, 2012), and chap. 3, n. 9 above.

Revelation (one reference), and the Gospel of John (four references).[5]
Even more than Matthew (one quotation and three references) and
Luke (two quotations and one reference), John mirrors the experi-
ence and worship of the first Christians. The use of the Scriptures in
Sacrosanctum Concilium invites at least six comments.

1. Baptism and Eucharist

As befits a document on the liturgy, texts are quoted or at least referenced which concern baptism, the Eucharist, singing and praying
together, and preaching. First, as baptism means sharing in the dying
and rising of Christ, *Sacrosanctum Concilium* cites Romans 6:4 (no. 6 n.
16); since such union with Christ means becoming the adopted sons
and daughters of God, the constitution quotes Romans 8:15 (no. 6).
Although a range of New Testament texts are pressed into service,
curiously no appeal is made, however, to the classic trinitarian formula
for baptism (Matt 28:18).

Second, a footnote (no. 9 n. 18) cites Paul's statement that eating
the Supper of the Lord means proclaiming the death of the Lord until
he comes (1 Cor 11:26). Another classic testimony to the Eucharist as
"the breaking of bread" is taken from Acts 2:42 (no. 6).

Third, the constitution recalls various biblical witnesses to the early
Christian practice of meeting to pray and sing together: the praying
together attested by Acts 6:4 and 1 Thessalonians 5:17 (both quoted
in no. 86), and the assembling to sing psalms and hymns encouraged
by Ephesians 5:19 and Colossians 3:16 (referenced in no. 112 n. 42).
Fourth, Romans 10:14-15 (quoted in no. 9) and Acts 2:42 (quoted in
no. 6) support preaching and teaching in the context of the liturgy.

2. The Other Sacraments

When dealing with the sacraments other than the Eucharist, *Sacrosanctum Concilium* mandates various revisions, including a revision of

---

[5] No. 5 of SC speaks of the Church being born from the side of Christ dead
upon the cross—a clear reference to John 19:34 and to the way John Chrysostom,
Augustine, and other fathers interpreted the flow of blood and water from the
side of the pierced Christ. The reference to John is clear, even if the constitution
does not add a footnote.

the rites and the formulae of penance (no. 72) and of the anointing of the sick (no. 73–75). But in neither case is any reference to Scripture made, unlike the Council of Trent. In one and the same session (1551) Trent spelled out at length the theology and practice of both penance and extreme unction (as the anointing of the sick and dying was then called) (DzH 1667–1719; ND 1615–59). Trent's teaching on penance quotes twelve passages from the Bible, while its teaching on extreme unction quotes four; both sections contain various echoes of the Scriptures. The sections on penance highlight John 20:22: "Receive the Holy Spirit. If you forgive the sins of any, they are forgiven them; if you retain the sins of any, they are retained" (DzH 1670, 1684, 1710; ND 1617, 1627, 1650). The teaching on extreme unction highlights James 5:14-15: "Are any among you sick? They should call for the elders of the church, and have them pray over them, anointing them with oil in the name of the Lord. The prayer of faith will save the sick, and the Lord will raise them up; and anyone who has committed sins will be forgiven" (DzH 1695–96; ND 1636–37). Three of the four "canons" added to Trent's three chapters on extreme unction refer to the passage from James, while the first canon maintains that James "promulgates" a sacrament instituted by Christ (DzH 1716–19; ND 1656–59). But in chapter 3 of *Sacrosanctum Concilium* the Second Vatican Council did not set itself to offer anything like a full-scale treatment of the institution and nature of sacraments (other than the Eucharist) and of various sacramentals (e.g., funeral rites). Instead, the constitution sketched some guidelines toward revising the existing rites. Hence the absence of any scriptural reference is understandable.

But we should not overlook a further reason for the "biblical" difference between Trent and Vatican II. In the mid-sixteenth century the Reformers had raised pressing questions about the number of sacraments and what their being "instituted by Christ" meant. They allowed only two "evangelical" sacraments (baptism and Eucharist), with the practice of penance retained, as least as far as Philipp Melanchthon and the influence he exercised on the *Augsburg Confession* (nos. 11 and 12) went.[6] Driven by the desire to retain seven sacraments, Trent argued its

---

[6] For a critical edition of the *Augsburg Confession*, see Robert Kolb and Timothy Wengert, eds., *The Book of Concord: The Confessions of the Evangelical Lutheran Church* (Minneapolis: Fortress, 2000), 27–105.

case by appealing to the Scriptures, as did the Reformers. Hence that Council marshalled as many biblical texts as possible—introducing, for example, witness to the anointing of the sick practiced by the twelve when sent on a trial mission by Jesus (Mark 6:13; see DzH 1695; ND 1636). On the basis of that text, Trent taught that "extreme unction is truly and properly a sacrament instituted by Christ our Lord," and added, on the basis of James 5:14, that it was "promulgated by the blessed apostle James" (DzH 1716; ND 1656).

Vatican II, however, met in a century when many other Christians had led the way in fostering relations between Churches and hopes for Christian unity. Such pioneers as Cardinal Désiré Joseph Mercier (1851–1926), Abbé Paul Couturier (1881–1953), Cardinal Yves Congar (1904–1995), and St. John XXIII (pope, 1958–1963) brought a sea change among Roman Catholics and a commitment to the ecumenical movement. In a new, irenic atmosphere, Vatican II was not bent on arguing a biblical case against other Christians. Hence when *Lumen Gentium* completed what *Sacrosanctum Concilium* had said by expounding the way in which the seven sacraments nourish the life of the Church, the constitution described gratefully how Catholics experience their sacramental life, and cited the Scriptures only in the case of the anointing of the sick and matrimony (LG 11).

In the case of the anointing, when *Lumen Gentium* 11 referred to James 5:14-16, unlike the decree from Trent, it reminded those who suffer that, by joining themselves to the passion and death of the risen Lord, they contribute to the good of the People of God and referred them to four appropriate texts (Rom 8:17; Col 1:24; 2 Tim 2:11-12; 1 Pet 4:13). In its teaching on extreme unction, Trent had limited its vision of what the sacrament does for the sick and dying by saying that it "confers grace, remits sin, and comforts" those who are suffering (DzH 1696, 1717; ND 1637, 1657). Vatican II, however, briefly sketched a biblical spirituality for the sick (LG 11), a spirituality that would be taken up later (LG 41) and massively developed by John Paul II in his 1984 apostolic letter on the Christian meaning of human suffering.[7]

The account of marriage offered by the Council of Trent in 1563 insisted on the sacrament being instituted by Christ, its indissoluble nature, and various "canonical" matters. Once again the polemical

---

[7] *Salvifici Doloris*, in AAS 76 (1984), 201–50.

atmosphere and changes introduced by Reformers put the Scriptures at the center of the debate and kept any married spirituality to a minimum. Trent quoted the Bible six times and referred to it ten times (DzH 1797–1812; ND 1804–19). Citing Ephesians 5:32 and "the great mystery" of Christ and his Church symbolized by the union of man and woman, it noted only briefly how the sacrament of marriage confers grace and sanctifies the spouses (DzH 1799; ND 1806). For its part, *Lumen Gentium* 11 refers to Ephesians 5:32 and 1 Corinthians 7:7 but no other biblical texts. It leaves behind any polemic arguments over the Scripture and develops an image of the family as "the domestic church" in which "by word and example parents should be the first heralds of faith for their children." *Lumen Gentium* will later offer a spirituality for married people when it describes their being called to holiness (no. 41). At the end of the Council *Gaudium et Spes* was to spell out at length the dignity and values of married love (nos. 47–52).

3. The Jewish Scriptures

There is one relative "absence" in *Sacrosanctum Concilium* that might catch our attention. The whole of the liturgical constitution contains only two explicit appeals to the Old Testament. First, the constitution refers to Isaiah 11:12 in support of calling the Church "a sign lifted up among the nations" (no. 2 n. 5). Second, when presenting the incarnate Son of God, *Sacrosanctum Concilium* speaks of his being "anointed by the Holy Spirit to preach the good news to the poor and heal the contrite of heart" (no. 5 n. 8). Footnote 8 refers to Isaiah 61:1 and to a verse in the gospels (Luke 4:18) which quotes the passage from Isaiah. Despite the abundant material on sacrificial and other cultic activity found in Deuteronomy, Exodus, Leviticus, and other books of the Old Testament, the Jewish Scriptures at first glance feature explicitly only twice in *Sacrosanctum Concilium*.[8]

Nevertheless, one should not overlook a global reference to the book of Psalms: among the liturgical presences of Christ, the constitution lists his presence when "the Church makes petitions and sings psalms

---

[8] One should also note the way in which SC 5 quotes Heb 1:1: "At many times and in various ways [God] spoke of old to the ancestors through the prophets." These words embody a global appeal to the Old Testament history and Sacred Scriptures.

[*dum supplicat et psallit Ecclesia*]" (no. 7). Further, when underlining "the supreme importance of the Sacred Scripture for the celebration of the liturgy," *Sacrosanctum Concilium* mentions specifically only the psalms (no. 24).

A further (this time indirect) reference to the psalms comes in chapter 6 ("Sacred Music"). Footnote 42, attached to no. 112, directs the reader to Ephesians 5:19 ("you sing psalms and hymns and spiritual songs among yourselves, singing and making melody to the Lord in your hearts"), and to Colossians 3:16 ("Let the word of Christ dwell in you richly; teach and admonish one another in all wisdom; and with gratitude in your hearts sing psalms, hymns, and spiritual songs to God"). However "hymns" and "spiritual songs" are to be distinguished, in both passages singing psalms takes pride of place. Chapter 6 of *Sacrosanctum Concilium* ends by prescribing that the texts for sacred music should be "drawn principally from the Sacred Scriptures and from liturgical sources" (no. 121). While composers have over the centuries set to music the *Magnificat*, the *Benedictus*, the Lord's Prayer, and some other New Testament texts, it has been verses of psalms and whole psalms that have entered massively into Gregorian chant and other forms of sacred music.

Naturally chapter 4 of *Sacrosanctum Concilium* on the divine office (nos. 83–101) attends to the psalms; they form the staple biblical prayers for singing or reciting the office (nos. 90–91). This chapter opens by silently quoting from no. 144 of the 1947 encyclical *Mediator Dei*, saying: "Jesus Christ, the High Priest of the New and Eternal Covenant, when he assumed a human nature, introduced into this land of exile the hymn that is sung in heaven throughout all ages. He unites the whole community of humankind with himself and associates it with him in singing the divine canticle of praise" (no. 83).[9] In the same

---

[9] In a chapter on the divine office the encyclical had said: "The Word of God, when he assumed a human nature, introduced into this land of exile the hymn that in heaven is sung throughout all ages. He unites the whole community of humankind with himself and associates it with him in singing this divine canticle of praise" (*Mediator Dei*, 144; ND 1225). Without adding a reference, SC quotes this passage, significantly replacing "the Word of God" by a title that evokes Hebrews, "the High Priest of the New and Eternal Covenant." For a chapter dedicated to the divine office and appearing in a document on the liturgy, it seems more appropriate to use a priestly title for Christ than "the Word of God," which readily evokes John's statement on the incarnation ("the Word was made flesh"). In "The Con-

section (no. 144), the encyclical had cited Augustine's *Expositions of the Psalms*: "it is the one Saviour of his [mystical] body, our Lord Jesus Christ, Son of God, who prays for us, who prays in us, and who is prayed to by us as our God. Let us therefore recognize in him our *voice* and in us his *voice*" (85.1; emphasis mine). Augustine understood the singing or reciting of the psalms to be the *voice* of the whole Christ: the head and body/members.[10] Without referencing either *Mediator Dei* or Augustine, the liturgy constitution speaks of the divine office as "the voice of the Bride herself addressed to the Bridegroom [*vox Ecclesiae ad Christum*]." The document adds at once: "it is the prayer that Christ [addresses] to the Father with his Body [*vox Christi ad Patrem*]" (no. 84). It returns to the language of "voice" when it says: "the divine office is the voice of the Church, that is, of the whole mystical body publicly praising God [*vox Ecclesiae ad Patrem*]" (no. 99).

In presenting the psalms as the voice of Christ addressing the Father, Augustine and *Sacrosanctum Concilium* took their cue from the New Testament. The Letter to the Hebrews applied psalms in that way. Using the words of Psalm 22:22, Christ speaks to God the Father: "I will proclaim your name to my brothers and sisters; in the midst of the congregation I will praise you" (Heb 2:12). On his coming into the world, the Son picks up the language of Psalm 40:6-8 and says to the Father: "sacrifices and offerings you have not desired, but a body you have prepared for me; in burnt offerings and sin offerings you have taken no pleasure. Then I said: 'See, God, I have come to do your will'" (Heb 10:5-7).[11]

---

stitution in the Making," in *Vatican II: The Liturgy Constitution*, ed. Austin Flannery (Dublin: Scepter Publications, 1964), Pierre-Marie Gy writes: "The Constitution relies considerably on the great encyclical of Pius XII [*Mediator Dei*] and time and again it uses its very terminology, without quotation marks or reference. Only in the case of biblical, liturgical and patristic quotations are references given" (17–26, at 22). This claim has to be seriously modified, however. Several times SC cites passages from the Council of Trent, puts them in quotation marks, and provides the reference (e.g., no. 6 n. 19; no. 7 n. 20; no. 77 n. 41).

[10] On the psalms being "the voice of Christ to the Father [*vox Christi ad Patrem*]," as well as the *voice* of the Church about Christ to the Father [*vox Ecclesiae ad Patrem de Christo*]" and "the voice of the Church to Christ [*vox Ecclesiae ad Christum*]," see Balthasar Fischer, "Le Christ dans les Psalmes," *La Maison Dieu* 27 (1951): 86–113.

[11] See Harold W. Attridge, "Giving Voice to Jesus," in H. W Attridge and Margot Fassler, eds., *Psalms in Community* (Atlanta: SBL; Leiden: Brill, 2004), 101–12.

4. Richer Scriptural Readings

Sacrosanctum Concilium mandated a richer selection of Scripture readings for the divine office (no. 92). Here it followed what it had already prescribed for the celebration of the Eucharist: "the treasures of the Bible are to be opened up more lavishly so that a richer table of God's word may be prepared for the faithful. Thus a more representative part of the Holy Scriptures will be read to the people in the course of a determined number of years" (no. 51).

5. The Bible and Tradition

All in all, the liturgical constitution, imbued as it is with the Sacred Scriptures, exemplifies admirably the aim Vatican II set itself of "religiously hearing the Word of God and faithfully proclaiming it." Right from its first promulgated document, the Scriptures "nourish and rule" the teaching of the Council. At the same time, as the "supreme rule of faith" the Bible is to be followed and interpreted "together with Sacred Tradition."[12]

While *Sacrosanctum Concilium* contains thirteen quotations from the Bible and thirty-three references to it, it also contains a further twelve quotations, drawn from liturgical texts (seven), the Council of Trent (three), and the fathers (two), as well as ten references, drawn from liturgical texts (two), the Council of Trent (two), and the fathers (six). This spread of quotations and references mirrors something of the long and rich Christian tradition, which embraces (a) the law of praying that is the law of believing enshrined in the liturgy, (b) the fathers of the Church as early, privileged interpreters of the divine self-revelation in Jesus Christ, and (c) Trent as the sixteenth-century Council that dedicated most attention to the institution, nature, and administration of the sacraments. Significantly, seven of the twelve quotations from traditional sources concern the Eucharist, whereas five out of ten such references also do so. As Vatican II taught, through tradition "the

---

[12] The Book of the Gospels enthroned at Vatican II, a Latin copy from the fifteenth century, does not simply contain the text of the four gospels but opens with some concordance tables prepared by Eusebius of Caesarea, a letter of St. Jerome, and Jerome's prologues to the gospels. A preface by the Venerable Bede accompanies the Gospel of John. All of this suggests how representatives of the tradition received and interpreted the Scriptures.

Church in her doctrine, life, and worship perpetuates and transmits to all generations everything that she herself is, everything that she believes" (DV 8). The liturgy and, specifically, the Eucharist remain the heart of Christian tradition, both as the action of the Church and "the content" of what is handed on.

6. *Sacrosanctum Concilium* as Hermeneutical Key

These achievements support Massimo Faggioli's decision to base his hermeneutics of the entire Council on the liturgical constitution.[13] *Sacrosanctum Concilium* embodied and reproposed the centrality of the Scriptures (taken with and interpreted by tradition), and this led to a rediscovery of the central image of the Church as the worshipping People of God (no. 33). The constitution quoted 1 Peter to picture the Christian people as being "a royal priesthood" (1 Pet 2:9; see Exod 19:6) and so prepared the way for a major theme to be developed in *Lumen Gentium* and other documents: through baptism (all Christians) and ordination (the relatively few ministers), the faithful share in Christ's triple function as priest, prophet, and king (see below). In doing all that, the liturgy document initiated Vatican II's procedure of *aggiornamento* through *ressourcement* or retrieval—in this case retrieving the biblical theme of the people of God being priests, prophets, and kings/shepherds.

The liturgy constitution also initiated the Council's outreach to other Christians (UR), followers of other faiths (NA), and the whole world (GS). As we saw in chapter 5, it adumbrated this universal outreach by restoring the "prayer of the faithful," and justified this change by recalling 1 Timothy 2:1-2. Thus the Scriptures inspired a change in the liturgy, which involved retrieving an early liturgical tradition, a change that led to a universal outreach to "the others."

Lumen Gentium

The Dogmatic Constitution on the Church, while being more than twice as long as the liturgy constitution,[14] shows a similar desire to

---

[13] Massimo Faggioli, "*Sacrosanctum Concilium* and the Meaning of Vatican II," *Theological Studies* 71 (2010): 337–52; see also his *True Reform*, passim; see chap. 3 above.

[14] Published almost a year later, LG draws support from SC three times, and in two cases refers to the picture of heavenly worship found in the book of Revelation

be shaped and nourished by the Sacred Scriptures. It quotes biblical texts seventy-six times, and refers to the Scriptures 357 times, with such quotations and references occurring in every chapter. Despite an early statement about "the Church being wonderfully prepared in the history of the people of Israel" (no. 2), *Lumen Gentium* quotes the Old Testament only eight times and refers to it only eight times. Yet the Old Testament provides, as we shall see, encouragement and material toward developing various images of the Church.

Like *Sacrosanctum Concilium*, the constitution on the Church interprets and applies the scriptural texts within the context of tradition. In fact, *Lumen Gentium* cites teachers of the faith from Clement of Rome and Ignatius of Antioch right down to John XXIII and Paul VI. Naturally *Lumen Gentium* retrieves much from Augustine, Cyprian, Irenaeus, Leo the Great, and numerous other fathers of the Church. Every chapter contains at least one patristic *reference*, whereas *quotations* from the fathers appear in chapters 1–4 and chapter 8. In all there are 121 references and nineteen quotations, the heaviest concentration coming in chapter 3 ("On the Hierarchical Constitution of the Church and, in particular, on the Episcopacy," with forty-seven references and five quotations) and chapter 8 ("The Blessed Virgin Mary Mother of God in the Mystery of Christ and the Church," with thirty references and five quotations).

Since the fathers of the Church often delivered their teaching by commenting on biblical texts, their contribution to Christian tradition may be distinguishable from the inspired, scriptural witness but is rarely separable from it. This close alignment with the Sacred Scriptures defines many of the patristic quotations and references introduced by the documents of Vatican II. *Lumen Gentium*, for instance, refers to Cyprian's commentary on the Lord's Prayer (no. 5 n. 4), Origen's commentary on Matthew (no. 6 n. 5), John Chrysostom preaching on Ephesians (no. 7 n. 8), John Chrysostom preaching on John's gospel (no. 13 n. 9), and Ambrose commenting on Psalm 38

(no. 50 n. 18; no. 51 n. 25; see also no. 28 n. 68). On LG, see Peter Hünermann, "*Lumen Gentium*," in *Herders Theologischer Kommentar*, vol. 2 (2004), 269–563; Gérard Philips, *L'Église et son mystère au IIe Concile de Vaticane: histoire, texte et commentaire de la Constitution "Lumen Gentium,"* 2 vols. (Paris: Desclée, 1967).

(no. 21 n. 22). Frequently Vatican II's appeal to patristic authorities scarcely remains apart from an appeal to the Scriptures.

Lumen Gentium refers to a number of ecumenical councils and, in particular, to the First Vatican Council (1869–70); there are twenty-one references to that Council, with eighteen of them occurring in chapter 3. Vatican I, after debating and promulgating its teaching on papal primacy and infallibility (DzH 3050–75; ND 818–40), had intended to issue a complete constitution on the Church. But its work was abruptly terminated when the withdrawal of French protection brought an invasion and the loss of the papal states. The dogmatic definitions regarding the authority of the pope left a one-sided view of the Church's life and structure. *Lumen Gentium* set itself to integrate the teaching of Vatican I into a fuller vision that we will come to below.

Lumen Gentium refers to a number of popes, with the overwhelming majority of these references drawn from modern times. It recalls, for instance, teaching coming from Pius IX, Leo XIII, Pius X, Benedict XV, Pius XI, Pius XII, John XXIII, and Paul VI. Pius XII enjoys the most citations, with the constitution referencing him forty-two times and quoting his words twice (no. 27 n. 58; and no. 37 n. 7). His encyclicals *Mystici Corporis* of 1943 and *Mediator Dei* of 1947 provide sixteen of these references, eleven to the former encyclical and five to the latter.

Some liturgical witness is cited, like texts from the *Roman Missal* and a few hymns. Several theologians from the Middle Ages and later centuries feature among the witnesses of tradition: in particular, Thomas Aquinas with thirteen references, which include six in chapter 5 on "The Universal Vocation to Holiness in the Church."

Like the Sacred Scriptures themselves, the traditional matrix in which those Scriptures are understood, interpreted, and actualized is never off display. Past tradition is constantly retrieved, as the Council goes about its business of updating and renewing the Church's faith and practice, while "devotedly hearing" and "faithfully expounding" the word of God.

Let me now offer four examples which show the teaching of *Lumen Gentium* being "nourished and ruled" by the Scriptures: the mystery of the Church; the collegial authority of the bishops; the universal call to holiness; and respect for the religious situation of those who follow other faiths. These examples will throw light on the way in which Vatican II regularly turns to and draws on the biblical witness.

1. The Mystery of the Church

The first chapter of *Lumen Gentium* does not attempt to describe the institutional structures of the Church but to ponder her mystery. Ultimately never fully knowable, the inexhaustibly deep truth of the Church may be glimpsed in a variety of ways.

Lumen Gentium cites (no. 6) various images drawn "from pastoral life or from agriculture, or from building, or from family life and betrothal." The vivid language of Isaiah and Ezekiel pictured God as a shepherd caring for his flock. The New Testament takes up this imagery to portray Christ as "the good shepherd" (John 10:11) and "chief shepherd" (1 Pet 5:4), who "leads and nourishes" his sheep and "has given his life" for them (John 10:11-15). Thus *Lumen Gentium* cites four sacred authors and weaves together different strands of a major biblical theme to produce its initial image of the Church as the flock of Christ.

Some words from Paul, "you are God's field" (1 Cor 3:9) lead *Lumen Gentium* to open up thoughts about agriculture and what can be grown—in particular, "the ancient olive tree, whose holy root were the Patriarchs, and in which the reconciliation of Jews and Gentiles has been effected" (Rom 11:13-26). This image of God's community as an olive tree into which the Gentiles have been grafted once again evokes the whole story of salvation history, as does the associated image of "the chosen vineyard, planted by the heavenly Farmer" (Isa 5:1-7; Matt 21:33-43). The parable of the vineyard and its tenants (also recorded by Mark 12:1-12 and Luke 20:9-19) brings *Lumen Gentium* to recover an associated parable developed in John's gospel, where "Christ is the true vine who gives life and fruitfulness to the branches, namely us, who through the Church remain in him and without whom we can do nothing" (John 15:1-5). By introducing an olive tree, a vineyard, and a fruitful, life-giving vine, the constitution uses related scriptural themes to fill out the cryptic, metaphorical statement that Paul makes to the Church of Corinth: "you are God's field" (LG 6).

Paul produces another metaphorical picture of the Church: "you are God's building [*oikodomē*]" (1 Cor 3:9). *Lumen Gentium* completes this picture by reminding its readers that the gospels record Christ drawing on Psalm 118:22 to call himself "the stone [*lithos*] which the builders rejected," an image taken up elsewhere in the New Testament (Acts 4:11; 1 Pet 2:7).The apostles have built the Church "on that foundation" (1 Cor 3:11), from which "it receives strength and cohesion." The constitution presses on immediately to recall various, related names for the Church: "the house [*oikos*] of God (1 Tim 3:15) in which his family resides, the dwelling-place [*katoikētērion*] of God in the Spirit (Eph 2:19-22), God's tabernacle [*skēnē*] with human beings (Rev 21:3), and, especially, the holy temple [*hierateuma hagion*], into which the baptized 'are built like living stones [*lithoi*]' (1 Pet 2:5)." *Lumen Gentium* enlarges the building image for the Church by introducing the picture of the Church as "the new Jerusalem" or "holy city coming down from heaven" and "prepared like a bride adorned for her husband (Rev 21:2)" (LG 6).

Citing the closing scene of the book of Revelation summons up the related images of the Church as "our mother (Gal 4:26)" and the "spotless spouse of the spotless Lamb (Rev 10:7; 21:2, 9; 22:17)." No. 6 of *Lumen Gentium* reaches its close by citing the language of Ephesians about Christ loving the Church as his bride, handing himself over to death for her sake, "sanctifying her," and "nourishing and cherishing her" (Eph 5:25-26, 29).

When taking stock of how *Lumen Gentium* enunciated images of the Church drawn from sheep farming, the cultivation of olives and vineyards, the construction of buildings, family life, and marriage, we can see how the Council followed the advice it was to give to those who teach dogmatic theology (OT 16). It first appealed to biblical themes and a range of texts to present the mystery of the Church before moving on to provide more elaborated teaching about the Church as the Body of Christ (LG 7) and the People of God (LG 9–17). Yet even then, when developing those two central images, the constitution continued to refer to and cite the Sacred Scriptures. These images are nothing less than two major biblical themes.

In assembling the scriptural witness to the Church as the Body of Christ, *Lumen Gentium* quoted six passages from the Pauline corpus, made seventeen references to it, and cited no other biblical sources. This implied silently endorsing the common view among exegetes that the apostle Paul had introduced this image for the Church, perhaps drawing the image from philosophical thought about the organic unity of human society and the whole cosmos.[15]

[15] See James D. G. Dunn, *The Theology of Paul the Apostle* (London: Continuum, 2002), 533–64.

By dedicating an entire chapter to "the People of God" (also called "the messianic People," "the new People of God," "the one People of God," "the holy People of God," or, simply, "the People"), the Council compellingly highlighted that image for the Church and, in one or other of those six forms, used it fourteen times. This chapter added a further image, the Church as "communion" (nos. 9, 13 [three times], and 15). The theme of the Church "as a communion of life, love, and truth" (no. 9) was to prove popular in the post–Vatican II situation, not least at the 1985 Extraordinary Synod of Bishops.[16] The same chapter of *Lumen Gentium* also spoke (metaphorically) of the Holy Spirit dwelling in the Church as in a temple (no. 9).[17] This prepared the way for ending the chapter on a trinitarian note and calling the Church "the People of God, the Body of the Lord, and the Temple of the Holy Spirit" (no. 17). The whole of chapter 2 is richly biblical, containing twelve quotations from the Scriptures and fifty-three references to them, with six quotations coming from New Testament epistles and twenty-seven references being made to them. Along with the epistles, the witness of Acts (six references) also remains essential for those reflecting on "the People of God."

2. The Collegial Authority of the Bishops

A change that *Lumen Gentium* introduced and that caught the imagination of many commentators was its teaching about all the Catholic bishops around the world forming with the Bishop of Rome a college (nos. 22–23), like "the one apostolic college constituted by St. Peter and the rest of the apostles" (no. 22). This teaching expressed the organic unity between pope and bishops and their joint responsibility for the universal Church.

The reference to Peter and the other apostles forming an apostolic college might have been supported by citing appropriate examples from

---

[16] See Jean-Marie-Roger Tillard, "Final Report of the Last Synod," in *Synod 1985: An Evaluation*, ed. Giuseppe Alberigo and James Provost (Edinburgh: T. & T. Clark, 1986), 64–77, at 71–73.

[17] LG could have cited here what Paul says about the Church as the temple of the Holy Spirit (1 Cor 3:16-17), a metaphor the apostle might have drawn from the Essenes who lived at Qumran. See Joseph A. Fitzmyer, *First Corinthians* (New Haven, CT: Yale University Press, 2008), 202–3; Anthony C. Thiselton, *The First Epistle to the Corinthians* (Grand Rapids, MI: Eerdmans, 2000), 315–18.

the first half of the book of Acts, not least the account of the Council at Jerusalem (Acts 15:1-29). Instead *Lumen Gentium* appeals, on the one hand, to the promise made to Peter in Matthew's gospel that he would be "the rock and key-holder of the Church (Matt 16:18-19)" and his being constituted "the pastor of the entire flock (John 21:15-19)." Then *Lumen Gentium* notes, on the other hand, that "the task of binding and loosing, given to Peter (Matt 16:19), was also bestowed on the college of the apostles united to its head (Matt 18:18; 28:16-20)" (LG 22).

In Matthew 18:18, however, Jesus is speaking to his disciples at large and not, specifically, to the twelve apostles.[18] The verse shows that Peter's authority to "bind and loose" or to regulate behavior authoritatively (by forbidding or permitting certain things)[19] is not limited to him alone but is shared—with an indefinitively large group of other disciples and not simply with a clearly defined group of apostles and their "episcopal" successors, if we might speak anachronistically. Elsewhere the evangelist records the calling and commissioning of "the twelve disciples," whom he also calls "the twelve apostles." Jesus authorizes them to preach the kingdom of heaven, work miracles, and firmly protest against those who do not receive them (Matt 10:1-15). But nothing is added here about any authority to "bind and loose." Matthew 18:18, however, yields at least the conclusion: the evangelist understands the authority "to bind and loose" to be somehow shared with other followers of Jesus and not the responsibility of Peter alone. The verse occurs in a section dedicated to the way in which the community of disciples should deal with sinners and meet to pray together (Matt 18:15-20). In that sense the statement about "binding and loosing" enjoys a kind of "collegial" setting.

What of Matthew 28:16-20? The passage describes how the eleven disciples, now called "the eleven" rather than "the twelve" after the

---

[18] On Matt 18:18, see Ulrich Luz, *Matthew 8–20*, trans. James E. Crouch (Minneapolis: Fortress, 2001), 454–57; John Nolland, *The Gospel of Matthew* (Grand Rapids, MI: Eerdmans, 2005), 748. On the meaning of "binding and loosing," see Luz, *Matthew 8–20*, 364–65; Nolland, *Gospel of Matthew*, 677–82.

[19] Craig A. Evans may well be correct in arguing that, while "binding and loosing" normally "refer to forbidding and permitting," the reference here is to "convicting and acquitting"; *Matthew* (Cambridge: Cambridge University Press, 2012), 334; see 314–15.

defection of Judas, keep a rendezvous on a mountain with the risen Christ. With solemn authority ("all authority in heaven and on earth has been given to me"), Jesus charges the group to make disciples of all nations, baptize them with a trinitarian formula, and teach them to obey all that Jesus had commanded—that is to say, the whole way of life he taught, teaching gathered together not least in the Sermon on the Mount (Matt 5–7). This "college" of official witnesses to Jesus obviously includes Peter among the eleven, as one whom Matthew knows to be the head of that group. But the scene lays its emphasis upon a collegial commission, a shared responsibility to evangelize the world, and an assurance that the risen Lord will be with them "always, to the end of the age." Here we might risk using later language and speak of "one apostolic college," constituted by Peter and ten other apostles, and jointly charged to preach the good news to all nations and do so until the close of human history.[20]

The heart of the good news was, of course, Jesus' resurrection from the dead and the sending of the Holy Spirit. In the two articles dedicated to the collegial character and unity of the bishops, *Lumen Gentium*, however, never explicitly mentions the resurrection. The constitution could have strengthened its biblical appeal by recalling Luke's picture of Peter, right from the day of Pentecost, speaking with and for an apostolic "college" or official group of Easter witnesses in announcing the good news: "This [crucified] Jesus God raised up, and of that all of us are witnesses" (Acts 2:32). Peter stands "with the eleven" (Acts 2:14) and proclaims a resurrection of which "we [plural!] are witnesses" (Acts 3:15). As with Matthew 28:19 ("all nations"), the audience for this collegial preaching is universal, not only "the whole house of Israel" (Acts 2:36) but also the diaspora Jews who have come from "every nation under heaven" (Acts 2:5-11). The latter group of Jews represent their homelands and the Gentile inhabitants of those lands. The Easter message from the apostolic college of witnesses should go out to "all the families of the earth" (Acts 3:25).[21]

---

[20] On Matt 28:16-20, see Ulrich Luz, *Matthew 21–28*, trans. James E. Crouch (Grand Rapids, MI: Eerdmans, 2005), 614–36; and Nolland, *Gospel of Matthew*, 1258–72.

[21] On these passages from Acts, see Joseph A. Fitzmyer, *The Acts of the Apostles* (New York: Doubleday, 1998).

Although not expressed in the narrative style of Acts, a sense of collegial witness to Jesus' rising from the dead also comes through the list of Easter witnesses listed by 1 Corinthians 15:5-8. "Cephas" or Peter comes first, but he is joined by "the twelve," more than five hundred believers, James, "all the apostles," and finally Paul himself. All these witnesses share, "collegially," the task of proclaiming the good news of Jesus' resurrection (1 Cor 15:11). The Pauline "college" that testifies to the resurrection obviously extends beyond "the eleven" who receive the great commission at the end of Matthew's gospel.[22]

John 20 offers another "collegial possibility" when the risen Jesus confers on "the disciples" the authority to retain and forgive sins (20:23)—that is to say, discern the responses of people to him and pronounce judgment on their righteousness. The authority to forgive or retain sins recalls the disciples being authorized to "bind and loose" (Matt 16:19; 18:18). But John moves beyond authoritative teaching or judging in the Church to the worldwide mission for which the risen Jesus empowers the disciples through the gift of the Holy Spirit.

The chapter in John mentions the twelve (20:24) once, and names two of them, Peter and the absent Thomas. But "the disciples," while including the twelve, go far beyond them. Chapter 20 highlights "the disciples," using that expression seven times, naming three of them (Mary Magdalene, Simon Peter [referred to as one of two disciples in 20:10], and Thomas), and speaking of a fourth as "the other disciple" (20:2-4, 8). Peter, while prominent as a witness of the empty tomb (20:2-10) and the leader of the twelve, shares, "collegially," with the other disciples the authority to retain and forgive sins.[23]

On balance, the biblical underpinning for the collegial authority of the bishops "with" and "under" Peter remains slight in the two relevant articles (LG 22–23). This is understandable in the situation in which the final text of *Lumen Gentium* was elaborated. Those who championed collegiality needed to provide, not so much biblical witness,

---

[22] On 1 Cor 15:5-11, see Fitzmyer, *First Corinthians*, 549–54; Thiselton, *The First Epistle to the Corinthians*, 1197–1213.

[23] On John 20:1-29 in general and John 20:23 in particular, see Craig S. Keener, *The Gospel of John: A Commentary*, vol. 2 (Peabody, MA: Hendrickson, 2003), 1167–1212, esp. 1206–8; and Andrew T. Lincoln, *The Gospel According to John* (London: Continuum, 2005), 488–504, esp. 500–501.

but arguments and nuances to satisfy the one-sided defenders of papal primacy who flatly queried collegiality.

The footnotes which accompany articles 22–23 of *Lumen Gentium*, rather than appealing to the New Testament as such, create a broad landscape of witnesses from the third to the twentieth century: from Cyprian (three references), Tertullian, Dionysius, the First Council of Nicaea, Eusebius of Caesarea (two references), Hilary of Poitiers, Celestine, Leo the Great, Gregory the Great, the Fourth Lateran Council, the Council of Florence, the First Vatican Council, Leo XIII, Benedict XV, and Pius XII (two references). There are naturally no references to the Council of Constance (1414–18) or to the Council of Basle (431–49). Tainted with "conciliarism" or the view that supreme authority is vested in an ecumenical council independent of the pope, they might obscure what Vatican II wishes to convey about the joint responsibility of pope and bishops for the universal Church.

3. The Universal Call to Holiness

We saw above how *Lumen Gentium* began expounding the mystery of the Church by weaving together different strands of a major biblical themes. Likewise it upholds the vocation to holiness that touches all members of the Church by citing the gospels on the teaching and example of Jesus and drawing on various New Testament epistles (LG 39–42). The chapter includes nine biblical quotations and thirty-six references to the Scriptures, with ten of the references and five of the quotations coming from the Pauline corpus, and the Old Testament providing neither quotations nor references..

Surprisingly no use was made of the "thrice holy" of Isaiah 6:2-3, which the book of Revelation quotes (4:8) and which entered the Latin eucharistic prayer as the *Sanctus* and the Eastern liturgy as the *Trisagion*. But the constitution remains silent about this. The absence appears even more surprising as the chapter opens by citing the Roman Missal and recognizing how the *Gloria in excelsis* celebrates the Son of God, together with the Father and the Holy Spirit, as "alone holy" (LG 39).

This absence belongs with a startling, wider absence of the Jewish Scriptures, which make the holy otherness of God a central theme. Chapters 17–26 of Leviticus offer a "Holiness Code," through which God calls the people to live holy lives: "You shall be holy, for I the Lord your God am holy" (Lev 19:2). Vatican II's chapter on the call to holiness quotes the Sermon on the Mount: "Be perfect, therefore, as your heavenly Father is perfect" (Matt 5:48; quoted by LG 40), an injunction that roughly parallels the Old Testament's call to complete holiness (Lev 19:2) and obedience (Deut 18:13). *Lumen Gentium* speaks of "the holiness of the People of God" (no. 40) but neglects the chance to support this theme by appealing to the call to holiness of the People of God found in Leviticus, Deuteronomy, and elsewhere—not least in the prophetical books.[24]

As well as presenting the New Testament teaching that is relevant to the call to holiness, the constitution ranges widely in the witnesses it retrieves from the Christian tradition. There are sixteen references to the fathers of the Church, including Ignatius of Antioch (two), Origen (three), John Chrysostom (three), and Augustine (three). Thomas Aquinas is referenced four times, and three twentieth-century popes are referenced: Pius X (once), Pius XI (four times), and Pius XII (five times).

4. The Religious Situation of Other Faiths

A fourth example of how *Lumen Gentium* was "nourished and ruled" by the Scriptures involved understanding "the religious others" in the light of Christian faith (no. 16). An earlier article framed the scope of what would be said there. Holding that, through Christ's redeeming work, "all human beings are called to the new People of God" (no. 13), the Council reflected on how, "in different ways," they "belong [*pertinent*] or are ordered [*ordinantur*] to catholic unity." This is true, no matter whether "they are Catholic faithful, or others who believe in Christ, or lastly all human beings without exception [*omnes universaliter homines*], called by God's grace to salvation" (LG 16).Thomas Aquinas prompted this language about all members of the human race being "ordered" variously to "catholic unity" under Christ, who is the head not only of the Church but also of all human beings, albeit "in different degrees."[25]

---

[24] The Council might have quoted 1 Peter which cites God's repeated exhortation, "be holy for I am holy" (1 Pet 1:16; see Lev 11:44, 45; 19:2; 20:7).

[25] LG 6 n. 18 refers to *Summa Theologiae*, 3a.8.3 ad 1. Without referencing Thomas again, the closing sentence of LG 17 also follows him by calling Christ "the head of all."

In considering how "those who have not yet received the gospel" are "ordered to the people of God for different reasons," *Lumen Gentium* 16 distinguished (a) Jews, (b) Muslims, (c) other believers in God, and (d) those who, through no fault of their own, have not yet come to an explicit knowledge of God.

Apropos of (a), the constitution selected some of the privileges listed by Romans 9:4-5 to speak of "the people to whom the covenants and promises were given and from whom Christ was born according to the flesh."[26] Then it aligned itself with Paul by stating that "according to the [divine] election, they [the Jews] are a people most dear on account of the fathers; for the gifts and calling of God are without regret [*sine poenitentia*] (Rom 11:28-29)" (LG 16). This was the first time in the history of Catholic Christianity that an ecumenical council had ever spoken well of the Jews. In its 1442 decree for the Copts, the Council of Florence declared: "the holy Roman Church . . . firmly believes, professes, and preaches that no one remaining outside the Catholic Church, not only pagans, but also Jews, heretics, and schismatics can become partakers of eternal life but they will go to the eternal fire prepared for the devil and his angels" (DzH 1351; ND 810). Before Vatican II, no ecumenical council had ever cited Romans 9:4-5 and 11:28-29. The Council found its scriptural warrant in the classical texts of Paul about God's irrevocable election of Israel.[27] In the longer treatment of the Jewish people that appeared a year later in *Nostra Aetate*, the Council once again quoted Romans 9:4-5 (no. 4), and in a reference to Romans 11:28-29 recalled the use of that verse in *Lumen Gentium* 16 (NA 4 n. 11).

In 1274, the Second Council of Lyons met shortly after the fifth and final major crusade failed to recover the Holy Land. In that context the Council began by dismissing the blasphemous and faithless Sara-

[26] Here I repeat some material from chapter 5 above, but with a different aim: to illustrate the Council's use of Scripture and not simply to retrieve its teaching on those who follow other faiths.

[27] Rom 9:4-5 entered what would become the text of LG, thanks to the schema elaborated by Gérard Philips that, from February 1963, became the basis for a revised draft; after emendations were received, Rom 11:28-29 entered the text in 1964. *Constitutionis Dogmaticae Lumen Gentium Synopsis Historica*, ed. Giuseppe Alberigo and Franca Magistretti (Bologna: Istituto per le Scienze Religiose, 1975), 71.

cens as "the impious enemies of the Christian name."[28] It was only in the twentieth century that an ecumenical council, Vatican II, offered some positive teaching on Muslims. It was a teaching that highlighted common ground: the divine "plan of salvation also embraces those who acknowledge the Creator, in the first place among whom are the Muslims. They profess to hold the faith of Abraham, and together with us they adore the one, merciful God who will judge human beings on the last day" (LG 16). While describing Muslims as those "who profess to hold the faith of Abraham," the Council agreed that they "acknowledge the Creator," "adore with us the one, merciful God," and also share with Christians the expectation of a general judgment "on the last day." A year later in the Declaration on the Relation of the Church to Non-Christian Religions, Vatican II filled out its positive picture of Islam (NA 3). But neither *Lumen Gentium* 16 nor *Nostra Aetate* 3 attempted to recruit biblical texts: for instance, some statement by Paul about the faith of Abraham (e.g., Rom 4:1-22).

After the Muslims, the same article of *Lumen Gentium* turns to (c), other believers in God: "nor is this God distant from others who in shadows and images seek the unknown God, since to all he gives life and breath and all things (see Acts 17:25-28) and [since] the Saviour wishes all human beings to be saved (see 1 Tim 2:4)." Because God is both the Creator who gives life to all human beings and the Savior who wishes all to be saved, the Council holds that the divine presence also embraces all God-seekers, even if it is "in shadows and images" that they seek the unknown God.[29] Hence "those who through no fault [of their own] do not know Christ's Gospel and his Church and who, nevertheless, seek God with a sincere heart and under the influence of grace, try in their actions to fulfil his will made known through the dictate of their conscience—these too may obtain eternal salvation."

We meet here two key biblical passages, already discussed in chapter 5 above. The second (1 Tim 2:4), echoed by Pope Gregory VII when writing to a Muslim king of Mauretania (ND 1002),[30] had been

---

[28] *Decrees of the Ecumenical Councils*, ed., Norman P. Tanner, vol. 1 (London/Washington, DC: Burns & Oates/Georgetown University Press, 1990), 309.

[29] After emendations were received, in 1964 Acts 17:25-28 and 1 Tim 2:4 were added to what would become the definitive text of LG; see Alberigo and Magistretti, *Synopsis Historica*, 72.

[30] This letter, written in 1076, was referenced by NA 3 n. 1.

quoted by the First Vatican Council in its Dogmatic Constitution on
the Catholic Faith, *Dei Filius* (DzH 3014; ND 124), and then quoted
at Vatican II by *Sacrosanctum Concilium* 5. It would be quoted by the
conciliar documents twice more and referenced twice more.[31] It was
in *Lumen Gentium* 16 that Acts 17:25-28 was referenced for the first
time by an ecumenical council in the history of Catholic Christianity.
In the last session of the Council, *Ad Gentes* (no. 3) would refer to Acts
17:27, and *Gaudium et Spes* (no. 24) would quote Acts 17:26.

Finally, apropos of morally upright atheists (d), *Lumen Gentium* 16
adds: "whatever *good* or *truth* is found among them is considered by
the Church to be a preparation for the Gospel, and given by him [the
incarnate Word] who enlightens all human beings so that they may
at length have life" (emphasis added). *Nostra Aetate* was to recognize
the "goodness and truth" and enlightenment by the Word in those
who followed other religious faiths. *Lumen Gentium* 16 followed the
example of Pope Paul VI. By a few months he had anticipated, in no.
107 of his first encyclical *Ecclesiam Suam*, the positive teaching on
Islam to come in *Lumen Gentium*. He wrote of Muslims "whom we
do well to admire on account of those things that are true and commendable [*vera et probanda*] in their worship."[32] Here the paired blessings acknowledged by the pope may point toward John's language
about the Word being full of "grace and truth" that he has come to
share (John 1:14, 17). Even more clearly *Lumen Gentium* picked up this
double-sided terminology when speaking of Christ, who through the
visible community of the Church "communicates truth and grace to
all [human beings]" (no. 8). In the same article the constitution also
used such Johannine-style terminology when speaking of "the many
elements of sanctification and truth" to be found among Christians
not united with the Bishop of Rome.

When reflecting on the religious condition of "others" in terms of
"whatever good or truth is found among them," the Council proposed
two distinguishable but inseparable dimensions of the divine self-communication that has blessed them: salvation ("good") and revelation

---

[31] 1 Tim 2:4 is quoted by the Declaration on Religious Liberty, *Dignitatis Humanae*
(no. 11), the Decree on the Church's Missionary Activity, *Ad Gentes* (no. 7); the
text is referenced by NA (no. 1 n. 2) and the Decree on the Ministry and Life of
Priests, *Presbyterorum Ordinis* (no. 42 n. 21).

[32] AAS 56 (1964), 609–59, at 654.

("truth"). The Johannine language of revelation and salvation (in that order) followed at once when our passage in *Lumen Gentium* introduced "enlightening" (revelation) and "life" (salvation). The following year the final documents of the Council included a similar double terminology inspired by the prologue to John, and did so in the order of revelation first and salvation second. In non-Christian religions the Council found elements "of what is true and holy" (NA 2). Six weeks later the Council followed the same order: missionary activity "purges of evil associations every element of truth and grace which are found among peoples" (AG 9). Thus not only in *Lumen Gentium* but also in *Nostra Aetate* and *Ad Gentes*, John's language about "grace and truth" enjoyed some echoes, when the Council spoke about "religious others." In a christological context *Ad Gentes* expressly quoted the verse to speak of Christ "the new Adam," who is "the head of a renewed humanity," being "full of grace and truth" (no. 3). *Dei Verbum* introduced its chapter on the New Testament by speaking of the Word being made flesh and dwelling among us "full of grace of truth" (no. 17). John 1:14 is referenced, along with seven other quotations, to support the teaching that Christ is "the mediator and fullness of all revelation" (DV 2 n. 2).

Apropos of John 1:9 ("He was the true light that enlightens everyone coming into the world"[33]), we saw above that *Lumen Gentium* 16, albeit without referencing this verse, echoed it and stated that the incarnate Word "enlightens all human beings." The following year *Nostra Aetate* would also echo the verse, but once again without adding a reference, when it described the Church's attitude to other religions: "it is with sincere respect that she considers those ways of acting and living, those precepts and doctrines, which, although they differ in many [respects] from what she herself holds and proposes, nevertheless, *often reflect a ray of that Truth, which illuminates all human beings*" (AG 2; emphasis added). It was left to *Gaudium et Spes* to quote from John's prologue the words about "the true light which enlightens every human being" (no. 57).

Thus not only in *Lumen Gentium* but also in other documents Vatican II effectively appealed to the language of "grace and truth"

---

[33] These words might also be translated as "the true light, which enlightens everyone, was coming into the world," but that would not affect the Council's appeal to the verse as witnessing to Christ who enlightens all human beings.

and "the true light enlightening every human being." No previous ecumenical council of Catholic Christianity had quoted or referenced those words from John. Vatican II made these texts central when it cited biblical witness that could apply to the religious situation of those who follow other faiths.

5. Further Questions

When reviewing ways in which *Lumen Gentium* was formed and nourished by the Bible, I limited myself to four examples: the mystery of the Church, the collegial authority of bishops, the universal call to holiness, and respect for those who follow other living faiths. Obviously further examples could be examined.

A major theme that entered into the Council's new vision of the Church was the triple office of Christ as priest, prophet, and king/ shepherd, prefigured, as we saw, in *Sacrosanctum Concilium* (see chap. 3 above). Given its scope as a document on the Church, *Lumen Gentium* did not set itself to explore and define the triple office of Christ himself. It concerned itself rather with illustrating how others participate (through baptism and then, in the case of some, through ministerial ordination) in his priestly, prophetic, and kingly roles. Distinguishing "the common priesthood of the faithful" from "the ministerial or hierarchical priesthood," the constitution adds that "each in its own proper way shares in the one priesthood of Christ," which is a "royal priesthood" (no. 10). *Lumen Gentium* completes the threefold scheme when it moves on to say that "the holy people of God also shares in Christ's prophetic office" (no. 12). The constitution opened the way for further conciliar documents to repeat and develop the teaching about sharing in the triple office of Christ: *Unitatis Redintegratio* (no. 4); *Christus Dominus* (nos. 12–21); *Apostolicam Actuositatem* (nos. 2, 10); *Ad Gentes* (no. 15); and *Presbyterorum Ordinis* (nos.1–6).

Vatican II broke new ground by spelling out the ways in which the baptized and then the ordained participate in the redemptive function of Christ as priest, prophet, and king/shepherd. While belonging to the renewal or bringing-up-to-date (*aggiornamento*) of the Church's life and doctrine, the teaching on the priestly, prophetic, and kingly character of Christian discipleship is also a spectacular example of the Council retrieving (*ressourcement*) matters from the Scriptures and the long tradition that interpreted and actualized the biblical witness. But it would require at least a monograph to explore the biblical (and traditional) underpinnings for Vatican II's teaching on priest, prophet, and king.[34]

Lumen Gentium introduced a related theme, which merits scholarly attention, when it retrieved teaching from St. Paul about the special gifts or charisms that the baptized receive from the Holy Spirit and exercise for the good of the whole Church (nos. 7, 12, 30, 33–35; see AA 3). While Cardinal Ernesto Ruffini contested this teaching, thanks to Francis Sullivan, some American bishops, and others, this biblical theme about the charisms conferred on the faithful entered the final text of *Lumen Gentium*.[35]

Four Conclusions

This examination of the first two constitutions approved and promulgated by the Second Vatican Council has shown, first, a serious and constant engagement with the inspired word of the Scriptures. Add too that many of the quotations from the Church fathers and references to them, especially in *Lumen Gentium*, involved texts in which Cyprian, John Chrysostom, and others were expounding biblical texts. Their witness merged more or less seamlessly with the scriptural witness.

Vatican II's desire for its deliberations to be "nourished" and "formed" by the Scriptures supported and led to a highly important decision. The Council mandated a richer selection of biblical readings for the divine office, for the administration of the sacraments, and, above all, for the celebration of the Eucharist. Since the Council had opened itself "more lavishly" to "the treasures of the Bible," it wanted all the faithful to be fed "at a richer table of God's word" (SC 51).

Second, we saw how the sea change in attitudes toward the followers of other faiths involved Vatican II in appealing to such texts as Acts 17:25-28, Romans 9:4-5, Romans 11:28-29, John 1:9, and John 1:14, which no previous council had ever invoked. Attention to previously neglected scriptural witness helped inspire new teaching. We

---

[34] In *Jesus Our Priest: A Christian Approach to the Priesthood of Christ* (Oxford: University Press, 2010), Michael Keenan Jones and I explored the scriptural and traditional witness to the priestly function of Christ in which his disciples share.

[35] See Francis A. Sullivan, "Vatican II and the Charisms of the Faithful," in *Vatican II: Forty Personal Stories*, ed. William Madges and Michael J. Daley (Mystic, CT: Twenty-Third Publications, 2003), 94–97.

find other such examples of development in teaching being inspired by long neglected biblical witness. No ecumenical council had, for instance, appealed to Genesis 1:26-27 and what it said about human beings "created in the image and likeness of God" until the promulgation of *Nostra Aetate*. This declaration echoed the Genesis doctrine about all people being created in the divine image, and drew a practical conclusion: there is no basis for any discrimination that offends against or curtails "human dignity and the rights that flow from it" (no. 5). "Human dignity" would become the title of the Declaration on Religious Liberty promulgated a few weeks later on December 7, 1965. *Gaudium et Spes* (also promulgated on the same day) would insist on "the extraordinary dignity of the human person" and the basic rights that flow from that dignity (no. 26; see no. 29).

Third, we noted above how Vatican II encouraged teachers and students of theology to press beyond single biblical texts or passages and attend to biblical themes that recur and do so even frequently (OT 16). The Council put into practice its own advice: for example, in weaving together different scriptural strands to illustrate the image of the Church as the flock of Christ (LG 6). *Lumen Gentium* would adopt the same method in other contexts (e.g., no. 20 nn. 4 and 5). Later documents of the Council were to follow suit and bring together a varied witness to major biblical themes (e.g., DV 2 n. 2; AG 2 n. 3; AG 4 n. 12; PO 2 n. 1). Various biblical themes of theological and ecclesial relevance helped to build up the documents, as much or even more than the witness of individual verses or passages.

The contribution that Pieter Smulders, a *peritus* at Vatican II, made even before the Council opened, anticipated the use that would be made of biblical themes. During August and September 1962 he wrote for the papal nuncio at The Hague a long critical evaluation of the schema, *De deposito fidei pure custodiendo*. Smulders drew on numerous exegetes and theologians to demonstrate the broad biblical witness to the history of revelation and salvation, a rich witness that the schema had neglected but that would eventually undergird scripturally the Dogmatic Constitution on Divine Revelation and, in particular, its opening chapter (DV 1–6).[36] The biblical approach championed by

---

[36] For a remarkable series of articles by Jared Wicks on the contribution of Pieter Smulders, see chap. 1, fn. 17 above.

Smulders prefigured the way in which the Council let the Scriptures nourish and form its documents.

A fourth feature that characterizes the conciliar use of the Bible concerns its limited use of the Jewish Scriptures. As we observed above, the two constitutions we scrutinized contain relatively few references to the Old Testament or quotations from it. We noted how the universal call to holiness might have been enriched by using Leviticus, Deuteronomy, and prophetic books. We could add further examples. At the end of no. 8, *Lumen Gentium* describes the Church as being "simultaneously holy and always in need of purification." A few lines later, no. 9 opens the chapter on the People of God by speaking of the people of Israel. The prophets and others constantly witness to the way in which, while God's election and grace made that people holy, they were in regular need of conversion and purification. Some quotations or at least biblical references to that effect could have vividly dramatized the picture of the Church as *simul justa et peccatrix* or *semper reformanda* (UR 6).

But, all in all, this partial examination of the Council's performance serves to vindicate the claim to hear the word of God "religiously" and "faithfully" proclaim it (DV 1). Substantially Vatican II practised what it preached about the Scriptures being "the supreme rule of faith" (DV 21). The Council genuinely did its work under the aegis of the Book of the Gospels.

Chapter 10

Concluding Reflections

In his spiritual testament, dated March 17, 2000, John Paul II wrote: "For a long time to come it will be granted to new generations to draw on the riches which the Council of the twentieth century has blessed us with." Two generations have passed since the Second Vatican Council ended in 1965. Its teaching is still being received and tested; trajectories it initiated or at least encouraged are still continuing.

The Second Vatican Council has aimed to explore theologically some important aspects of the teaching of Vatican II. Through the practice of both *ressourcement* and *aggiornamento*, the Council went about renewing the apostolic identity of the Church and her outreach to the world. For the first time in the history of Catholic Christianity, it introduced fresh teaching on major themes (e.g., about all the baptized sharing in the triple function of Christ as priest, prophet, and king/shepherd), as well as recalling for the first time and applying some key texts from John, Luke, Paul, and other biblical witnesses. It mandated far-reaching changes in the life of the Church, both *ad intra* and *ad extra*. Some of that teaching is still far from being implemented satisfactorily: for instance, the collegial authority of all the bishops and proper respect for the life of the local churches. Over-centralization has clearly hampered such developments.

This book has necessarily been selective. Its chapters have attended closely to only five of the sixteen documents of Vatican II: *Sacrosanctum Concilium* (in chaps. 2, 3, 4, 5, and 9 above), *Lumen Gentium* (in chaps. 1, 2, 5, and 9), *Nostra Aetate* (in chaps. 2, 5, and 6), *Dei Verbum* (in chaps. 1, 7, and 8), and *Ad Gentes* (in chaps. 1 and 5). Attention to two further texts, *Perfectae Caritatis* (in chaps. 1 and 2) and *Dignitatis Humanae* (in chap. 2), was more or less confined to the principles they invoked in mandating change. Carefully examining these seven documents can convey, however, a sense of the remarkable contribution made by the Council.

Hopefully the book has succeeded in illustrating the rich teaching of Vatican II and how its documents interlock. In particular, the chapter on *Sacrosanctum Concilium* (chap. 3 above) set itself to trace the complex ways in which the liturgy constitution, the first document to be approved by the Council, anticipated and initiated teaching on at least twelve topics. The "law of praying" proved itself to be the "law of believing."

Through the Second Vatican Council, the bishops of the world tackled a very large agenda, and came up with an extensive plan to reform the Catholic Church, both in herself and in her relations with "others." Far from being a mere exercise of speculative reason, their teaching exercised motivational reason that aimed to inspire the practice of faith. That teaching consistently raises the question: what was the Council's impact? What did it bring the Catholic Church to do or leave undone?

For this reason I include a short appendix concerned with a specific case of reform, a long overdue reform that constitutes a regrettable example of what still needs to be done in the aftermath of Vatican II.

Finally, the subtitle for this book, *Message and Meaning*, has been chosen as a further call to action against those who misinterpret what the Council taught. Ralph Martin, for instance, in his recent *Will Many Be Saved? What Vatican II Actually Teaches and Its Implications for the New Evangelization*, egregiously misrepresents Vatican II's teaching.[1]

To begin with, the subtitle is misleading, and not simply because two long (and interesting) chapters on the views of Karl Rahner and Hans Urs von Balthasar about the final salvation of human beings, together with the notes to these chapters and an appendix on von Balthasar, make up well over one-third of the book. (That could have "justified" a different subtitle: *What Karl Rahner and Hans Urs von Balthasar Actually Held*.) Far from examining the full scope of the Council's teaching on human salvation, Martin's work, when he directly examines the conciliar texts, concentrates on *Lumen Gentium*

---

[1] Ralph Martin, *Will Many Be Saved? What Vatican II Actually Teaches and Its Implications for the New Evangelization* (Grand Rapids, MI: Eerdmans, 2012).

16, and attends only very briefly to a few other passages: notably *Ad Gentes* 7 and *Gaudium et Spes* 22. He ignores so much relevant material that the existing subtitle could be changed to: *What Lumen Gentium 16 Actually Teaches*, or, perhaps even more accurately, to *What the Last Three Sentences of Lumen Gentium 16 Actually Teach*.

These three sentences follow a positive account of four groups who have not or have not yet accepted the gospel and been baptized: (a) Jews, (b) Muslims, (c) followers of other faiths and philosophies, and (d) those who, through no fault of their own, have not yet reached an explicit knowledge of God. With an eye primarily on the fourth group, the Council recognized the "good and truth" that is found among them as "a preparation for the Gospel and given by him [the incarnate Word] who enlightens all human beings so that at length they may have life." Then come the three sentences (two in the original Latin) with which Martin is concerned above all:

> But very often deceived by the Evil One, human beings have become vain in their thoughts and have exchanged the truth of God for a lie, serving the creature rather than the Creator (see Rom 1:21, 25). Or else, living without God and dying in this world, they are exposed to final despair. Hence to promote the glory of God and the salvation of all these, the Church, mindful of the Lord's command, "preach the good news to every creature (Mark 16:16)" takes zealous care to foster the missions.

Martin interprets this passage as teaching that "the conditions under which people can be saved who have never heard the gospel are very often, in fact, not fulfilled."[2] As he puts his view later, "the Council's *main teaching in LG 16*" is that "'very often' the possibility of people being saved without hearing the gospel is not realized."[3]

In an article of thirty-nine lines in the official (Latin) edition that I am using, the last ten lines are alleged to be the "main teaching" of the whole article. To begin with, this article has spoken positively of the Jews and Muslims as included in "God's project of salvation." Then the article looks at the followers of other faiths and philosophies who, "through no fault of their own, knew neither the Gospel of Christ nor the Church." If, "under the influence of grace," they try

[2] Ibid., xii.
[3] Ibid., 198; emphasis added.

to do God's will as they know it through their conscience, "they can attain eternal salvation." As regards the fourth group, those who, through no fault of their own, have not yet reached even "an explicit knowledge of God," but, "with the help of divine grace" strive to lead an upright life, "divine providence" does "not deny them the helps necessary for salvation."

After expounding in this positive way the possibility of salvation for various non-Christian groups (who together remain the majority of human beings), the article insists on the need to evangelize the world. In doing so, it invokes St. Paul's teaching in Romans (about the universal prevalence of sin) and echoes what he wrote about those who grieve because they lack Christian hope (1 Thess 4:13). Christians should do their very best to bring all these "others" the good news, which can help them to serve the Creator and die in the hope of sharing in Christ's resurrection.

Martin simply moves beyond what Vatican II states here, when he claims an impossibility and maintains that very often people who have never heard the gospel *cannot be saved*. If they live deprived of the conditions under which they can be saved, that means that they will not be saved and will finish up damned for all eternity. If they cannot be saved, they will not in fact be saved. This is a frightening thesis, tantamount to the extreme Augustinian view that God creates a *massa damnata*: the majority of the human race are simply predestined to hell.

In arguing for this chilling thesis, Martin ignores much of "what Vatican II actually teaches." *Sacrosanctum Concilium* fails to appear in his volume and yet, as we have seen above, it is deeply concerned with human salvation. The remarkable article 83 begins: "Jesus Christ, the High Priest of the New and Eternal Covenant, when he assumed a human nature, introduced into this land of exile, the hymn that in heaven is sung throughout all ages. He unites the *whole community of humankind with himself* and associates it with him in singing the divine canticle of praise" (emphasis added). This union of all people with the incarnate Christ takes place whether they know about it or not, and it is a union that fulfills a very basic condition for people to be saved. Martin likewise fails to consider what *Ad Gentes* taught about "the seeds of the Word" sown by God and "hidden" everywhere: in particular, in "religious traditions." This teaching pointed to the "secretly present" Christ, the "author" of the elements of "truth and grace" found "among the nations" (nos. 9, 11, 15, 18).

In dealing with *Gaudium et Spes*, Martin interprets in a minimalizing fashion article 22 and its statement that through the Holy Spirit, all human beings can be united with the crucified and risen Christ.[4] He passes over in silence further important teaching on the Holy Spirit that we find in the same constitution. The Spirit gives all human beings "the light and strength" needed "to respond to their supreme calling" (no. 10); through the Spirit the risen Christ is at work in the hearts of human beings everywhere (no. 38). This theme of the Holy Spirit's universal activity was taken up by Pope John Paul II, not least in his 1990 encyclical *Redemptoris Missio*. Martin pays some attention to that encyclical but ignores what the pope wrote about the Spirit operating "at the very centre" of each person's "religious questioning," and about "the Spirit's presence and activity" which affect "not only individuals but also society and history, peoples, *cultures and religion*" (no. 28; emphasis added). In short, Martin fails to factor in the universal presence and activity of the Holy Spirit, which provide the second, very basic condition for the salvation of human beings at large.

I admire and share Martin's passion to encourage Catholics and other Christians to become much more actively concerned with their mission. But a seriously deficient interpretation of the Second Vatican Council should not be offered as a way of inspiring such fresh commitment to evangelization.

It may seem strange to conclude a book on the Second Vatican Council by sharply rejecting a recent publication. But Martin's book comes recommended by four cardinals and produced by a leading religious publisher in the United States. This and other such recent books highlight the need to examine what Vatican II "actually" did teach and so to reclaim that teaching.

---

[4] Martin, *Will Many Be Saved*, 9–10.

The Reform of the Congregation for the Doctrine of the Faith[1]

In a celebrated address to the Roman Curia on December 22, 2005, Pope Benedict XVI proposed that the teaching of the Second Vatican Council should be applied through a "hermeneutic of reform"—that is to say, through a method of interpretation that would continue to reform and renew the Church in different aspects of her life.

On July 2, 2012, it was officially announced that Bishop Gerhard Ludwig Müller of Regensburg would take over the Congregation for the Doctrine of the Faith (CDF) as its new prefect. Might this change be an opportunity to apply a hermeneutic of reform to the CDF?

As a member of the International Theological Commission Bishop Müller belonged to a subcommission of seven theologians who produced a 100-page study on the diaconate. Published in late 2002, *Le Diaconat: Évolution et perspectives*, despite some official disclaimers, concluded by leaving open the question of ordaining women to the diaconate. A friend of Gustavo Gutiérrez, the founding father of liberation theology, Bishop Müller co-authored with him *On the Side of the Poor: The Theology of Liberation*.

How should the CDF serve the Church in general and the cause of life-giving theology in particular? What would the CDF look like if Bishop Müller set himself to renew it by a "hermeneutic of reform"?

In an article originally published in German, translated into English for *Doctrine and Life* 48 (1998): 451–66, and summarized by the *Tablet*

---

[1] Two weeks after Bishop (now Cardinal) Müller was appointed to head the CDF, a version of this appendix was published in *The Tablet* (July 14, 2012).

(January 16, 1999), Ladislas Orsy, a Washington-based canon lawyer, proposed in detail some desirable reforms of the CDF. He argued that its procedures leave much to be desired from the point of view not only of ordinary justice but also of the Church's own canon law. So far as I know, there has never been an official response to Orsy's article.

What detailed reforms might one envisage? Let me make six suggestions. First, the CDF is meant to be the last court of appeal and not the first tribunal to handle cases of doctrine. Its workload might be reduced by automatically sending back unsolicited complaints and asking the authors of such complaints to take up matters with their local bishop. If they remain dissatisfied with their own diocesan authorities, they could appeal to the doctrine commission of their national bishops' conference. If they are still not satisfied, they have the freedom to appeal to the CDF, *provided* that they supply a full documentation which proves that their complaints have already been heard by the local and national authorities of the Church and which records the response(s) they received from those authorities.

Such a procedure would honour the principle of subsidiarity, one of the ten principles guiding the composition of the 1983 Code of Canon Law. That principle means that activities and decisions which naturally belong to a lower level of responsibility should not be taken at once to a higher level. The practice of subsidiarity promotes the healthy flourishing of the worldwide Church, a flourishing that can only be harmed when individual Catholics quietly take issues straight to some Vatican office and regularly receive an immediate hearing.

Second, as Orsy pointed out, a universally accepted principle of justice supports the right to a fair hearing. That means the right of the accused to be present from the outset, to meet their accusers (face-to-face, if possible), to be given in writing well beforehand the accusations, and to be represented by someone of their own choice. Nothing poisons the atmosphere more than a lack of transparency which tolerates anonymous delators and keeps proceedings secret, while for months the accused may know nothing at all about what is building up against them. Everyone, including unfortunate theologians who may be obscuring or misrepresenting "the faith that has come to us from the apostles," have a right to a fair hearing.

A few years ago the CDF itself may have realized that it was not putting into practice the principle of a "fair hearing," or at least not practising it fully. Up to 2002 in the "historical notes" that accompanied the CDF, the *Annuario Pontificio* (Papal Yearbook) carried the observation that "in all the proceedings there is granted the widest possible chance of defence." But this sentence disappeared in the same section of the *Annuario Pontificio* for the following year.

Third, a priest who served for many years as a consultor on the CDF admitted to me that he "wondered whether the CDF had done more harm than good." His hesitancy might have been fuelled by a lack of balanced membership. Faced with a one-sided selection of his fellow consultors, he could hardly describe them as what they are meant to be: "theologians of diverse schools." Notoriously, when an institution is not strengthened by appropriate diversity, it lacks the internal criticism that can lend more balance and wisdom to what it does and what it publishes.

Recently with a view to writing a contribution for the forthcoming *Oxford Handbook of Ecclesiology*, I was re-reading numerous books of the New Testament and commentaries on them. Repeatedly warnings about false teachers and the harm they could cause, or were actually causing, turned up in the letters of Paul, the general epistles, and elsewhere. At the same time the authors of the New Testament accepted a healthy diversity. They proved shining models of a principle which Saint John XXIII retrieved from St. Augustine and which found its place in the closing chapter of Vatican II's Pastoral Constitution on the Church in the Modern World: "let there be unity in what is necessary, freedom in what is doubtful, and charity in everything" (GS 92). Whenever an appropriate and justified diversity of theological views remains unrepresented, those who work at the CDF or act as its consultors run the clear and obvious risk of confusing their personal theological views with matters of revealed doctrine. Peter and Paul differed in secondary matters but were utterly united in their faith in the risen Christ for whom they eventually gave their lives. They never misrepresented real unity as if it involved a package of uniform opinions.

Fourth, Pope Paul VI wanted consultors of the various Vatican offices to be changed every five years or at least every ten years. Yet some consultors at the CDF have regularly been kept on for many years—a practice that can only encourage investing their own opinions with false authority.

Fifth, as prefect of the CDF, Bishop Müller will preside over two advisory bodies, the International Theological Commission (ITC) and the Pontifical Biblical Commission (PBC). Over the years all three bodies have published documents on a variety of topics: from the ecclesial vocation of theologians to the interpretation of the Sacred Scriptures in the Church; and from issues concerned with the person and work of Christ to the new evangelization. Frequently the texts coming from the ITC and, especially, the PBC have handled their sources more skilfully, argued their case more compellingly, and, in short, produced more convincing documents than those coming from the CDF itself. Would the CDF enhance its standing by authorizing and publishing as its own the texts of the PBC and the ITC?

Sixth, in the past some at the CDF have promoted meetings on key questions that drew together theologians and other scholars of various (legitimate) schools of thought. The late Édouard Dhanis, for instance, facilitated an international meeting on the resurrection of Christ and gathered the proceedings in a large and valuable volume, *Resurrexit* (Vatican Press, 1970). I would be delighted to see the CDF following such an example by positively promoting theology that would be both creatively faithful and pastorally effective in the multicultural and fast-changing world of today.

In an apostolic letter of January 2001, *Novo Millennio Ineunte*, St. John Paul II recognized that there was "much more to be done" in "the reform of the Roman Curia" (no. 44). Two years later in *Pastores Gregis* (no. 59) he reiterated this point, using the same language. Pope Benedict XVI firmly endorsed a "hermeneutic of reform." Dare we hope that the new prefect of the CDF might examine critically the running of that institution and implement reforms that would have a healthy and life-giving impact on the Church and the whole theological community?

Select Bibliography

Alberigo, Giuseppe, and Joseph A. Komonchak, eds. *History of Vatican II*. 5 vols. Maryknoll, NY: Orbis Books, 1995–2006.

Congar, Yves. *My Journal of the Council*. Translated by M. J. Ronayne and M. C. Boulding. Collegeville, MN: Liturgical Press, 2012.

———. *True and False Reform in the Church*. Translated by P. Philibert. Collegeville, MN: Liturgical Press, 2011.

Congar Yves et al., eds. *L'Église et Vatican II*. 3 vols. Paris: Cerf, 1966–67; up to 1970, twenty-one further volumes appeared in this series of commentaries on the Council documents.

Faggioli, Massimo. "Concilio Vaticano II: bollettino bibliografico (2000–2002)." *Cristianesimo nella storia* 24 (2003): 335–60.

———. "Concilio Vaticano II: bollettino bibliografico (2002–2005)." *Cristianesimo nella storia* 28 (2005): 743–67.

———. "Council Vatican II: Bibliographical Overview 2005–2007 " *Cristianesimo nella storia* 29 (2008): 567–610.

———. "Council Vatican II: Bibliographical Overview 2007–2010." *Cristianesimo nella storia* 32 (2011): 755–91.

———. *True Reform: Liturgy and Ecclesiology in Sacrosanctum Concilium*. Collegeville, MN: Liturgical Press, 2012.

———. *Vatican II: The Battle for Meaning*. Mahwah, NJ: Paulist Press, 2012.

Heft, James L., and John O'Malley, eds. *After Vatican II: Trajectories and Hermeneutics*. Grand Rapids, MI: Eerdmans, 2012.

Hünermann, Peter, and Bernd Jochen Hilberath, eds. *Herders Theologischer Kommentar zum Zweiten Vatikanischen Konzil*. 5 vols. Freiburg im Breisgau: Herder, 2004–5.

Lacey, Michael J., and Francis Oakley, eds. *The Crisis of Authority in Catholic Modernity*. New York: Oxford University Press, 2011.

Lamberigts, Mathijs, and Leo Kenis, eds. *Vatican II and Its Legacy*. Leuven: Leuven University Press, 2002.

Latourelle, René, ed. *Vatican II: Assessment and Perspectives*. 3 vols. Mahwah, NJ: Paulist Press, 1988–89.

Noonan, John T. *A Church That Can and Cannot Change: The Development of Catholic Moral Teaching*. Notre Dame, IN: University of Notre Dame Press, 2005.

O'Collins, Gerald. *Living Vatican II: The 21st Council for the 21st Century*. Mahwah, NJ: Paulist Press, 2006.

O'Collins, Gerald, and Michael A. Hayes, eds. *The Legacy of John Paul II*. London: Burns & Oates, 2008.

O'Malley, John W. *What Happened at Vatican II*. Cambridge, MA: Harvard University Press, 2008.

———. "'The Hermeneutic of Reform': A Historical Analysis," *Theological Studies* 73 (2012): 517–46.

Quinn, John R. *The Reform of the Papacy*. New York: Crossroad, 1999.

Rush, Ormond. *Still Interpreting Vatican II: Some Hermeneutical Principles*. Mahwah, NJ: Paulist Press, 2004.

Vorgrimler, Herbert, ed. *Commentary on the Documents of Vatican II*. 5 vols. London: Burns & Oates, 1967–69.

Wicks, Jared. "Still More Light on Vatican Council II." *Catholic Historical Review* 98 (2012): 476–502.

Biblical Index

Index of Names